ALL KINDS OF LOVE:
Experiencing Hospice

Carolyn Jaffe
Primary Care Nurse and Co-Founder
Hospice of Metro Denver

and

Carol H. Ehrlich
Chairperson Emerita, Audiology and
Speech Pathology
The Childrens Hospital, Denver

Death, Value and Meaning Series
Series Editor: John D. Morgan

Baywood Publishing Company, Inc.

Library of Congress Catalog Number: 96-48015
ISBN: 0-89503-147-7 (Paper)

Library of Congress Cataloging-in-Publication Data

Jaffe, Carolyn.
  All kinds of love : experiencing hospice / Carolyn Jaffe, Carol H. Ehrlich.
      p.   cm. - - (Death, value, and meaning series)
  Includes bibliographical references.
  ISBN 0-89503-147-7 (paper)
  1. Hospice care.   2. Death.   3. Terminally ill.   I. Ehrlich, Carol H. II. Title.   III. Series.
  R726.8.J34 1997
  362.1'756- -dc21   96-48015
                                                            CIP

DEDICATION

To Carolyn's patients and their families who,
through their own poignant odysseys,
gave both of us much to nourish our lives.

Foreword

Rabbi Dr. Earl A. Grollman

After working in the field of crisis intervention for nearly three decades, I am more than ever convinced of the importance of truth and experience. The power they hold for transmuting distortions into accuracy, misunderstanding or shallow understanding into real grasp, and apathy into fire in the belly, cannot be overestimated.

The insights gained from Jaffe's many years of hospice nursing reflect the kind of truth I have come to value—the kind that has this power. Her stories bring alive the concerns, the surprises, the victories, the disappointments, the mistakes, the uncertainties, the joys, and the pain that are part of one's dying. They reveal in a variety of ordinary could-be-me lives the problems and solutions, the successes and failures people experience in coping with dying. They present authentically the needs and reactions of persons at the end of life and those of their loved ones. They show what is helpful in the responses of health professionals serving them, and lay bare the inadequate, the harmful.

There are good deaths and bad deaths. In these stories we see what hospice and a good death can mean.

All hospice workers hear frequently, "I admire you. But, to tell the truth, I couldn't do it. Being with dying people is just too morbid. How can you do it?"

Jaffe's experiences in the first eight chapters of this book and her personal story in Chapter 9 shed light on the motivations and feelings of persons who do this unusual work. We read and begin to understand how and why anyone could spend a career helping people die.

There is much for health professionals, hospice workers, and families to learn from these readable accounts.

Jaffe and Ehrlich have followed each of their narratives with notes containing valuable information and provocative opinions—their own and others. The *Notes* are the factual and editorial frames for the pictures, a handle, if you will, with which to deal with the issues in each story. Matters of public and private concern regarding death and dying are explored from their fresh point of view.

Each contribution to the literature adds to the debate about dying. Like the tide's deposits of sand to the growing dune, each one will help to shift society's attitude about death away from denial to acceptance. *All Kinds of Love* will lend its power to that movement.

I commend this unique volume to you. *All Kinds of Love: Experiencing Hospice* will make a difference in your life.

Preface

Ira R. Byock, M.D.

The subjects of dying and care for the dying have finally attracted the attention of the public and the health-care professions. As this preface is being written, America is reeling from studies documenting that prevailing medical practices often ignore the preferences of patients, limit their options, and, most disturbing, add to their suffering. People who work in the field of end-of-life care, and who teach palliative care in medical and nursing schools, live with a sense of urgent need for strategies that will bring about effective change.

Heated discussions of what the core problem is dominate a bumper crop of conferences and symposia on improving care for the dying. Those attending usually agree that real change in standards of care will only occur when professional attitudes toward dying and public expectations of end-of-life care shift. But change on this scale seems beyond anyone's scope. Experts in clinical care, health policy, and ethics have mounted a host of initiatives directed at improved medical education, certification of clinical proficiency, and development of practice protocols and standards.

On occasion, I have mustered the courage to express my belief that, as important as these efforts are, even collectively, they will probably prove insufficient. After struggling with these questions for years, I have come to the conclusion that the power to change public and professional attitudes lies within the stories of people's experiences in dying. Such notions can sound plausible in small circles, late at night (over sufficient red wine). Yet, they have been met in scholarly gatherings by a chorus of learned colleagues assuring me that effective change can only occur through the cumulative weight of stringent scientific research. I respectfully disagree.

It is true, of course, that research is needed. Studies that are well-designed, reproducible, and statistically reliable are necessary to carefully define existing problems, evaluate the efficacy of existing interventions and test the efficacy and practicality of proposed therapeutic innovations. Needed most of all is research that explores the subjective nature of the dying experience. Quality of life research, for instance, must focus not only on functional status, nor only on the evaluation of pain and other symptoms, but must extend to interpersonal, emotional, and even spiritual realms. Without question, issues of meaning, life satisfaction (or dissatisfaction) and the degree to which a person senses that his affairs are in order and that he is ready to leave this life all have an impact on the quality of the dying experience. Quantifiable measures for the full range of human experience with dying must be devised.

But, in calling for research, it is necessary to understand that experimental design has inherent limitations. The very process of research carries assumptions which act as a lens to focus—but also to limit—the perception of reality. The tools chosen to measure change within the confines of clinical studies prospectively determine which aspects of human experience can be inspected. It is essential that the precise nature of what is being measured by these instruments is carefully defined or there is risk that the results will be misinterpreted. Studies of patients with end-stage illness, for instance, often utilize the Karnofsky or ECOG functional scales as indicators of "quality of life." They reflect the presumption that as people's functions decline, their quality of life will correspondingly diminish. If this were strictly true, however, every non-ambulatory and, especially, every bed-bound patient would report a predictably abysmal quality of life. As the stories of *All Kinds of Love: Experiencing Hospice* richly show, this is not the case.

What other assumptions might be limiting our ability to identify the root cause of the crisis of terminal care? Within the conceptual model of medicine dying is understood as a clinical event; medical students are still taught to approach the dying patient by defining a set of medical problems to be solved. The preponderance of palliative-care research reinforces this problem-based approach to patients. Yet, for the person dying and for the family, the experience of dying extends beyond the purview of medicine; it is more basic and more pervasive. Dying is a part of living and while it entails a series of medical problems to be dealt with, the fundamental nature of dying is experiential.

Dying is a part of living. Dying is fundamentally a personal experience. The simplicity of these two statements belies their profound implications. Persons are multidimensional beings. Body, mind, spirit, and soul, thoughts and feelings, past, present, and future, meaning and purpose, conscious and subconscious, values and beliefs, likes and dislikes, shame and pride, family and friends all are part of a person. While news of an incurable condition can dramatically alter an individual's perspective, the person dying experiences life in the same moment-to-moment fashion as do those of us who, as yet, do not think of ourselves as dying.

All Kinds of Love beautifully and powerfully reveals these truths. The stories herein allow us to peer into the poignant human process that unfolds within the community of family, professionals, and volunteer caregivers that forms around the person dying. We observe instances of non-physical suffering as well as the surprising personal growth that can occur at life's end.

Subtle features of dying are also revealed. We see the benefit that flows both ways in acts of caring. Subtler still, we witness that, even at life's end, responsibility between people continues to be mutual. The dying person retains rudimentary responsibilities: to make his needs known, to communicate his preferences, and to allow himself to be cared for. These qualities are central to understanding the human experience of dying, yet elude most research designs.

When I think about the American society's attitudes and expectations regarding dying, the image of an enormous ocean liner comes to mind. At present, the passengers who collectively comprise the culture of America venerate youthfulness, vitality, independence, power, and material possessions and, not surprisingly, recognize no value to life in the decline. Once a person's cancer or heart or lung condition is deemed terminal, all aboard presume that life is over and the best to be hoped for is relief from suffering.

It is no wonder that this ship is headed in the direction of assisted suicide and euthanasia as a way of pre-empting death, thus avoiding the physical discomfort, emotional strain, and social isolation of physical and functional decline. In so doing society continues to steam away from the more fundamental issues of dying and the ongoing need to care for all our dying fellows.

If the course of American culture is to change, it will do so slowly as the underlying knowledge, values, attitudes, and expectations of its citizens mature and as they begin to look at new horizons. Direction must shift toward recognizing that dying is a time of inherent importance and potential value within the life of an individual. Furthermore, both the caring professions and the general public must recognize that care for the dying is a fundamental responsibility that human beings have toward one another. Such responsibility is part of the basic fabric of community and, by extension, it is an integral part of what makes people human. In shirking that responsibility society shakes its very foundation and places itself in peril.

I believe that the problems of care for the dying would dissolve if, as a national community, we could perceive how simple and straightforward are the alternatives. The stories in *All Kinds of Love* highlight what is possible: Care that delivers on a commitment to provide comfort. Care that allows the person control over his decisions and life. Care that is genuine, loving, and unabashed. Care that is creative.

So often mention is made that in years gone by people died at home, surrounded by family and their closest friends. In this nostalgic vision, dying was known and not so frightening. *All Kinds of Love* provides contemporary examples of care to look at and learn from, wholesome images that are real and relevant to all of us today.

The core deficit that is preventing America from effectively dealing with the crisis of end-of-life care is a lack of imagination. As ethereal as that may seem, the imagination to which I refer is a concrete, requisite step toward effective change. Whether we are hospice professionals or family members of the person dying, our ability to help the person to die well turns on our ability to imagine a positive outcome that incorporates the fact of his progressive decline and ultimate demise.

By helping our culture imagine how things can be different, *All Kinds of Love* offers a point on the compass toward which we can direct our efforts. This book contributes to the critical re-storying of America with tales of people in the authentic, human act of dying. In the stories it tells and the humanity it reveals, *All Kinds of Love* will prove as valuable as the most heavily funded, scientifically exacting research. It deserves to become course material for public and clinical education at all levels. Through the stories it tells, aspects of symptomatology, ethics, and psychosocial intervention can be explored.

It would be inaccurate to say that *All Kinds of Love* is simply a book about dying. It is also a book about the courage and commitment of families and friends. It is about care that goes beyond management of symptoms, care that is imaginative and nurtures personal opportunity at the end of life. And it is about the uniquely human emotions of honor and celebration.

To all who honor the full breadth and depth of human life, the publication of *All Kinds of Love* is, itself, cause for celebration.

Acknowledgments

Our project never would have been completed without the Hospice of Metro Denver (HMD), the program which motivated and generated this book. We are indebted to HMD; it deserves the respect and admiration we give it.

Our deep and real gratitude toward the patients and their families who live in this book is best expressed by our hope that the stories may provoke thought and give insight, strength and inspiration to others who face life-threatening illness, either in their families or as professionals serving those families.

There are many who have willingly aided us with their counsel and support. We thank them with great feeling, for they strengthened us and our work by their participation.

Dr. Earl A. Grollman provided the initial encouragement we needed to get the project rolling, and he did it unselfishly. We are indebted to him in a special way.

Another inspiring supporter was Ira R. Byock, M.D., who graciously agreed to write the preface for this book. He has lived the experiences described in these stories himself, and he responded with understanding which bouyed our spirits. We thank him for his generosity.

Alan S. Feiner, M.D., has provided a special quality of support in patient care which has enriched us and must be recognized in this book.

Much appreciated technical assistance was given freely by Perry Dole, Rabbi Grollman, Sandy Kuka, R.N., William Lamers, M.D., Edward Myers, Lori Odom, M.D., Joanne Pearson, P.N.P., and Robert Weisser. Warren Hamilton and

Ralph Hansen assisted us by cajoling a recalcitrant computer and printing the manuscript, providing essential help when we needed it.

The Hospice of Metro Denver, Hope Hospice in Fort Myers, Florida, and Samira Beckwith in particular, the Community Hospice of the Roaring Fork Valley in Aspen, Colorado, and Marie Butler, Marie Brown and Lou Cunningham in particular, Barry Mink, M.D., and Jackie Mastrangelo and John Freeman, M.D. of the Orthopedic Associates of Aspen have graciously helped us locate references and literature and encouraged us in many ways, and we thank them.

Our readers did much to shape our project into what it is today. We want to thank Barbara Aiton, Ruth Arent Anderson, Alice Demi, D.N.Sc., Alicita Hamilton, Deborah Hoffman, Gail Holstein, Joseph Kordick, Dottie Lamm, Bernie Lane, Nicky Mead, Louann Miller, Barbara Raizen, Esther Shapiro, Ph.D., Roswitha Smale, the generous, talented and hardworking members of the Island Writers on Sanibel Island, Florida, and the writers' workshop in Aspen, Colorado, the Aspen Writers' Conference, and our children, Mindy Jaffe, Rabbi Evan Jaffe, Richard Ehrlich, Gloria Ehrlich, and Peter Ehrlich, who read and commented on parts of the manuscript at one of its many stages.

We are grateful for critiques done by Betty Anholt, Bruce Berger, Karen Chamberlain, Ted Conover, and Barbara Schoichet. Their expertise helped us over some stumbling blocks, and Karen Chamberlain in particular lent her considerable talent and a great deal of time because she believed in the project. We lack words to thank each one of them.

Our editor, John Morgan, has been our friend; we have valued his support and ideas which have strengthened the book. Bobbi Olszewski from Baywood Publishing has been a jewel with her production help.

To our husbands, Marvin Jaffe, M.D. and Max Ehrlich, goes our greatest appreciation. They understood, and their support never flagged. *All Kinds of Love* holds a large chunk of theirs.

Table of Contents

Hospice Is . . .*

- A professional holistic care service to patients with terminal illness and their families. Hospice service can be given at home or in a dedicated hospice program within a hospital or nursing home (usually on a separate floor or in a separate wing), or in a free-standing hospice facility.
- Care that is based on an attitude of acceptance of death as a part of life.
- Care that is guided by the patient and his or her goals rather than by others' rules or prescriptions.
- Care that preserves dignity and is given with respect and compassion. It is the outcome of warm human relationships between the care providers and the patient and family.
- A caring, dedicated effort to encourage the patient and his[1] family to recognize and express their feelings about dying, both before and after death.
- Care that uses a creative flexible approach to control of distressing symptoms (especially pain) and whatever other problems the patient and family may encounter.

---

*This description is that of the authors and not an official statement of any organization.

[1] We believe in and support the equality of men and women. However, we ask our readers to please accept the outdated "he, him, and his" when it appears in our writing, reflecting either or both genders. We use these words rather than gender-free language in order to avoid distracting from our essential message for the sake of another, important as that one is.

- A program that provides liaison between the family and all the professionals and agencies involved, so the family doesn't have to manage everything alone.
- Care provided by a team which may include physician, registered nurse, nurse's aide, home health aide, family counselor, chaplain, nutritionist, therapists, and volunteers.

Introduction

Carolyn Jaffe
with Carol H. Ehrlich

Retirement beckons me. After fifty-one years of nursing, I should be thinking of taking a rest. My hair is white, and although my will to work continues, my body has begun to resist. Soon I will retire—but first I have a mission.

For the past twenty-one years I've been deeply involved in hospice. I worked for two years to start the first hospice program in Denver. During the nineteen years since then I've been a primary-care nurse in that program. Before I retire I want to share with you what I have learned—about the end of life, families and hospice. I want you to know so that one day, if you choose, you may enrich your lives—or your friends' or your patients'—with the help of hospice. That is my mission.

You probably already know that hospice is a support system for persons facing death and loss. I hope that, through the stories in this book, the lives of my patients and their families will help you understand what hospice really means. You can experience in them the transformation hospice produces in lives and memories when death comes, as it must to everyone.

I learned the value of hospice the hard way. Earlier, I had been a nurse in a hospital intensive care unit where death visited often. For many years there I watched patients, families, and staff professionals fight desperately for life, adapting even in the worst of circumstances to the accepted definitions of life=success, death=failure. When a patient recovered, the staff and family celebrated. When it was clear the patient would die, we all saw and felt the failure.

None of us on the staff could cope with that sense of failure, especially when it happened over and over. We backed off. We told ourselves if the patients could not be saved, there was little more we could do for them. We cut back our commitment and care, reserving our energies for the patients who might recover. (WE meant everyone in the health-care system, not just the nurses. WE included doctors, nurses, and allied health professionals.) Failure—impending death—most often meant the patient and family were abandoned to manage alone the best they could.

The hospice view is different. We revere life, all of it. We accept dying as part of life. Hospice programs continue nursing care, help in the home, and most important, emotional support through the dying and bereavement period. We guide our families through the time of dying so they can face the unknown, and feel the solace of acceptance, completion, and farewell. We help them to find new meaning in the patient's last days. Hospice can be a rich blessing to any of us when life draws to a close.

For this book my friend, Carol, and I have selected stories from the more than 600 patients and families I have been privileged to serve, and from a couple of patients my colleagues in hospice have nursed. (For the sake of simplicity we have used "Janice Miller" as the nurse's name in all stories.) We have disguised these patients, changed their names, and combined some of their experiences in order to show you the variety of ways hospice can help and the values hospice brings. Therefore these stories are, in a sense, constructed; however, they are about real people and real events, not fiction.

We have deliberately not written our book in a series of clinical reports, which would have been once removed from our readers, but rather in a way that will allow you to be right there, inside the stories. We want you to engage, to be privy to the thoughts and feelings of each person—to feel them as they did— to see and hear—to know what they knew. Whenever possible, we have used their own words drawn directly from the context of events. Where conversations were created, they are faithful to the spirit of the persons and events and what I knew about them. They are authentic. We hope you can lose yourself in the stories and live them yourselves, for then you will know under the skin what hospice is all about.

While the stories contained in this volume don't pretend to describe the activity of every hospice in the land, they do reflect the core philosophy and effort of the hospice movement. Some programs may be more fully expressed, some less, depending on resources and circumstance, but the essence is the same. They are hospice.

We have chosen to follow the stories with Notes containing information about some of the issues raised in the stories. The information in some cases relates the history or current controversies about these issues; it also fleshes out facts about and interpretations of the issues. We offer this not as a complete or comprehensive discussion, for to do that would require many volumes, but as a broad screening of solid information that will be helpful to practitioners, volunteers, and families alike. We hope our work will advance a healthier view of death and dying and a broader understanding of hospice than currently exists in this country. We hope you will find it both illuminating and useful.

CHAPTER 1

All Kinds of Love

Each new patient referred to me offers a new challenge. Will he present problems I can handle? Will I be able to help?

The tools I bring to my assignment start with an open mind. I must accept the new person as he is—not judge him, not assume anything that pigeon-holes him. I have learned the hard way how mistaken I can be. Preconceptions can ruin any chance for a good supportive relationship to grow.

Even though all human beings have the same basic needs and feelings, we are all very different. The patients I see have their own ways of dealing with what they want and need. They talk differently. They smile or don't smile. They complain or keep their feelings inside.

There's a staggering variety of backgrounds out there. I can't make judgments about what people are like, or what they mean by the way they act—not unless they grew up in my own family. Even then I wouldn't bet a lot on it. So I start out fresh every time. When I meet a new patient he's a unique, special person, and we go from there.

One thing I know for sure. Bright or dull, rich or poor, eccentric or normal, beautiful or ugly—all people need love and understanding, and want to give it in return. Each one has his own way of expressing this. There are all kinds of love.

AGGIE

"I'll cook up some spuds 'n hot dogs, howzzat?" Ray stood at the kitchen sink, turning to look through the doorway at his

5

sister who lay propped against a cushion on the sofa in the next room. Broad ladder-like shadows from the old venetian blinds in the window striped a path across a faded floral carpet to the end of the sofa, dimming the brightness of the late afternoon western sun entering the room.

"Yeah, okay." Aggie yelled back, never looking away from the TV. For her, eating was just a necessary part of living, one she managed for the most part on the job. She was a bus-girl at the local cafeteria, and the short-order type of meals her brother prepared on the weekends failed to attract her interest. She waved off a fly buzzing around her face, and remained engrossed in the wrestling match she was watching.

Aggie Gerhard, plain and wide of face and body and simple in tastes, and Ray, hard-working and leathery-skinned with a premature stoop to his shoulders, had only each other as they approached middle age. Neither had ever married. They shared the small dingy house and the uninspired meals Ray was able to cook, suffering from a steady diet of greasy fried foods, without motivation or knowledge to change to something better.

Outsiders could not tell how much support they received from each other. Neither one spoke very often; they saved their words for elementary messages about the essentials of daily living. Television programs filled the void, and even they were limited to soaps, and sometimes sports. World and local news, books and ideas were not the stuff of their existence.

For twenty years since their last parent died they had lived this way—dreary, perhaps, to the outside observer, but dependable and acceptable to them who had known nothing else. They neither looked forward to change nor imagined what change there might be. At eleven o'clock every morning, five days a week, Aggie trudged off to the cafeteria in her starched white shirt and black pants, returning after eight in the evening, tired and footsore, but unlamenting. Ray worked the evening shift at a cross-town service station, sleeping then, often without removing the day's accumulation of dirt, from midnight until eight o'clock. Their lives meshed during breakfast, weekends, and their occasional matching days off.

The notable and solitary drama in Aggie's life was her Elvis fantasy, lived out with a surprising collection of memorabilia from "The King's" career. A scrapbook of newspaper clippings, most of his records, including some originals which she prized but never played, an almost new poster she had purchased at a garage sale three years earlier, a wide assortment of busts and full-length Elvis liquor bottles on some shelves next to the TV, and every issue of an Elvis Presley fan club newsletter since it began in 1958: these were the symbols of romance that provided her few moments of magic in an otherwise humdrum life. What she did with these treasures when she disappeared into her bedroom was known to her alone, and the secret would likely die with her. Aggie had neither the skills nor the inclination to communicate, even with Ray, with whom she had shared a home for the entire forty-two years of her life.

Plain as Aggie was, she was a flower compared to her brother. Short, square, with an over-large head carried at a forward tilting angle and shoulders bent forward to support it, he could only be described as brutish-looking. Worse, odd dark-colored lumps stood out wherever his skin was visible, making him appear diseased and ugly. Seeing him produced shock, even after repeated encounters. Only Aggie could have known his simple goodness. He was her brother and she was incapable of seeing him solely as a physical image. In fact, it is doubtful she saw the image at all. He was her family, dull and devoid of conversation, but dependable and good to her. They relied equally on each other for stability in their lives.

Their routine was interrupted in the spring of her forty-third year when a pain in Aggie's right leg, first mild and eventually intense, forced her to seek help. Some months earlier she had slipped from a step-stool, falling against some bricks stacked against the kitchen wall. She assumed the pain was simply the result of the bruise from that fall. The clinic at City Hospital found she had a malignant tumor.

The tumor was excised and a course of radiation therapy completed, and Aggie tried to resume her work. The pain returned, however, and she had to give up her job.

No longer bound by her work-a-day schedule, she spent most of her waking hours on the living room sofa, TV blaring amidst the clutter and dust of months of housekeeping neglect.

Ray did nothing to clear the grease from the kitchen or the pop and beer cans from the growing heap in the corner of the porch, but he provided her care. He saw that she had food to eat, and when she needed to go to the clinic, he took her there. He would hoist her arm around his neck as he did this day, and half-carry her to his relic of a car, spilling her the best he could into the passenger seat. Once at the clinic he would repeat the procedure, getting her in to see the doctor.

Aggie carried a plastic-coated card to identify herself at each clinic visit. It was a help. She didn't have to sign in, which would have required the laborious writing of her name, address, phone number, and "None" where the form requested insurance information. The card did it all for her. This day the admissions supervisor was called when Aggie's lack of insurance was noted, and upon learning she had no source of income, he shook his head. He promised to come back to the desk for her when the doctor finished his examination.

She was wheeled down the hall to the out-patient clinic and told to wait until her name was called. An X-ray orderly eventually came for her, and her leg was filmed.

The resident physician in oncology studied her X-rays. He scowled, then called the chief resident. "Looks bad. What do you think?"

The chief resident pursed her lips, measured some shadows on the X-ray and sighed. "It's growing fast. We better get it right away."

"Yeah."

The two doctors considered Aggie's options, then the chief resident spoke. "That leg has to go. Too much risk any other way. D'you want me to tell her?"

"No . . . I will. We'll schedule the first opening they have in the OR. I'll call the clerk. Thanks." He picked up the phone to call the orthopedic operating room. The chief resident turned and left.

The young doctor went to see Aggie in the examining room. She sat on the table, head bent down resting on her fists, her straggly dishwater-colored hair hanging limply on her neck.

"Are you here alone, Ms. Gerhard?"

Aggie looked up. "No, Ray's here. He's out there watching TV." She pointed in the general direction of the hospital lobby.

A nurse went to get Ray. He followed her back and slouched into a chair near the examining table on which Aggie sat. The resident stood over them and began to lay out his ominous findings and recommendations.

"Your sister's tumor has begun to grow again," he said, looking narrowly at Ray, "and with her history and the location of the new growth, we now expect it to grow faster. I do not believe radiation treatment will stop it. We must keep it from spreading into the rest of her body."

The doctor shifted his weight and cleared his throat. "There is only one answer, and there's no good way to put it." His eyes suddenly focused on the floor. "We must amputate her leg."

Ray paled. The lumps on his skin stood out in stark relief. Aggie, listening from her position as a forced outsider, had become angry as the physician spoke exclusively to her brother. With this news she flushed beet-red.

"In a pig's eye, you must!"

The resident's attention jerked to her. He stared, his mouth hanging open. For a moment no one breathed.

"You heard me. Nobody's takin' my leg off. No way!"

"But you will surely die . . ."

"So I'll die. I'll die with my boots on." With that she swung herself around to a sitting position and addressed her brother.

"C'mon Ray. Get me home."

Ray blinked twice and rose to his feet. He looked quickly at the doctor, then without a word raised Aggie's arm around his neck, hoisted her off the examining table and half-carried her through the doorway. The dumbfounded resident stared after them, papers in his outstretched hand, watching in disbelief as the two made their way toward the exit.

The admissions supervisor had been waiting for Aggie. Wheelchair in tow, he made a beeline to the main entrance before she and Ray could escape, and with authority stopped them to move Aggie into the chair. In seconds he wheeled her off to his cubicle near the business office. Uncomprehending, Ray stood stock-still in his grease-darkened work clothes and watched Aggie disappear.

"Now, I need to ask you some questions so we can do something about your bills, Miss Gerhard. How do you live? Where does your money come from?"

Aggie appeared not to hear him. Still angry at the young doctor, she couldn't switch her mind from the events in the examining room. Her adrenalin raced; it was hard to concentrate on the questions. "I used to bus tables at Green's Cafeteria before I got the tumor," she finally managed.

"And now?"

"Ray buys the food 'n' stuff."

"How did you pay the hospital when the tumor was removed?"

"I didn't."

The supervisor placed both hands on his desk and pushed himself away, his jaw tight. He went into the business office and pulled Aggie's record up on the computer screen. Upon seeing the numbers, he swore under his breath. Nothing had been paid on her bill—ever. He went back to his cubicle where she sat staring at the wall.

"Ah. . . ." He stopped, eyed her coolly, then started again. "Miss Gerhard, has anyone ever spoken to you about Medicaid?"

"What's that?"

The supervisor squirmed, then settled back into his chair.

He proceeded to describe the rules and requirements of the Medicaid program, often confusing Aggie with technical jargon and long complex sentences. She finally grasped the idea that with her lack of money, she could get public support for her medical care.

"That's great." She half-smiled. "They'll pay for everything?"

"No, Miss Gerhard, you still don't quite get the picture." His voice rose a notch, and he spoke through a tight obligatory smile. "We have to fill out some application papers, and there is usually quite a long wait before the application is approved. If it's approved, then Medicaid will pay. In the meantime we must work out some arrangements for paying the old bills and any more you get until your application is approved."

An hour later Aggie was wheeled out to the lobby where Ray waited, watching television. The application had been filed, and she had a copy of her hospital bill in hand, reduced from $31,600 to $1,500 by the formula the hospital used for indigent patients. It was left to Aggie and Ray to find a way to pay off the amount she still owed.

The two of them went home in silence. They couldn't comprehend all that had happened. Hearing the doctor say Aggie's leg should be amputated, then learning they had to pay $1,500 to the hospital, left them in shock. Amputation was unthinkable, and the debt was much larger than their supply of unassigned money allowed. They had no way to deal with the events of this day.

The one thing Aggie understood was that following some unknown waiting period Medicaid would pay her bills. She and Ray passed the hospital statements back and forth between them uncertainly that evening, folding and unfolding the papers. Ray finally stuffed them into a kitchen drawer. "Medicaid's gonna pay," Aggie stated simply. "Medicaid's gonna pay." With that she went to bed.

It took almost a month for the clinic system to catch up with Aggie. An energetic woman in sensible low-heeled shoes appeared at the door one morning and was greeted by Ray, dressed in rumpled pajamas. The smells of burnt bacon, coffee, and an unventilated sickroom wafted out with him as he opened the door and stood silently examining the visitor.

"I'm Betty Sanderson, a social worker from the clinic at City Hospital. The doctor asked me to talk with your sister. May I come in?"

Ray did nothing to set the woman at ease. His dull expression, hunched posture, and total silence menaced rather than aided her. Finally he stood aside for her to enter. Once inside, she waited for him to point the way to Aggie, which he did with a minimal nod of his head.

After introducing herself, Miss Sanderson tried to determine how much Aggie understood about the condition of her leg and the serious implications of rejecting amputation. It was a one-sided conversation. Aggie had neither the ability to grasp the arguments Miss Sanderson faced her with nor the desire to respond. She had only one position. No one was going to cut her leg off. There was no point in discussing it.

Miss Sanderson gave up after twenty minutes. She rose from her chair, casting a distressed look down at the uncooperative client on the sofa, and turned toward the door. "I'll be back next week. I'm leaving a phone number where you can reach me." With an economy of words and movement, she was gone.

Aggie put the visit out of her mind, and it was with some effort that she recalled the conversation when Miss Sanderson returned a week later. It was like starting over again.

"Have you had a chance to reconsider your decision, Aggie?"

"Yeah, and no one's gonna take my leg off." Aggie's face was haggard. She had been suffering worse pain, and was in no mood to go over the subject again.

"The doctor will be very disappointed." Miss Sanderson fished in her briefcase for a card, letting out a resigned sigh. "However, you should have a plan to get some help. This card has the name of a hospice; they can provide it. Don't lose the card, because you're not going to be able to take care of yourself. And your brother can't do it alone." Her lips were a grim line in an otherwise expressionless face as she let herself out the door.

Within a month that advice had to be put to use. Ray dialed the hospice phone number, reading from the social worker's card he dug out of the junk drawer in the kitchen. He was nervous and frightened. He couldn't stand watching Aggie suffer. He felt awkward and uncomfortable helping her bathe and dress. Aggie's problems overwhelmed him. He was forced to call hospice for help.

Aggie and her care were referred to me.

Ray was out when I arrived. After ringing several times I pushed the front door open and called. "Hellooo!" From the interior I heard Aggie yell back, "Come in."

Aggie lay on the sofa in the living room, head and shoulders elevated on a soiled cushion so she could see the TV. The dried remains of her breakfast lay on dishes next to her on the floor. I moved them and pulled a chair up to her side so I could face

her at eye level. "I'm Janice Miller. I'll be your hospice nurse."
I reached out to shake hands. She made no effort to respond.

"I'm here to help you, Miss Gerhard, but first I want to see
how you're doing. Then I must learn what you need from me." I
clipped a history form into my board and uncapped my pen.
"Now—I have some questions. Then I'll look at your leg."

Aggie waited silently. I began my assessment. To each of my
questions Aggie responded in monosyllables, offering nothing
more. The exam and interview, as I wrote in the chart, revealed
"a middle-aged woman with remarkable loss of muscle tone and
an enlarged right thigh. She says little, won't look at me directly,
doesn't seem disturbed about me or exam. Watchful, but not
hostile or upset." I wondered how long it would take to be able
to communicate with her.

When I concluded my work, Aggie volunteered her only comment beyond the limited responses she had been obliged to
make. She said it with some pride. "I'm gonna get Medicaid.
Medicaid's gonna pay."

I nodded. "Thank you for telling me, Aggie."

Aggie never did look at me, but there was a shy smug smile
on her face as I stood up to leave.

"I have to go now, but I'll be back tomorrow. I'm going to
bring a home health aide with me so we can give you a boost
with some of the household chores. That'll help. Is there anything you want before I leave?"

Aggie just shook her head.

Feeling a tacky pull on the soles of my shoes with each
step as I moved to the kitchen sink to wash my hands, I already
knew of one task that was long overdue. The aide might not
be thrilled, but she was going to start by washing the kitchen
floor.

As it turned out, both Jenny, a sturdy cheerful home health
aide, and Elizabeth, a more mature composed volunteer who
ran the finance committee on our Board of Directors, accompanied me the next day. Jenny made a quick inventory of the
refrigerator and cupboards, then headed for the store. Aggie
needed some decent food. It fell to Elizabeth to wash the floor. I
held my breath, wondering how she would react. I didn't need

to worry. She smiled at me and moved to the kitchen to carry out her task, a momentary hesitation her only visible sign that this work was unaccustomed.

We three women became frequent visitors in the Gerhards' home. We were an eclectic trio, Jenny just emerging into her twenties, muscular and plain-spoken, Elizabeth middle-aged, tall and slim and always poised, and I, a white-haired and more ordinary, but determined woman. Each of us followed a different schedule, so usually only one of us was there at a time. Ray admitted us readily when we arrived, but quickly made himself scarce. Aggie didn't object to our coming. Although she had little to say, and was reluctant even to look at us, her shy attempts to cooperate when we fussed over her suggested it was all right for us to be there.

I gave Aggie large amounts of medication for her pain, which grew as the days went by. Elizabeth, an incongruous new part of the household in her smart flannel blazers and slacks, was moved at seeing this suffering but stoic woman lie hour after hour watching the television. She showed up one day with a gift.

The gift was totally unexpected; it changed Aggie's life. I watched her that day when it came. Her eyes widened as Elizabeth entered the room.

Elizabeth held out toward her a tiger-striped short-haired cat. She set it down and the cat picked its way daintily around the perimeter of the room, sniffing and scratching as it went. Finally it reached the sofa on which Aggie lay. There it stopped, arched its back and rubbed against the rough brown and tan-striped upholstery. Elizabeth withdrew to the kitchen to prepare a litter box she had brought along with her.

Silently Aggie watched the cat, then inched her hand down toward its back. A small slow smile formed on her face. The cat purred. Under the curve of Aggie's hand it moved, warm and smooth, back and forth. Elizabeth held her breath, watching through the kitchen doorway.

The cat paused, turned several complete circles as it looked around, then headed through the door to the litter box. Aggie watched with interest, and when it lowered its haunches she let out a chuckle. "He knows where to piss—would y'look at that!"

Elizabeth turned to me and smiled.

The weeks went by and Aggie's condition gradually worsened. At frequent intervals she reminded me, "Medicaid's gonna pay." It was important to her, not being a dead-beat.

"That'll be fine," I tried to reassure her. "Don't worry about it now. Everything is taken care of."

Fortunately, hospice has a fund to help take care of people when they can't pay. We have an annual campaign for contributions for this purpose. In any event, since Aggie was unable to do anything about her financial problems, there was no reason to let her worry.

In rereading the chart one day, I discovered that Aggie's forty-third birthday was approaching. I mentioned it to Jenny. "Let's have a birthday party for her," she exclaimed. "I'll bet she's never had one in her whole life!"

Elizabeth and Jenny worked on the party preparations, and good-hearted Ray put up balloons and crepe paper before going to work the night before the party. For Aggie, he would have done anything we asked.

"I let myself in at eight o'clock and tiptoed to the sofa," Jenny told me later the next day. "Aggie was awake, so I sang 'Happy Birthday' to her. She kind of jumped, and got all red in the face, and you know that funny little smile of hers?"

I nodded, remembering.

"She lay there with her mouth crooked up on one side like she does, and when I finished singing, all she could say was 'Is this my birthday?' Yes, I told her, and I started to laugh. She seemed more embarrassed than anything. I probably shouldn't have laughed, so I leaned over and squeezed her face between my hands and said 'You're wonderful, Aggie.' She smiled again."

At noon Ray, Elizabeth, and I arrived with flowers, tuna salad, birthday cake, and ice cream, and repeated the song. While Aggie ate little and remained quiet amid the gaiety, we knew by the gleam in her eyes that she was touched.

Then for the first time since her hospice care began, Aggie opened up. She talked about herself. We listened, fascinated. She spoke haltingly.

"Ray takes good care of me. I remember one time he even taught me to use a gun."

Someone gasped. "A gun! Whatever for?"

"When I worked at the cafeteria I had to walk home at night. Sometimes guys'd drive by, and they'd slow down and yell at me. Once they stopped and got out of the car, and I got scared and ran all the way home. I told Ray. He said I should carry a gun. So we got one, and he taught me how to shoot it."

"Did you ever have to use it?" Jenny's eyes were riveted on Aggie.

"Well, sort of. I mean, I didn't really shoot it. See, these two guys stopped me one night, and they were givin' me the business. And I pulled the gun out and pointed it at 'em." She stuck her forefinger out, waving it back and forth at the remembered hoodlums. "I said, 'Which one of you motherfuckers wants it first?' and, boy, you shoulda' seen 'em run!" She let out a quick laugh from deep in her throat. "They never bothered me again."

Not one of us knew what to say. We sat there, speechless, until Elizabeth had the presence of mind to go to the kitchen to get the ice cream.

One day in the middle of summer the mailman, whose deliveries to the household were generally limited to junk mail, knocked on the door and handed Ray a large envelope. It carried an official state government insignia, and was addressed in typewritten characters to Aggie.

Jenny told me she had to read the letter to her several times since it was in formal and rather technical language. Finally Aggie began to smile. It was, of course, the approval of her Medicaid funding for which she had waited with such anticipation. It was a vindication of her promises, a reward for her trust. It was the means by which she would avoid the humiliation of being a charity case. Jenny said Aggie could hardly contain herself until I arrived that afternoon.

"It came! It came!" she crowed, waving the envelope weakly at me when I walked through the door. "I told you Medicaid'd pay!" She absolutely beamed.

"That's great, Aggie. That's just super. We knew you'd get it, didn't we?" I gave her a little hug.

Taking weekly measurements of Aggie's thigh, I watched its girth increase. It reached forty-five inches around, much larger than her trunk, and she could no longer move to the bathroom or into her bed at night. I brought in a commode from hospice supplies and set it next to the sofa.

"Ray," I explained when he awakened that afternoon, "The fluid is building up more in Aggie's leg. Walking is too hard for her now. She can stay on the sofa." Ray looked soberly at me. I continued, "I brought in a commode so she won't have to move to the bathroom. I'll need you to empty the commode when you are alone with her, and Jenny or I will bathe her right here."

"She's getting worse, huh?" His eyes opened wide.

"Yes, Ray," I said as gently as I could. "We're going to make another change, too. Remember I taught you to inject the morphine into the top side of her leg, above the tumor?" Ray nodded. "We can't do that any more. The fluid pressure in her leg won't let the medicine in. From now on, I want you to give her shots either in the other leg or in one of her arms. Come. I'll show you."

Ray followed me and watched silently as I selected a site on Aggie's arm and administered the morphine injection. When I finished, he turned and walked back to the kitchen. Beads of perspiration covered his upper lip.

One day late in the summer the skin covering the swollen thigh cracked open, and from then on Jenny and I had to keep it covered with sterile dressings. The pus oozing from her leg smelled bad. At the same time, her appetite disappeared. The more wasted her body became, the larger her leg grew.

I was scheduled to leave on a three week vacation trip. I knew there was little chance Aggie would still be alive when I returned, and while she had given no sign that she wanted to talk about her inevitable fate, I had to let her know I cared. So I stayed longer on my last day. I pulled a chair up to the sofa and sat down.

"Aggie, I have to be gone for three weeks, and I've arranged for another nurse to come in my place. She'll take good care of you." I reached for her hand.

"I'm going to miss you, my dear. Just in case we won't have a chance to talk again, I want you to know I'm glad I've known you." Aggie pulled her hand back. "You have courage and strength, and I admire you," I continued, trying hard to make her understand. "You're a special person. I want you to remember that—will you?" I reached forward to give her a hug. Aggie said nothing, the expression on her face closed, dull. I couldn't know whether she received the love I was trying to send.

I left. I thought often of Aggie while I was traveling. I even shopped for a gift for her, hoping there would still be time to give it.

The night I returned I called Jenny. "Has Aggie died, Jenny?"

"No, and you better watch out," Jenny warned. "Aggie's mad at you. Oooee! Is she mad at you!"

"Good heavens! What on earth for?"

"You thought she was going to die, and that made her furious. She made sure she didn't die while you were gone. Nobody was going to set her time before she was ready!"

Early the next morning I drove out to see Aggie, fearing I'd be met by a tempest. I rang the bell, opened the door and called. There was no answer. I went in. Aggie was stretched out on the sofa, looking straight ahead. She said nothing, but I could tell what she was thinking. "You were wrong, dammit—I didn't die" was written all over her face.

I reached for her hand. She withdrew it. I reached again. This time she allowed me to touch her.

"I was wrong, Aggie."

She sniffed.

"I'm glad you're still here. I brought you something."

Aggie let her glance move to my hands in which I held a bright Israeli scarf. She sniffed again. I unfolded the scarf and laid it around her emaciated shoulders. Neither of us said a word. I can never be sure I was forgiven.

I came to see Aggie on each of the next three days, each time describing her deterioration in the chart. Then Ray called me about two o'clock the following morning.

"Janice, I give her the morphine shots like you showed me, but she still hurts awful bad. I need help. You think you could come over?"

I was there in twenty minutes. Ray peered anxiously at me in the doorway. "I give her the last shot an hour'na half ago."

"You did fine, Ray." Although Aggie wasn't due for it, I went to her and prepared another injection. It was the only relief available. Ray hovered over us as I shot the morphine into her arm.

Then Ray and I pulled chairs up to the sofa and sat with Aggie, Ray at her head and I beside him. I took Aggie's hand. I wanted to reassure both of them.

"We're here, Aggie. We've given you more medicine, and it will make you comfortable. . . . We'll stay with you. Lie very still and just breathe in the quiet."

Aggie closed her eyes and seemed calmer for a time, then moved restlessly in the confining sofa. Ray sat bolt upright, vigilance in his face. She shifted her shoulders and arms several times, then was quiet again.

After half an hour, Aggie looked at me, a question in her eyes. "You are coming close to the end of all the pain, Aggie. You are coming close to death, and it is your friend. Soon you'll be at peace, with no more hurting and no more problems. Ray is going to be all right. He's here with you, and he wants you to relax."

Ray reached out and touched Aggie's shoulder, and she half-smiled. Gradually her tension eased. Soon she was still, looking more comfortable. As she quieted, her breathing slowed and her color became more gray than pink.

After a time her breathing changed. No longer deep and slow, it became shallow and rapid. Ray breathed in tandem. He moved tensely in his seat. Aggie's gray color darkened. It was apparent she was near death. Her pulse was weak and sporadic.

"Is she . . . gone?" Ray's voice was hoarse.

Aggie took two or three breaths, and he knew the answer. For another hour Aggie repeated this pattern, a breath or two or three and then a minute's pause. Another breath, another pause.

Aggie's hands and arms had become cold to the touch, her fingernails blue. She stopped breathing for what seemed an eternity, then gave one final small gasp with a long drawn-out release of air. Her body relaxed. A peaceful look came into her face.

Ray held his breath, continuing to stare at her. "She's going . . . she's leaving. I can feel her. . . ." Ray's face was filled with awe. He spoke without seeming to realize what he said. He sat there, gazing at her for a long time. I did nothing to break the silence.

Then I leaned over and kissed Aggie. Ray had been almost immobile, watching Aggie die. With my action he came alive, free to touch his sister. He reached for her hand, then put his rough fingertips to her cheek, awkwardly at first, then with more ease. I left them alone and went to the kitchen to call Aggie's doctor and the coroner.

Ray was in the same position when I returned. I reached out and touched him. "She's at peace, Ray. You were so kind and good to her. You took fine care of her so she could be in her own home, with her own things. That meant a lot to her. . . ." I waited, but he didn't stir. I continued. "She knew you loved her. What a wonderful brother and friend you've been!" Ray still didn't move.

"Would you like to get in touch with any friends to tell them Aggie has died?"

He leaned back and sighed, shook his head, and continued to sit where he was.

"The funeral director will be coming soon. I need to do some things here, Ray. Why don't you go fix a cup of coffee?"

At last he left. I cleaned Aggie and dressed her in a fresh gown. Soon the funeral director arrived. Ray helped move his sister from the worn sofa to the gurney on which she would be moved. Then, a bleak expression on his mottled face, he watched the man wheel his sister out.

When I finished clearing the sickroom paraphernalia, I found him back in the kitchen, staring out the window, stroking Cat in his arms.

"I'm going now, Ray." He turned to me, and I laid my hand on his arm. "You've been a good brother to Aggie, and you'll always have that to remember. She loved you.

"It's going to be hard for a while. I want you to call me or the other people at hospice if you want to talk, or if you just want to be with someone. We're there for you. And I'll call you in a few days. Take good care of yourself."

He nodded, and a small grunt escaped his lips. He reached out and for a quick second put one arm around me. I hugged him, then turned to leave.

The last thing I saw as I walked to the door was Aggie's sofa, a permanent and deep sag down its middle, a small Elvis liquor bottle bust poking out of one corner and the Israeli scarf draped across the back.

NOTES:
Unique Hospice Team; Relating to Families

Aggie and Ray's experience with her illness and death varied strikingly from what it might have been as the low-income citizens they were, recipients of health care under public indigent and low-income care systems. Indeed, it varied markedly from the experience of many families, whatever their income, who spend their final weeks or months in and out of hospitals and nursing homes, receiving the care deemed by medical authorities to be what they need. Income is not the critical factor. The dramatic difference exists because hospice care is unique among health-care delivery systems.

What makes hospice different from all other care can be specified only in part. Ask any patient or family who has known true hospice care after experiencing other forms of health care, or ask any member of a hospice team who has had prior work in a hospital, nursing home, visiting nurse, or home nursing setting, and the answer will be vehement, perhaps awe-struck. You will be given a variety of answers; these people will describe different constellations of happenings, but they will all agree that hospice has a special remarkable quality not available in any other venue.

Hospice is comfort care, not care for cure. Hospice care is patient-centered. The voice that counts belongs to that patient, not to the physician or nurse, as in the medical model. The patient chooses his or her path for the days, weeks, or months of remaining life. This much is known about hospice, and can be stated in so many words.

What is more difficult to describe in a sentence or two is the nature of the care and why it is that way; why it is so special.

The answer is bound up in two concepts. One is a holistic perspective, the other a dedicated, ongoing team. The two concepts are tightly interwoven. The whole patient and his family are the focus, that is, the patient's physical being and his and his family's psychosocial selves and spiritual selves, not just the patient's body—or worse, body part. This comprehensive focus changes the nature of care entirely. The person and his significant others are affirmed as whole human beings of value for whom the care is given.

Hospice care encompasses the patient's physical concerns: pain, infection, fatigue, sleeplessness, dizziness, nausea, inability to eat or swallow, shortness of breath and trouble breathing, stomach cramps, uncontrollable diarrhea, or any other distressing symptoms that can arise. It encompasses his capacity for activities of daily living, and the family's health around him. It takes in the patient's and family's psychosocial needs for support. It includes an awareness of and response to their yearning for an uplift of the spirit, for meaning from their lives and the dying they are experiencing. Hospice care is all of this. Furthermore, it is all of this in a unity, not in pieces. It is an acceptance of the whole person, with his family, and a caring about their broad needs.

This acceptance of the whole person in hospice care permeates all the members of a team. The team may include the nurse, an aide, and a volunteer, as Aggie's and Ray's on-line team did. The physician (either the patient's own or the medical director if the patient is no longer being cared for by his or her own doctor), social worker, and chaplain are on the team, either on-line or behind the scenes in staff conferences. Others are included as needed: nutritionist, therapist, psychologist, or psychiatrist. Each person plays his part, not in a narrow, role-defined way, but with an open and aware appreciation of the patient and family's total needs and priorities. Professional boundaries are not important. Meeting needs is the primary goal of all. The initial orientation to this holistic approach together with frequent team meetings keeps hospice care tuned to human beings, not physical ailments.

Dame Cicely Saunders, founder of the modern hospice movement, made nursing the philosophical and theoretical basis for hospice care [1]. She was educated first as a nurse, then added social work, medicine, and pharmacy to her vitae. She referred to herself as "a nurse with extras." Her hospice nursing model contrasts sharply with a medical model in the words *holistic* rather than *reductionistic*, *caring* instead of *curing*, *self- and team-care* instead of *physician-controlled care*, *symptom management* rather than *disease management*, *inclusion of family* rather than *focusing only on the patient*, and *maximizing quality of life* instead of *extending life*.

Continuity adds its magic to hospice's comfort care. Team members are the patient's own; once connected, they can identify with each other and build the trusting relationship necessary to produce comfort. Time is spent with the patient and his family not just to carry out a task, but with the purpose of meeting their needs. Teaching the member of the family or the friend who becomes the caregiver how to give a bed bath, for example, may be the nurse's responsibility; he or she will spend the extra time needed to talk with the caregiver and patient about and respond to any worries or problems uncovered in the process. Threaded throughout these interactions is the nurse's example of an accepting view of death which helps to shape the caregiver's and patient's attitudes [2]. Visits are open-ended in order to permit this support. Reimbursement is structured to allow patient-oriented, not task-oriented care, with a per-diem rather than per-hour rate.

Clearly, this broader view of the role of the nurse, the aide, the physician, the social worker, the chaplain, and others who may participate in the team, requires that they be competent in human interactions and teaching as well as in their own professional arenas.

An integral part of this unique comfort care is building self-confidence in the patient and caregiver, for hospice aims to enable them to care for themselves and each other as much as possible. They are not consumers of health care, being acted upon—thereby being put in a weak or infantilized role—but full participants in the team. Hospice is not their savior, but their friend and objective helper.

It is important, then, to consider what the patient and his family want and need from the hospice team. When asked, the answers have a common ring to them.

> I'd like a doctor (or team member—authors' comment) to scan *me,* to grope for my spirit as well as my prostate. Without such recognition, I am nothing but my illness[1] [3, p. 61].

> Be honest with me; listen to me. Give me hope. Let me be in control. Accept and support me. Know what you are doing. Don't encourage me to cry, but understand if I do. Don't give me routine reassurance. (Drawn from various patient comments.)

Successful care, that is care which will help the patient and his family and result in a positive experience at the end of life, must respond to these wishes.

The primary care nurse holds a large responsibility in hospice care. His or her skill and competence and human responsiveness will often set the tone of the hospice/patient and family relationship.

We consider empathy to be a helpful part of a good nurse-patient relationship [4]. Empathy is the projection of one's own personality into that of another, a sensing of what the other is experiencing. It has been described with four components: emotive, moral, cognitive, and behavioral [5], and alternatively, emotional, cognitive, communicative, and relational [6]. We know empathy when we feel it, distinguishing it from sympathy and sentimentalism, neither of which is desirable.

Empathy, in its best sense, is a positive social quality. It is not manipulative; that is, an empathic response is not aimed at accomplishing some objective from the person responding. Empathy is pure; it happens because of the nature of the persons involved, like a gift. Empathy balances subjectivity with objectivity, closeness with distance, and conscious thought with

---

[1] Anatole Broyard, from *Intoxicated By My Illness,* Clarkson Potter Publishing Company. Used with permission of Crown Publishing Group.

intuitive feeling. Patients and their families know they are heard and valued when they feel an empathic response.

Empathy requires knowing the patient, both his typical pattern of response and him or her as a person. Knowing the patient comes from listening, from caring enough to be willing to be involved, from participating in the relationship and the clinical context [7]. Janice and her team came to know Aggie in just these ways.

A commitment is negotiated in the course of building an empathic relationship [8]. Typically and ideally, the patient asks questions to determine if the nurse is a good person, a good nurse, and whether the nurse will care about him. If satisfied, the patient makes overtures to the nurse. On the other side, the nurse looks at the patient to see if he has special needs, and whether their personalities might click. If that is positive, the nurse may offer personal information to establish a common ground, and with a mutual lowering of the guard, may offer humor. And so the relationship builds. The process may be swift or take some time, and may occasionally be elusive, but when achieved, empathy in the relationship between patient and hospice worker adds crucial value to end-of-life care.

The first author has known these trusting relationships with her patients; she knows the comfort and value of being able to express and receive honest feelings and thoughts. Patients with advanced disease have been able to ask their difficult questions, to let out their true worries and talk them through. She felt the patients' trust in order to answer their questions, sometimes with painful answers, perhaps with uncertain answers. Even when there can be no answer, this climate of trust and the necessary skills are important for an honest and helpful discussion [9]. The core of the trust is telling the truth, which hospice nurses are adept at doing [10].

Relationships in the generic health-care setting between a nurse and a patient can have different qualities: clinical, therapeutic, connected, or over-involved [8]. Our relationships in hospice aim at being connected. Our nurses regard the patient first as a person, like herself or himself—not as a "case"—in order to achieve a connected relationship. In that relationship, the nurse can intercede for the patient, buffer him, and in general be his advocate. The patient in a connected relationship believes the nurse will go the extra mile, and he respects the nurse's judgment and feels grateful. The nurse believes his or her care makes a difference to the patient. The trust, the empathy, the reward to his spirit, all help the patient. The response, the connectedness, the success in helping, all reinforce the nurse [8, 11]. The relationship becomes one of the spirit, of their shared humanity.

The length of time in which the nurse and patient can build this relationship will, of course, affect its quality. A patient's length of stay will depend on how early in his illness he is referred to hospice; what his functional status is; how much of his hospice time is spent in the hospital as opposed to actual hospice care; whether he is in a home, free-standing, or hospital hospice; whether caregiver support is available; and what comprises the nurse's patient care mix.

(Rumblings within the hospice community and among enlightened physicians portend earlier referrals and extension of the hospice-type comfort care to persons beyond those terminally ill.)

Because hospice care is directed to the at-home caregivers as well as the patients, team members need to build empathic relationships with them as well. Quality of life for the caregiver is enhanced by hospice support of his or her physical, emotional, social, and financial needs, and is directly affected by that caregiver's perception of the patient's quality of life. Hospice workers, patients, and caregivers become one unit in this end-of-life journey, and the care program recognizing that provides a uniquely effective service [12].

While nursing goals may be pursued more freely within hospice than any other setting because it is a nursing model of service, and therefore has intrinsic rewards for the nurse [1], the commitment in a good hospice relationship can make the nurse vulnerable—to fatigue, to rejection, to disappointment. It is not a nine-to-five job. Burn out can occur—although one study found hospice nurses show less emotional exhaustion and experience a greater sense of personal accomplishment than did critical care and hospital oncology nurses [13, 14]. We believe energy regenerates with the caring, connected relationships in hospice, out of a source greater than the nurses' own selves alone.

Selection of persons to be hospice nurses is done carefully in order to avoid problems of failure and burn out. Certain characteristics are necessary in addition to competence in the traditional nursing skills of managing complicated pumps, tricky medications, diet, bowel regularity and skin care, to mention a few [15]. Special qualities include assertiveness and ability to operate productively without role restraints, to function under stress and to make decisions and accept responsibility for them. Can this person work in a team? Deal with not being appreciated? Work with the pain of death? Balance his own life with his work, and avoid over-involvement and its handmaidens, rescuing, and codependency?[2] [16].

Once selected, nurses have found it helpful to have resources available to them which can support and recharge them. Hospice programs have arranged this with the provision of in-service meetings and formal retreats. Particularly when the staff of a hospice program grows large, annual retreats can be helpful to help workers rekindle passion and commitment, to discover ways to recover after a patient's death and to consider their ideas in the forum of others' experiences [17]. In addition, the availability of support personnel such as social workers and chaplains to nurses can mean help in their healing. These individuals can be a blessing when the days are hard.

Well-selected hospice nurses will have staying power if provided several other things: recognition, professional growth opportunities, the opportunity to participate in policy development, and occasional mental health days [16]. Nurse managers who are strong leaders willing to discuss work problems with the staff facilitate job satisfaction among the nurses [18].

Leonard et al. have recommended attitudes and behaviors of nurses caring for the dying which might well be extended to everyone on the hospice team, for they are worthy[3] [19]. They include:

---

[2] 1988 *American Journal of Hospital & Palliative Care*/Prime National Publishing Corp. Used with permission.

[3] Included by permission of *Cancer Nursing*.

1) Recognize the patient's and family's need for hope, control, accessibility, support, and normality.
2) Keep communications open.
3) Recognize and respect family characteristics, developmental stage and coping mechanisms.
4) Avoid preconceived ideas of how families *should* cope.
5) Inform the family of resources available to them.
6) Allow the family to make use of these resources, and not be coerced into them.

In one hospice program in 1982, Skorupka and Bohnet studied caregivers' perceptions of nursing behaviors in a home-care hospice setting, finding certain ones they regarded as most helpful and others least helpful out of a list of seventy-five behaviors[4] [20]. The most helpful, as determined by all care givers receiving service from this hospice, were:

1) Provide the patient with necessary emergency measures if the need arises.
2) Assure the patient that nursing service will be available 24 hours a day, 7 days a week.
3) Answer my (the caregiver's) questions honestly, openly and willingly.
4) Allow the patient to do as much for himself as possible.
5) Teach me (the caregiver) how to keep the patient physically comfortable.

The behaviors held least helpful by all caregivers included:

1) Pray with me.
2) Plan for me to talk about my feelings with other people facing the same problems.
3) Help me to understand what the loss of the patient will mean to me.
4) Help me to make funeral arrangements.
5) Cry with me.

---

[4] Included by permission of *Cancer Nursing*.

Using sixty of the same behaviors, a study ten years later found a somewhat different set of caregivers' perceptions of the most and least helpful nursing behaviors in a home-care hospice setting[5] [21]. That caregivers' list of most helpful nursing behaviors includes in descending order:

1) Listen to the patient and to what he wants.
2) Provide the patient with the necessary emergency measures if the need arises.
3) Assure me that the nursing services will be available 24 hours a day, 7 days a week.
4) Answer the patient's questions honestly.
5) Talk to the patient to reduce his fears.
6) Provide me with information necessary if a home death occurs.
7) Answer my questions honestly, openly and willingly.
8) Stay with the patient during difficult times.
9) Assure the patient that nursing services are available 24 hours a day, 7 days a week.
10) Teach me how to keep the patient physically comfortable.

The corresponding least helpful behaviors were:

1) Talk with me about my guilt.
2) Cry with me.
3) Help me to make funeral arrangements.
4) Attend the funeral when the patient dies.
5) Assist me in establishing a method for recording medications.
6) Teach me how to turn and position the patient.
7) Assist me in learning how to change the bed sheets with the patient in bed.
8) Recognize my need to talk about things unrelated to death.
9) Help me to face reality in my own way in my own time.
10) Assure me that the patient can be readmitted to the hospital if necessary.

---

[5] P. Y. Ryan, as published in The *American Journal of Hospice and Palliative Care.*

In the more recent study the helpful behaviors most often addressed the patient's psychosocial need, then his physical needs, and last the caregiver's psychosocial needs. In contrast, at least from the available data, the most frequent category of need met by nursing behaviors in the early study was patient physical need, then caregiver psychosocial, and last patient psychosocial need.

This reversal may reveal a complex change in values, skills, and health care realities over the ten-year period between studies. Hospice has been communicating its purpose through-out this time so presumably there is a better understanding now of its holistic philosophy. Human relationship skills and the need to address patients' psychosocial needs have grown in importance. And physical comfort has grown more achievable over these years, so perhaps it poses less of an unmet need.

Interestingly, the recent study added the hospice nurses' view of their own most and least helpful behaviors in a home-care hospice setting. They felt their most helpful behaviors were:

1) Assure the caregiver that nursing services will be avail-able 24 hours a day, 7 days a week.
2) Teach the caregiver how to keep the patient physically comfortable.
3) Help the patient to feel safe ventilating anger, sadness, anxiety, and other feelings.
4) Answer the patient's questions honestly.
5) Listen to the patient and to his wants.
6) Assure the patient that nursing services are available 24 hours a day, 7 days a week.
7) Teach the caregiver how to relieve the patient's symptoms.
8) Provide the caregiver with the information necessary if a home death occurs.
9) Help the caregiver to feel safe ventilating anger, sadness, anxiety, and other feelings.
10) Recognize when the patient needs to talk about death and dying.

Hospice nurses regarded the least helpful nursing behaviors as:

1) Describe how to keep the patient well groomed.
2) Assist the caregiver to provide a clean, neat environment for the patient.
3) Do not encourage the patient to have false hope.
4) Cry with the caregiver.
5) Pray with the caregiver.
6) Teach the caregiver to prevent long-term complications of bed rest.
7) Teach the caregiver how to adjust the diet as needed[6] [21].

Hospice nurses in this group clearly read their most important behaviors as meeting psychosocial needs, so long as basic physical needs are being met [21]. Their list of helpful behaviors is similar to the caregivers', except they regard as more important establishing a climate in which caretakers and patients feel safe to vent their feelings. Perhaps the families are not aware that is happening and so do not recognize it as a need, or perhaps that climate is not achieved as often as it should be. The authors agree strongly with the nurses in this study that establishing an accepting climate is crucial. It is the glue that keeps the various members of the effort together. It is the nutritional solution in the petrie dish which permits growth.

Defining the most and least helpful things hospice nurses do is helpful for programs providing their training, for nurses on the job, and for hospice administrators who must evaluate staff performance.

Another study found "critical nursing behaviors," a somewhat different slice through the globe of nursing, comprised of responding during the actual dying, giving comfort, responding to anger, facilitating personal growth, working well with colleagues, supporting quality of life during dying, and being responsive to the family [22]. In this study, the critical behaviors were identified by nurses and nurse educators.[7]

---

[6] P. Y. Ryan, as published in *American Journal of Hospice and Palliative Care.*

[7] L. F. Degner, C. M. Gow, and L. A. Thompson, as published in *Cancer Nursing.* Used with permission of Lippincott-Raven Press.

The authors find no fault with any of these lists. They contain important guidelines of behavior that are helpful for everyone involved. But good hospice nurses are first those who invest themselves in the philosophy of hospice, who are dedicated to making the end of the journey as rich and rewarding as possible for the patients and families they serve. The specifics of what they do can vary, as long as that foundation is there.

Some nursing care can be handled by persons less-trained than registered nurses. Certified Nurse Aides (CNAs) carry out important parts of the job, providing further competent coverage at lower cost. CNAs at the Hospice of Metro Denver (HMD) are required to have current certification and a valid driver's licence with $100,000 liability insurance (or the ability to get to the patient's home via public transportation), and must complete hospice training and attend all in-service training sessions, acquiring 12 Continuing Education Credits each year. They participate in team meetings. Following planning with the staffing coordinator and the primary care nurse, CNAs are responsible at Hospice of Metro Denver for providing many personal care services, according to federal and state regulations. They keep timely records of their care and provide miscellaneous support to the patient and family. They give no medications, and provide no supervision.

Home health aides and volunteers comprise other unique aspects of the hospice experience. We regard them as invaluable braces supporting the hospice tree, without which the branches would break. (Consider Elizabeth's contribution to Aggie and her brother.) Now numbering more than 65,000 in the United States [23], volunteers provide an enormous service as integral members of the hospice teams. Their service enriches the comfort care provided to patients and their families, and reduces the cost of this form of health care. Volunteers may assist with household and personal tasks, fitting into the dynamics of each situation. They can be the link between professional staff and members of the family, helping with their practical needs and providing emotional support [24].

Hospice home health aides and volunteers, men and women, are well trained. They must attend educational programs and be certified before beginning their work. Their programs orient them in some depth to the hospice philosophy and principles, and to what will be expected of them. The teaching aims to blend fact, methodology, creativity, and personal style in a way the volunteers can utilize so they can function under various and dynamic circumstances. The training is not a drill to teach and improve task performance. It is geared to inform and inspire, and to stimulate personal growth so the aide and volunteer can step in with a grasp sufficient to respond to the wide variety of needs with which they will be faced [25].

The National Home Caring Council of the Foundation for Hospice and Homecare in 1990 developed a "Model Curriculum and Teaching Guide for the Instruction of the Homemaker-Home Health Aide" (with the help of the Administration on Aging in the federal Department of Health and Human Services), which has provided guidance to local hospice organizations in planning their home health aide and volunteer training programs [25].

The Hospice of Metro Denver curriculum, as an example of what is required for certification of volunteers, includes roughly thirty hours of didactic and seminar training which must be completed before field training can begin. Lectures cover the history and philosophy of hospice, the mechanics of its operation, the holistic approach to pain control, interpersonal and family dynamics, team functioning, AIDS care, and presentations of personal stories. Training exercises include experience with team building and values determination. Short movies demonstrating home and in-patient care, and an opportunity for participants to know each other round out an intensive schooling from which volunteers can move with some confidence into their field training with staff members, and ultimately into their work. Even after all of that, volunteers are encouraged to attend in-service education and other programs offered by HMD.

Volunteers must have human qualities of warmth and caring, along with "people skills," and they need to be able to tolerate others' pain and suffering. Often the training program serves as a screening process: well-meaning students may realize as they learn about hospice that they are not cut out to be hospice volunteers. Those who proceed, by and large, become productive and successful volunteers.

Further screening has at times been regarded as necessary, because in spite of everything, a few volunteers do not work out satisfactorily. They may not have completed their own grieving over loss; they may not find the commitment workable in their lives; they may have had inappropriate reasons for volunteering.

An effort was made in 1981 to screen prospective volunteers using a psychiatrist-designed list of motivations for seeking such work. Applicants whose motivations were felt to be congruent with hospice work were accepted for the training program [26]. How much this is used, and how valid a tool it has been, is unknown to the authors.

Effective men and women volunteers were found in a recent study to be similar in some respects but different in significant ways. While all of the volunteers had sensing and judging traits, men in the group tended to be introverted and thinking, while the women were extroverted and feeling personality types [27]. Being aware that these gender differences may exist can be helpful in recruitment, training, placement, and retention of hospice volunteers.

When all works out and the volunteers are actively participating in their teams, they need feedback about their work. Without a good sense of how they are doing they can feel unsure of themselves, become hesitant and ultimately turn away from the work they had initially adopted with enthusiasm.

Most helpful is honest and direct informal feedback from the volunteer coordinator and the primary nurse with whom the volunteer works. A formal tool was devised in 1993, similar to a job performance evaluation in the commercial or industrial workplace, to enhance the assessment and provide tools for the volunteers' growth. Coordinators of volunteers from around the country developed criteria for satisfactory performance which were ranked in importance and grouped into four categories. The resulting performance checklist follows:[8]

---

[8] B. Lafer and S. Craig, as published in *The Hospice Journal*. Used with permission of The Haworth Press.

Commitment to the Program

1) Takes on cases when s/he is needed, according to agreement made with volunteer coordinator.

2) Works the number of hours per week agreed to with patient, family, or coordinator.

3) Makes home visits on the days and at the times expected by the patient or family.

Relationship to Patients and Family

4) Demonstrates the ability to be a good listener.

5) Does not preach or push his/her own religious ideas or practices.

6) Extends warmth and caring to patients and their families.

7) Behaves in a relaxed and calm manner around patients and families.

8) Sees the needs of patients and families and responds well to them.

9) Demonstrates the ability to remain engaged with the patient despite the physical or mental deterioration of that patient.

10) Does not try to take charge and get the family to do things his or her way.

11) Responds flexibly to changes in patient or family status.

12) Demonstrates the ability to cope with very stressful family situations.

13) Does not burden the patient or family with her/his personal problems or previous losses.

Team Member Functions

14) Demonstrates an acceptance of hospice philosophy and policies.

15) Reports any significant changes to the team immediately.

16) Complies reliably with required documentation.

17) Reports honestly and openly about cases to the volunteer coordinator.

18) Keeps hospice business confidential.

19) Keeps in touch with the volunteer coordinator or other designated team member to share and receive case information.

20) Consults with team members before making any changes in patient or family care.

21) Informs the volunteer coordinator, patient, or family when s/he cannot keep a scheduled appointment in sufficient time so that alternate arrangements can be made.

22) Demonstrates the ability to accept supervision and to learn from it.

23) Demonstrates the ability to accept support from and give support to team members.

Self Awareness

24) Does not get overly involved emotionally with patients or their families.

25) Knows when s/he needs a rest and tells volunteer coordinator.

26) Maintains professionally appropriate appearance and hygiene.

27) Able to say "no" when s/he knows that at some level s/he would resent saying "yes" to the patient, family or the volunteer coordinator [28, pp. 18-19].

This checklist, or a variation thereof, is used by many hospice organizations today.

Once found, a good volunteer must be nurtured in order to maintain his or her motivation. It helps if the volunteer's expectations in the work are met. Additionally, he or she must be made to feel like a valued team member. The feedback described above should confirm that [29]. Growth of a hospice program from a small, family-feeling operation to a larger, more diverse and geographically dispersed organization makes this sense of intimacy and belonging more difficult to maintain [30], so efforts should be strengthened when the program grows.

Maintaining a strong volunteer side of the program is essential. It can spell success or failure for a hospice organization.

Hospice social workers are important members of the team. They are flexible in their roles, generally providing support and services within the logistics plan of the particular hospice program. For example, social workers (often called family counselors) in some programs such as the Hospice of Metro Denver respond following the nurse's initial visit—routinely when children are in the family, and upon request of the patient when they are not. In some programs they may be the first person to see the patient and family. Whether they provide the first or later contact with the patient and family, their role is to explore with them their circumstances and feelings about admission to hospice in what would be labeled an *intake interview* in most health-care systems. From their first conversation, the family counselors gain insights about the family's strengths, potential problems, and resources that are added to the initial assessment for the team who will be working with the family. Then the social workers contribute to the ongoing planning that takes place in team meetings held during the service for any patient. They are on call during off hours, just as nurses are, for emergencies such as interpersonal crises, threats of suicide, etc. Social workers provide information and help with arrangements regarding insurance, contacting persons or agencies when needed. They also coordinate and conduct bereavement programs and support services.

In the Hospice of Metro Denver, social workers and chaplains plan and put on memorial services three times a year for both recently and more distantly bereaved families, at which the attendees are invited to share their memories.

Social workers may also provide support for nurses, aides, and volunteers under stress. Both patient and staff reap the benefits of having a social worker on the team.

The hospice chaplain also serves both the patient/family and the staff. Some of the most important issues faced by all persons trying to adjust to end-of-life realities are matters of the spirit. Many persons in this situation have within their own beings or circle of intimates the resources to resolve and deal comfortably with these matters, but some may be troubled and wish for help. When care is needed, they may call on their own clergyperson or the hospice chaplain. Hospice programs generally have a chaplain on staff or available to them when these needs arise. The HMD has valued its chaplain's help to patients, families, and to team members on many occasions.

Because comfort care can require attention to physical complaints—pain, infection, problems with eating, sleeping, or breathing or disability of some sort—the physician must be part of the team. No one else is equipped or authorized to prescribe medication for these problems. Most often the patient's own doctor continues to provide the service needed, and the valued doctor/patient relationship continues in the new context of the team. But we have occasionally been involved with patients who had no physician. They may have moved to be near a child or parent, or their physicians may have been reluctant to refer them for hospice care, so they chose to come independently, leaving their physicians. In these cases the medical director of the hospice program will assume responsibility, an essential part of the total hospice care.

The ease with which the nurse, the aide, the social worker, the chaplain, the physician, the volunteer, or any other member of the hospice team, can be called on to enrich a patient's care is part of what makes the hospice experience very different from other delivery systems, and very satisfying. No roadblocks interfere with their participation and service; not financial, as reimbursement is based on an overall per-diem rate; not organizational, as service is structured in the context of the team.

Combine the assets of the team with hospice's holistic approach to comfort care, and you have a special gift to the dying and their loved ones, indeed.

REFERENCES

1. N. Burns, K. Carney, and B. Brobst, Hospice: A Design for Home Care for the Terminally Ill, *Holistic Nursing Practice, 3*:2, pp. 65-76, 1989.
2. M. A. Mesler, Negotiating Life for the Dying: Hospice and the Strategy of Tactical Socialization, *Death Studies, 19*:3, pp. 235-255, 1995.
3. A. Broyard, *Intoxicated By My Illness and Other Writings on Life and Death,* Clarkson N. Potter, Inc., New York, 1992.
4. B. M. Raudonis, Empathic Nurse-Patient Relationships in Hospice Nursing, *The Hospice Journal, 10*:1, pp. 59-74, 1995.

5. J. M. Morse, G. Anderson, J. L. Bottorff, O. Yonge, B. O'Brien, S. M. Solberg, and K. H. McIlveen, Exploring Empathy: A Conceptual Fit for Nursing Practice, *Image: Journal of Nursing Scholarship, 24*:4, pp. 273-280, 1992.

6. C. A. Williams, Biopsychosocial Elements of Empathy: A Multidimensional Model, *Issues in Mental Health Nursing, 11*:2, pp. 155-174, 1990.

7. C. A. Tanner, P. Benner, C. Chesla, and D. R. Gordon, The Phenomenology of Knowing the Patient, *Image: Journal of Nursing Scholarship, 25*:4, pp. 273-280, 1993.

8. J. M. Morse, Negotiating Commitment and Involvement in the Nurse-Patient Relationship, *Journal of Advanced Nursing, 16*, pp. 455-468, 1991.

9. A. Faulkner and C. Regnard, Handling Difficult Questions in Palliative Care—A Flow Diagram, *Palliative Medicine, 8*:3, pp. 245-250, 1994.

10. J. Zerwekh, The Truth Tellers. How Hospice Nurses Help Patients Confront Death, *American Journal of Nursing, 94*:2, pp. 30-34, 1994.

11. K. Palmer, How Hospice Nursing Helped Me Choose Nursing, *Imprint, 38*:1, pp. 35-36, 1991.

12. S. C. McMillan and M. Mahon, The Impact of Hospice Services on the Quality of Life of Primary Caregivers, *Oncology Nursing Forum, 21*:7, pp. 1189-1195, 1994.

13. K. Mallett, J. H. Price, S. G. Jurs, and S. Slenker, Relationships among Burnout, Death Anxiety, and Social Support in Hospice and Critical Care Nurses, *Psychology Reports, 68*:3 Pt 2, pp. 1347-1359, 1991.

14. P. J. Bram and L. F. Katz, A Study of Burnout in Nurses Working in Hospice and Hospital Oncology Setting, *Oncology Nursing Forum, 16*:4, pp. 555-560, 1989.

15. L. Herbst, Quoted in K. Lubieniecki, Facing the Most Terrible Lord, *Hospice, 4*:3, p. 21, 1993.

16. E. Medoff, Strategies for the Retention of Hospice Home Care Nurses, *American Journal of Hospice Care, 5*:4, pp. 27-30, 1988.

17. B. Bailey, M. Carney, P. Grodski, and M. Turnbull, Holding Onto Ideals in the Face of Reality, *American Journal of Hospice Care, 4*:4, pp. 31-35, 1987.

18. A. V. Drennan and M. A. Wittenauer, Leadership Behavior of Nurse Managers and Job Satisfaction of RNs in a Hospice Home-Care Setting, *American Journal of Hospice Care, 4*:1, pp. 28-34, 1987.

19. K. M. Leonard, S. S. Enzle, J. McTavish, C. E. Cumming, and D. C. Cumming, Prolonged Cancer Death: A Family Affair, *Cancer Nursing, 18*:3, pp. 222-227, 1995.
20. P. Skorupka and N. Bohnet, Primary Caregivers' Perceptions of Nursing Behaviors that Best Meet the Needs in a Home Care Hospice Setting, *Cancer Nursing, 5*:5, pp. 371-374, 1982.
21. P. Y. Ryan, Perceptions of the Most Helpful Nursing Behaviors in a Home-Care Hospice Setting: Caregivers and Nurses, *American Journal of Hospice and Palliative Care, 9*:5, pp. 23-29, 1992.
22. L. F. Degner, C. M. Gow, and L. A. Thompson, Critical Nursing Behaviors in Care for the Dying, *Cancer Nursing, 14*:5, pp. 246-253, 1991.
23. D. S. Sharp, Hospice Heart and Soul, *Hospice, 4*:2, pp. 15-17, 1993.
24. M. Craig, Volunteer Services, *American Journal of Hospice and Palliative Care, 11*:2, pp. 33-35, 1994.
25. P. Lane, Using Adult Education Techniques to Teach—Not to Train—Home Care Aides, *Caring, 12*:4, pp. 50-58, 1993.
26. H. M. Houston, Screening Hospice Volunteers: Using a Psychiatric Nurse as a Consultant, *Hospital Topics, 59*:6, pp. 33-36, 1981.
27. J. Caldwell and J. P. Scott, Effective Hospice Volunteers: Demographic and Personality Characteristics, *American Journal of Hospice and Palliative Care, 11*:2, pp. 40-45, 1994.
28. B. Lafer and S. Craig, The Evaluation of Hospice Home Care Volunteers, *The Hospice Journal, 9*:1, pp. 13-20, 1993.
29. F. Chevrier, R. Steuer, and J. MacKenzie, Factors Affecting Satisfaction among Community Based Hospice Volunteer Visitors, *American Journal of Hospice and Palliative Care, 11*:4, pp. 30-37, 1994.
30. D. Field and I. Johnson, Satisfaction and Change: A Survey of Volunteers in a Hospice Organization, *Social Science Medicine, 36*:12, pp. 1625-1633, 1993.

CHAPTER 2

The Intimate Hour

Talking about death is taboo in our society. No one wants to hear about it. Maybe we hope that avoiding the words will invoke magic of some strange sort, putting off one's dying indefinitely. Whatever the reasons, we do not want to think about it.

Older people, those who are reminded of their own mortality by the loss of one friend after another and by their own visible aging, will sometimes reveal their feelings—haltingly, perhaps, in fragments of conversation. They cannot as effectively as the young keep the subject out of their minds. They simply wish to die peacefully in their sleep when their time comes. No awful things to go through first. Just live as long as you can feel all right, then one night go to sleep and not wake up.

I have often seen another desire, admitted grudgingly but fondly held. If our seniors must fall ill, they want to be at home when they die. No hospitals. No institutions. Be in the comfort of home with the people they love, where friends can come and go, where there are no rules. Be in control.

Of course that cannot always happen. Some people have no one at home to care for them, and sometimes the family is too scared or can't find a way to handle the load. In-patient hospice facilities have a definite place in this world, and when needed or wanted, they are enormously valuable.

MINNIE

"Minnie, the doctor will see you now."

Minnie was seated in a row of metal-armed red vinyl upholstered chairs lining the wall of the nearly empty waiting room. She looked up at the young woman in a white uniform standing in the doorway, then placed the magazine she had been leafing through on a rack beside her. Before getting up from the chair, she redid the mother-of-pearl combs meant to hold her grey hair back from her eyes. Stubborn, fine wisps immediately framed her face again, giving her an unsophisticated, grandmotherly look. She shrugged her shoulders, struggled to her feet and followed the woman back to the examining rooms.

Minnie's visits were routine. Every three months she returned for blood tests which monitored her arthritis medicine.

Too restless to stick with any of the stories in the magazines while she was waiting, she had picked up a brochure with a vivacious woman smiling at her from the cover. Inside she found the popular message urging women to examine their own breasts for unusual thickening or lumps after each menstrual period, along with a series of graphic instructions, a how-to-do-it guide. She had heard of the exam before but never knew exactly how it was done.

When her doctor saw her, Minnie remained preoccupied by what she had read, barely reacting to the stick of the needle as her blood was drawn. He encouraged her to be more regular about her exercises, and Minnie smiled automatically in response.

Upon returning home, Minnie went directly to her room to experiment with the instructions from the brochure. That was how she discovered the lump in her breast.

At sixty-two years of age, when thoughts of that part of her body were desultory at best, Minnie lay down on the bed with one arm at a time upstretched and began the vertical search of her breasts with her other hand. She came upon a strange resistance under her flattened fingers. Unlike the rest which was soft and compliant under the pressure, the breast tissue just below her left nipple was firm and thick. Her breath stopped short, and she explored her breast with her fingers once more. Surely she had imagined something! Moving slowly and deliberately, she reached the same point and stopped, probing a small mass beneath the surface. It felt about the size of the top half of a walnut, but much softer—more like an over-ripe peach to the touch. With less pressure there was scarcely a hint of something unusual in there; when she pushed down against her chest wall she felt the lump clearly.

Minnie's system went into SLOW. She reacted not with panic or hysteria, not with tears or fright. Her heart did not pound, nor did her adrenalin run. She was certain in the depths of her that she had breast cancer, and she was perfectly still—calm-still. Everything about her seemed to be on hold while her body decided how to handle this stunning change. It was as though she had known before she began the self-examination that the disease was lurking inside, that she would lose the breast, and that her years would be numbered. She did not cry out, or react in any way. She lay inert, wondering at her own non-response. It was a trick of the mind; she was fully aware of what she had discovered, but there was nothing there. She felt flat, strangely devoid of feeling.

She waited. With her eyes she traced the ivy-covered trellis on the slanted ceiling above her, an extension of the wall paper behind her bed. The small, walnut clock ticked on the night stand, a familiar meter that rose now, from the surrounding silence, out of its usual oblivion. The fragrance of lilac registered in her nostrils from a miniature pillow of sachet tucked into her lingerie in the drawer at her side. Nothing changed. After several minutes she rose like an automaton and dressed. As she moved into the kitchen to start the dinner routine she glanced into the mirror, expecting to see a change in her expression to correspond with the monumental change she might be approaching in her life. The face looking back at her reflected nothing. Nothing was different. But somehow she knew in her core that everything was different.

She washed lettuce and scraped carrots, shaped a hamburger patty with unthinking hands, and set a place at the table. She cooked her burger, seasoned it, gathered what she needed for her simple dinner and sat down to eat.

For sixteen years since her Leo's heart attack and eventual death she had carried on by herself, often eating alone in this same chair, watching the changing seasons through the window at her side. Her life, at first bereft and adrift, had become comfortable, busy with the homey things of house and garden, books and TV, and her daughter and grandchildren who lived nearby.

At this point there was nothing else to be done. It was dinner-time, so she sat and ate.

Not until later did her senses come alive. Dinner eaten, kitchen cleared, and some TV show she couldn't remember over, she moved woodenly through her bedtime preparations. Once in bed, against her will Minnie shifted her gown and reached again to feel the strange lump in her left breast. Questions came into focus. How long had it been there? Was it growing? What had made it start? What would she need to do about it? How would Jane, the mother of her grandchildren and the main object of her devotion, handle this news?

Then, like a surge of seawater, the enormity of her discovery washed over her. A sob welled out of her gut, and a long keening cry filled the room. She turned on her side, hugged the pillow into the hollow of her trunk, lowered her face into its softness, and wept. She gave herself over to the release, not fighting the tears and fear that poured out. They came and went in waves, a store of emotion with a life of its own. At last, her energy spent, she lay quiet and fell asleep. Tomorrow would have to take care of itself.

For the next two years Minnie fought the cancer her doctor confirmed within days of her discovery. He led the fight, backed by a large number of medical and allied health professionals. They operated on her, medicated her, radiated her; they altered her diet, administered hormones, and monitored her. Everything that could be done was tried, and Minnie participated 200 percent. She didn't want to die.

Her body did not respond the way they had hoped, however. The two-year effort and the disease took their toll. Instead of healing, the cancer spread to her spine. She suffered increasing pain and lost weight and strength, reaching the point where getting dressed exhausted her for the remainder of the day. She was profoundly tired—tired of hospitals and treatment and doctors and being sick. She finally called a halt; she would permit no more.

"Mom is like that, you know," Jane said to Howard as they sipped their nightly cocktails before dinner. The two of them sat reflecting on Minnie's painful efforts over the past two years to fight this disease. In and out of the hospital, undergoing one procedure after another to try to stop the cancer, she was forced to agree when her doctor decreed that independence was no longer possible. He wanted her to be in a nursing home.

This time of day was typically a relaxing, welcome hour. Jane's girls from her early marriage, twelve-year-old Amy and nine-year-old Beth, watched their favorite show, "One Day at a Time," in the family room. Jane and Howard, fresh from his after-work shower, retreated with highballs to a lounge on the enclosed porch, a garden-like space furnished in floral patterned wrought-iron furniture off the living room. For an hour they sat undisturbed, feet propped on matching upholstered ottomans, sharing their day's events. Jane supervised the processing of loans in a busy downtown office and Howard was the service manager of a large, noisy car repair shop, so they guarded this intimate hour jealously at the close of each day. It symbolized their compromise between dating and marriage, a long-term, live-in relationship. They cared deeply about each other, and over the years Beth and Amy had grown to love Howard as well.

"I expected her to rebel," Jane continued, undoing the clasp that held her shoulder-length, blond hair in a neat bun at the back of her head. "Mom really can't face living with the rules of a nursing home. She's been alone too long. She tolerated the hospital when she had to have surgery, but I knew she couldn't wait to get home." She raked her fingers through her hair, letting it settle where it would.

"I wish you could've seen her. First she learned she'd have an assigned roommate. Then they told her she'd be required to attend chapel. She just flipped! As sick as she is, she really put her foot down!"

"There's still a lot of spirit in the old doll, isn't there?" Howard laughed.

Neither one spoke for several minutes as they thought their private thoughts about Minnie and the profound changes in her life since she had first discovered the lump in her breast. They both admired her courage and ability to face facts. She had

coped so well with this threat to her life, agreeing to any treatment the doctors urged her to undertake, as a real fighter would
do. And she had had it all: removal of that breast, then the
other, chemotherapy, radiation, cobalt, hysterectomy, and some
new experimental drugs. But nothing had stopped the disease.

Jane and Howard knew by now, and so did Minnie, that she
would die. They realized what she wanted most was to decide
for herself what she would do—what she would allow to have
done to her. She had already paid a big price, losing her hair,
her appetite, and often her composure and dignity. Jane had
watched her proud mother change in recent months, now
shrinking in body and spirit when doctors and residents and
interns and nurses poked, punched, prodded, and talked over
and around her. It seemed the professionals were motivated to
try yet another treatment that might yield a cure, but they
made very little effort to recognize her fears and fatigue. It
wasn't enough that she had to suffer relapse and treatment
failure; she probably felt guilty in the presence of her caretakers
for not becoming whole before their eyes. The treatment had
become part of the illness.

"I can't bear the thought," Jane broke the silence. "Mom
doesn't have much time left, and she'll be so unhappy." She put
her drink down. "It's bad enough she's so sick. God. . . ." Her
voice trailed off.

Howard was silent, then sighed and stood up. He touched her
shoulder. "C'mon, Love," he rumbled softly in his deep, bass
voice. "Let's get the kids and eat dinner."

After the meal ended, Jane went to her desk in the bedroom
to go through the day's mail. Howard followed. He stopped, his
tall, athletic frame filling the doorway, and watched as she rif-
fled through the envelopes. "I've been thinking, Love. Would you
like to have your mom come here? I mean, it's a big house, and
the kids are crazy about her. . . . Maybe if you took some time
off. . . ."

"Oh," Jane gasped, turning to look at him, tears filling her
eyes. "Do you have any idea what you're saying?"

"It won't last forever," he responded gently. "Besides, I
know you. As close as you two are, you'd probably always blame

yourself for letting her go through that nursing home thing when she hates it so."

She nodded, two wet tracks running down her cheeks. "But, Howard, could you live with all of it going on right here in our house?" Her eyes bored into him as she started to think aloud. "We wouldn't have much privacy, and I might not have much time or energy for you, and I'm not sure I want to do this to the kids. They might react badly, and God . . . I don't know what else it would do! It'll change everything."

"Yes." He moved then, seating himself on the foot of the bed near her chair. "But your mom's very sick, and that's already changed everything." He reached for her hand. "Don't decide on the spot. I just wanted you to know it's okay as far as I'm concerned. I love you, y'know." He lifted her hand and held it to his cheek.

A week later the girls doubled up, and Jane moved Minnie into Amy's bedroom next to the family room. The adjoining bathroom was cleared of Amy's scattered adolescent collection of jars, tubes, bottles, and boxes and filled with medicines and hospital gear. It quickly took on the aura of a sickroom.

Jane had made the decision after a conference with the girls. Both Amy and Beth knew their grandmother was very sick.

"We'd have to be considerate of her, girls," Jane cautioned before they said yes or no. "She'll need quiet, so it would affect you . . . having friends over, playing your music so loud—things like that. And it'll be hard to watch her if she has a lot of pain. It won't be easy."

"How long would she be here, Mom?" Amy probed. The even features and tall slender body of her budding adolescent promised a beautiful young woman in a few years, and Jane looked at her thoughtfully before answering.

"It's hard to say. But she'll have to be somewhere, either here or a nursing home. She just can't handle it alone anymore." Jane stopped. There'd be time to talk about dying later, as the time approached.

Beth didn't hesitate. "I want Grandma here with us, not in any old nursing home. C'mon, Amy, say yes." Gamin-like Beth could be counted on to help her grandmother. They had always been close.

Amy remained quiet at first, then agreed, more by default than by affirmation.

The shadow flickering in Amy's eyes haunted Jane as she lay in bed that night. She tossed and turned, then finally decided to go ahead—to invite her mother into their home. She'd deal with Amy's reservations later, whatever they were.

Life in this expanded three-generation household seemed to settle quickly into its new routine. While Jane spent considerably more time at home, and the girls didn't get quite as much sleep as usual because now they could chatter together into the night, some things didn't change. They just shifted to include Minnie.

Cocktails were poured late each afternoon in Minnie's bedroom instead of on the porch, with the threesome now sharing the day's events—Minnie propped up in bed, Howard and Jane seated at one side in captain's chairs they brought in from the dining room just for the occasion. A small metal tray at the edge of the bed held their drinks and the mandatory dish of pretzels. Napping often so she could be rested, Minnie looked forward eagerly each day as the hour approached.

"We're going to have to watch you," Howard teased. "You're becoming an alcoholic before our eyes!" Minnie saluted him with twinkling eyes from the rim of her soda as she drained it, then laughed as she had not for many weeks.

Initially constrained and uncertain when her sick grandmother moved into the house, Beth soon bounced in with her stories of classmates and friends, teachers and tests, sometimes hovering over Minnie, but more often just being herself.

Amy, on the other hand, became quiet around her, spending less and less time at her side. She took frequent refuge in the room she now shared with Beth, who found her there one day, face down on her bed, crying.

"What's the matter, Amy?" Beth was baffled.

"GET OUT! JUST GET OUT!" Amy lifted her head only long enough to yell her away.

"Okay, okay. I didn't do anything, ferheavensake!" Beth backed out, slamming the door. She ran to the kitchen where

Howard stood, unloading groceries. "What's wrong with Amy, Howard? She's in our bedroom crying. She yelled at me like I'm a criminal, and I didn't even do anything!"

"Well, whatever it is, then, you must be in the clear. Let me go in and talk with her. Don't worry about it, Missy," he said, tousling her hair. She broke loose and made a mock face at him.

Howard went down the hall to the girls' bedroom and knocked on the door. All was quiet. He knocked again. This time he was met with a scream from within the room. "GO AWAY! JUST LEAVE ME ALONE!" Something hard hit the door; then he heard Amy crying.

Howard stood for some minutes with his hands on his hips. Finally, shaking his head, he retreated to the kitchen. Beth had left, saving him from admitting that Amy baffled him, too. Jane would have to look into the problem.

Minnie's doctor sent two newcomers to the household. They integrated quickly. Janice, a quick-moving, white-haired hospice nurse, and Elaine, an eager, young volunteer trained by hospice to assist the family, visited initially on a twice-weekly basis, then gradually more often. Janice followed Minnie's medications, reporting to the doctor when she saw the need to increase her morphine. She taught Jane how to bathe her mother and chart her temperature and medications. She spent time with both Jane and Minnie, answering questions and responding to their concerns.

Minnie liked Janice instinctively. Janice had a straightforward, no-nonsense style and good nature that appealed to her; moreover, they were close in age. The two women shared a perspective about life, neither being much for show. They both had an ease, a comfort that comes from years of living and learning what is important and what really doesn't matter.

One day Minnie pulled on the tail of Janice's shirt as she moved alongside her bed. "Janice, do you have a minute?"

"You bet!" Janice sat on the edge of the bed and took Minnie's hand. "What's on your mind?"

". . . I don't know where to start," Minnie began after an interval of silence. She chewed her lip solemnly, her wispy, face-framing hair in particular disarray. "I guess I'm not really a modern woman. I have a lot of trouble with this living together business—y'know what I mean?. . . without being married." She flashed an embarrassed half-smile. "I s'pose I'm old-fashioned."

"A lot of us are, Minnie. That's not so bad."

"I liked Howard from the day I met him," she continued, "but it was really hard when I learned he'd moved in with Jane." Minnie worked at the coverlet, smoothing it over and over. "That's a long time ago. I adore him—he's so good to her—but I didn't like it then and it still sticks in my craw! Personally, I wish they'd get married. I want to feel she's secure; d'you know what I mean?"

"Have you ever told Jane how you feel?"

"Not really. It's their business, y'know. They have to make their own decisions."

Janice felt the tension in Minnie's hand.

"Do you think Jane'd want to know how you feel? She loves you so much. You share everything else. . . ." Janice watched Minnie silently for a minute, then added, "It's not like you're trying to run her life."

Minnie digested that and brightened. "Do you think she'd hear it that way? I mean, if I said what I think, would she feel I'm telling her what to do?"

"I think she'd understand if you put it that way. She trusts you, you know."

Minnie's face was set with resolve when Janice left.

A couple of days later, Minnie motioned for Janice to come close so Jane, nearby in the kitchen, wouldn't hear.

"It worked, Janice." The whisper was conspiratorial. "We talked! She didn't get mad or anything. Like you said, I just told her how I felt, and I think she understood." Minnie radiated her joy.

"Oh, I'm glad, Minnie!"

"They may not do anything about it, of course, but I just told her it upset me, their not being married. It felt so good to get it out! Like lancing a boil." She chuckled. "She was wonderful. She really listened. She said she'd think hard about it. I love her so!" Minnie drew her knees up under the cover, thought for a moment, then added, "I still want them to get married, but it's Okay, I guess. They can decide."

Janice leaned forward and hugged her impulsively.

Elaine, meanwhile, split her schedule between household chores and time with the girls. She tried to help Amy and Beth adapt to a household that now had little time for them.

She and Amy were returning in the car from the post office one day when she heard a sniff. Looking over, she saw Amy wipe her eyes, head turned away toward the window, her face hidden by her long silky brown hair.

"Amy," Elaine said gently. "What is it?"

Amy shrugged. Elaine waited, then tried again.

"Something's bothering you, I can tell. Did something go wrong in school today?"

Amy shook her head, wadding her handkerchief against the side of her face.

"Are you having trouble sharing a room with Beth?"

"Uh-uh." Amy shook her head again.

"You're not sick or anything, are you?" It was unlikely, but Elaine had to ask.

"Uh-uh."

"Well, something's wrong. It usually helps to unload it. Why don't you try it out on me, Amy? I'm a good listener."

Amy sat tensely for seconds, then balled up her fists above her head and slammed them down on the dashboard in front of her. "I have to stay right here and watch her," she let out with a cry. "It's so gross! She's so skinny an' her hands shake an' her breath's bad an' it's . . ." Her words were lost in a paroxysm of sobs.

"Amy, Amy," Elaine reached out to touch the girl's shoulder, stunned. Amy rejected her touch with a convulsive jerk.

"She can't even eat right," Amy continued, the words now spewing forth out of control. "She drinks her food! And you can hear her swallow ger-lunk every time! It's so . . . gross!"

"You're having a really hard time, aren't you Amy? I had no idea . . ."

"You just don't know what it's like. I mean she's got my room, and we can't play the boom box loud enough to hear it . . . and I can't have my friends come over . . . they'd be grossed out. I HATE IT! It's so awful. IT ISN'T FAIR!"

Amy's outburst stopped in trembling silence. Elaine waited until it was clear she was through. "Have you told your mom?"

"Of course not." For the first time Amy lowered her handkerchief and shot a glance at Elaine. "How could I?"

"Well, you told me."

"That's different. I mean, Grandma's her mom. I couldn't say that to her."

"You've used good sense, Amy. That would hurt your mom. . . . Now, what are we going to do about it?"

Amy was silent. At last she offered, "Does Grandma have to live here?"

"I guess that decision's been made. She needs your mom now. And she needs to be here. She really doesn't want to be in a nursing home."

Amy's crying stopped, and she stared at Elaine for a minute, thinking hard.

"Well, then, maybe I could live somewhere else—with one of my friends."

"This is your home, Amy." Elaine reached over and squeezed her shoulder lightly. "Your mom wouldn't want you to move somewhere else." Elaine stifled a quick smile, then continued seriously. "I think you're just going to have to deal with it, Honey. Sometimes that's how life is. You'll have to find some way to be good to your grandma even though she's sick and you feel like this." Amy was quiet. "Do you think you can try?"

Amy leaned into Elaine's shoulder and hung her head. Finally Elaine heard her slow response. "Okay."

Amy didn't move, even to look up, until the car came to a stop, parked along the curb in front of the house. Then she opened the door and ran inside without speaking. Elaine, an anxious frown on her face, watched her disappear.

Amy spoke little and seemed subdued during the days that followed. She hung around Elaine when she was home, a mostly mute shadow. Gradually she came out of her shell.

A few days later Amy helped Elaine with the laundry, carrying her grandmother's clean gowns and bed linens into her room where she put them away in the dresser. "Thank you, dear."

Minnie roused from her sleep when the drawer shut. She smiled at her lanky granddaughter.

"It's O.K., Grandma." Amy dallied in the doorway.

"While you're here would you do something else? My geraniums need watering, I think. Could you . . . ?"

"Sure. I'll get water . . . be right back."

Amy grinned at Elaine, who was still in the laundry room, grabbed a watering can and filled it at the laundry sink. "Grandma's geraniums are dry," she explained over her shoulder as she headed back toward Minnie's room. Elaine shook her head, then smiled as she bent once more over the ironing.

The turning point came a few days later when Amy brought some gaily-colored crepe paper home from school and proceeded to fashion large flowers of every color which she attached to the walls and furniture in her grandmother's room. Minnie beamed. It seemed like the old Amy—that is, the young Amy, the way she used to be. "I love them, dear."

Amy laughed nervously, flipping her long hair back behind her shoulders. "Oh, it's nothing." She started to whistle, which is what she did when she didn't know what to say. She reached out her hand at the foot of the bed, placing it lightly on the small mound that was Minnie's foot under cover, and slid it up the bedspread alongside her entire length as she headed, whistling, back out of the room. Minnie's breath caught in her throat.

The next day Amy found her mother out on the back porch steps drinking a glass of iced tea, snatching a break from the sick room. "Come sit with me a minute, daughter-mine," Jane moved over to make room. Amy took the seat at her mother's side and looked up expectantly. Jane laid one arm around Amy's shoulders and drew her in close.

"How do you think Grandma looks, Sweetie?"

"Uh, she's awful thin. I guess okay."

"Can you tell she's weaker?"

"D'you mean she sleeps a lot? Yeah . . . But she seems okay. I mean she smiles and seems happy . . . I can't tell she feels sick." Amy rubbed her cheek against Jane's hand resting on her shoulder.

"I think she is happy," Jane said. "She likes being here with us. She feels close. When we do something nice, or include her in what we do, she feels loved. It's important. Even though it's not always easy."

Amy turned to study her mother's face. What did she know about her blow-up with Elaine? Jane's expression revealed no sign.

Jane went on. "She's going to die, honey. We're going to lose her." Jane gripped Amy tighter.

Amy's eyes widened. A dry swallow stuck in her throat. "How do you know?"

"Her disease can't be licked. It's just a matter of time." Jane's voice was low, and Amy strained to hear.

"When . . . ?"

"There's no way to know exactly, but Janice thinks it'll be soon. Within the month, probably. That's why this time is important. Like your paper flowers, Amy." Amy's lips parted, waiting to hear what came next. "You did a sweet, lovely thing for her, and you made her happy while there was still time. You'll always remember that."

Amy pressed closer to her mother, shivering suddenly. Jane put both arms around her. The embrace was warm—encircling her in love that left no room for the old ugly reaction to her grandmother. Without warning, Amy got to her feet and ran directly to her grandmother's room.

She went to the bed, leaned over and hugged the frail woman who lay there. Minnie's eyes opened wide; she took a quick breath, then turned and kissed Amy's cheek. They gazed briefly at each other, and Amy left as quickly as she'd come.

During the next weeks the girls were involved in a sister-school project across town, and they spent less time at home. On their race in and out, they stopped to see if Minnie was awake. Minnie welcomed their quick visits, if only to nod and smile.

Jane stayed with her mother for longer periods, while Elaine took over many of the household chores. Howard made Minnie's room his first stop on arriving home at the end of each day, then after he cleaned up he would return with a tray of cocktails. Their tradition continued, even when Minnie could only watch and listen.

Late one afternoon, Howard approached Minnie's room with their drinks. As he moved through the doorway he saw Minnie's arm extended over the side of the bed and the telephone receiver lying on the floor. Hurrying closer, he made out the name "Jane" sounding on her breath.

"Oh, man . . . JANE, COME QUICK!"

In the kitchen where she was talking with Janice, Jane heard the urgency in his voice and came running.

"Mom . . . " Jane sat down on the side of the bed and cupped her hands around Minnie's thin, white face. "Is it time?"

Composed and very still, a tiny smile hovering around her mouth, Minnie looked at Jane through nearly-closed eyes. Her fingertips touched her daughter's hand, and in unison, as if orchestrated by some unknown power, they spoke their last words to each other. "I love you." Minnie's final breaths passed through her lips, a quiet look of peace on her face. It was over.

Jane stayed for some minutes on the side of the bed, brushing Minnie's fine wisps of hair back from her face, moving her hand again and again over Minnie's brow. A mixture of joy and sadness filled her eyes.

Howard slipped out to get Janice, and when they returned he stood at Jane's side and took her hand. He steadied it, placing one of the cocktails within her grasp. He picked up another and handed it to Janice, then took the remaining one in his own hands. The three of them raised their glasses toward Minnie. They clinked and drank, bidding her farewell in the same intimate ceremony she had enjoyed so many evenings with them. Tears rolled down their cheeks in the silent tribute.

In time they called the girls into the bedroom. Beth stared wordlessly at her grandmother for several minutes from the foot of the bed, then moved up to sit next to Jane on the edge of the bed just as she had many times before. Amy went to Minnie's side and stopped, uncertain what to do.

"We can say goodbye to Grandma now, girls. It's over—she's all through being sick." Neither girl moved. "It's okay; you can touch her," Jane added, bending down to kiss Minnie on the forehead. "She loved you so much." First Amy and then Beth reached for Minnie's still warm hand and leaned over to kiss her cheek. Amy stayed, tears sliding down her cheeks, reluctant to take her leave.

When the farewells were finally complete, Janice said to Jane, "We'll need to call Minnie's doctor—and the funeral director. And we need to prepare her body and dress her. I'll make the calls; would you like to help with her and her dressing? I can do it, or we can do it together."

"Bless you . . . I think I want to be with the girls right now. But I hate to leave her. . . . "

"You can—you all can come back when I'm through. There's no rush. Take the time you want, Jane. She can stay with you for several hours if you like; the funeral home can wait that long. I'll see to it."

Jane and Howard left the room, and Janice made the necessary calls to the doctor and funeral home. Then she cleaned and dressed Minnie's body, gathered the linens, and started the laundry.

Jane and the girls returned to the bedroom—they couldn't stay away. They talked a little about their memories—at times with tears and at times with smiles. They held Minnie's hand and stroked her face, they walked around looking at her flowers and the view out the window, they touched her photos on the dresser, Amy brushed her hair.

After a while Howard joined them. "How about some tea, dear? It'll feel good going down." He folded his hand around Jane's shoulder and pulled her in to his side.

Jane rose from the side of the bed and embraced him.

"Yes . . . I would like that. Come, girls—I think we could all use something good going down." She and Howard led the way back to the kitchen. She stuck her head through the door as she passed the laundry, touched Janice's arm and whispered, "I think I am ready now. The people can come to get her."

In good time the funeral director arrived, and he transferred Minnie's body to the litter, covering her, head and all, with a blanket. He wheeled her to the door. The family stood, watching, and flinched when they saw the faceless mound.

"Wait—stay just for a minute!" Janice reached for the mortician's arm, stopping the motion of the litter. She ran from the hallway to the window in Minnie's bedroom. When she returned she carried two huge geranium blossoms on long stems and one of Amy's brightly colored paper flowers. She walked to the litter, turned back the cover so everyone could see Minnie's face, then tucked the blossoms into the cover. She smiled at the mortician. "Now she can leave."

"Oh, yes," Jane breathed in a small voice as she could see her mother's face once more, now adorned with the flowers she had loved so much.

The family stood close together as Minnie's body was wheeled down the sidewalk, composed and at peace. The litter was lifted into the van; the door closed and the van drove away.

NOTES:
Home Care; Institutional Care

With all of the stress of having Minnie in Jane's home during her final illness, the crowding, the discombobulation, Amy's unhappiness, the commotion of extra people functioning with the family, coming and going—with all of that, Minnie's home care was an inexpressibly rich blessing for all involved. They, like so many others in our experience, knew that blessing; they did not have to be told. From the intimacy of their final living together, from the caregiving that was not always easy, they achieved a depth of relationship that cannot be replicated in any other way. With the death, Jane and Howard and the girls knew the meaning of family in its fullest sense; they were left with loss, but also with the joy of love given and received.

Hospice care is available in a variety of other settings besides the home: in-patient hospice facilities, nursing homes, and hospitals. Each has its place; patients with different needs are at times best accommodated in one or another of them.

But we share the assessment of Anne Munley who describes home-care hospice as having the pace and atmosphere most conducive to comfort, the environment in which feelings can be shown and peace can come [1]. We believe with C. Everett Koop, who said when he accepted a board position at the San Diego Hospice, that people should be able to die in their own homes. He believed that families should not have to live with the memories of their loved ones in steel environments surrounded by respirators and machines. While his is an extreme description of other settings, his point is valid. Home is usually the best and most-favored place to live out one's end of life.

(This is true, despite the opinion of Derek Humphry, founder of the Hemlock Society and author of the suicide manual, *Final Exit*. He says hospice in-patient beds are in such short supply that the United States *has had* to go with home hospice—because of population size, distance, and financing problems, conceding ". . . however, there are some good ones." His description makes home hospice seem like a last resort, offering only respite care for the family member caring for the patient. He concludes that ". . . essentially, all we are speaking about here is good medical care for the dying," quite missing the central point of hospice [2, p. 34].

Humphry notwithstanding, there are problems that interfere with the achievement of home care for all dying patients who wish hospice service. First of all, not everyone has access to hospice, whatever the venue. While homecare and in-patient hospice are a reality in an increasing number of communities in the United States, many small communities and rural areas remain unserved, particularly in the South and West [33]. According to the National Hospice Organization, in 1995 there were 2,544 existing programs. A significant portion of the population is left without access.

Even in those communities where a home-care hospice program is available, some patients are unable to use it.

The biggest single impediment to the utilization of such a program is the live-alone patient who has no built-in caregiver to provide his or her day-to-day care. In 1992, the National Center for Health Statistics estimated that roughly one-third of the persons in the United States over sixty-five lived alone [4], so the impediment is substantial.

A caregiver is essential, providing many benefits. The most important of these is the comfort both the patient and the caregiver derive from their closeness, acted out in very concrete ways. Caregivers grow themselves, rediscovering and redefining themselves in the course of their labors, and having to confront a new reality that makes them ask probing questions about themselves—Who am I now? Where do I fit in this? Very commonly they are surprised and pleased by what they see [5]. In addition the caregiver facilitates decision making, which may be difficult for the patient to handle entirely alone. The presence of a caregiver enhances the patient's safety. And the work done by a caregiver significantly lowers the cost of the patient's care.

The hospice team cannot give total care. It was never intended to. The home hospice concept builds on the presence and participation of a caregiver in the home. With such a person there, the benefits of family reward, safety, decision making, and lowered cost can be reaped.

To some extent hospice volunteers can fill in around a part-time care taker. Such an arrangement has a potential risk, however, if the volunteer time is substantial. The hospice program would probably become liable for problems arising from the volunteers' activity; that is a risk most organizations cannot assume.

During the early portion of the hospice stay, hospice day care may offer some answers. While this unique program is not broadly available, it can be a helpful adjunct to other care for the live-alone dying patient [6].

Other efforts have been made to work around the absence of a full-time caregiver. Typically the in-home caregiver is elderly, caring for an ill spouse, or he or she may be an adult child caring for a child or elderly parent [7]. Substitutes for these caregivers have been suggested and tried.

Klingensmith and Novotny [8] and MacDonald [9] recommend seeking solutions from elements within the patient's environment, e.g., fellow members of a religious or other organization, or friends who would commit to a schedule in the patient's home. The first author has seen this work with an AIDS patient whose friends in a gay group functioned quite successfully as a "corporate caregiver." They were not only able to provide the care, they became his family. Admittedly, this arrangement is complex and may develop hitches.

Paid caregiver programs have been suggested by Beresford [10] and MacDonald [9] to meet this need. Persons hired to fulfill this role could be independent or part of an organization established to provide these personnel. The advantages of the latter are obvious; issues of bonding, benefits, and liability are automatically covered by the organization, thus simplifying matters for the patient. The disadvantages of any paid caregiver lie in the inability of the paid person to help with decisions and to relate to the patient with a spiritual tie.

Live-alone patients were compared with a similar group of "regular" home-care hospice patients in a study reported in 1994 which found that the live-alones can be safely and appropriately cared for at home with added service in case management, medical alert systems, lock boxes, and some additional services from hospice [4]. While they found it can be done, it was about 23 percent more costly than home-care hospice when a caregiver is present.

Another alternative is the relocation of the patient to a group home where someone is available to provide care [9]. The hospice team can function well with the patient in such a home. However, the environment and its occupants are to a greater or lesser degree unfamiliar to the patient, which may present a difficult adjustment for him, and the group home leader or director, the caregiver, would still be of little help with many decisions. In addition the caregiver likely cannot relate to the patient with a close spiritual tie.

The positive aspects for patients in a group home are that they have the chance to "adopt" a family in this more-intimate-than-institutional setting, and their safety and care are probably insured.

In-patient hospice programs offer a very satisfactory setting for dying patients under circumstances that contraindicate home care, particularly when those programs are fairly small and allow personal relationships to build between staff members and patients and their families. In-patient settings can be utilized for short periods, respite care, and as the end-of-life home for the patient, depending on the need. They include stand-alone hospice in-patient facilities, nursing homes and hospitals, the last two in a specific cluster of rooms, floor, or wing.

All Medicare-certified hospice programs offer both home care and in-patient care, either within their own programs, or when necessary, one part may be elsewhere by contract with another facility. The National Hospice Organization can be helpful in locating home care and in-patient programs (see Appendix C, pp. 317-328).

Genuine hospice philosophy is implemented best in a dedicated hospice program, where physical arrangements and training are thoroughly consonant with the hospice intent. Hospice care in a division of some other kind of institution may or may not adhere carefully to the tenets of hospice. To the extent it diverges, something is lost to the patient and his loved ones.

When hospice service in a nursing home or hospital is effective, it is marked by adequate training of its personnel in comfort care, use of a team to carry out its work, pain control strategies which work unhampered by old-fashioned biases like limiting morphine, and unwillingness to use the traditional medical response to patient crises [11]. Where these things are found in hospitals and nursing homes, hospice care should be quite satisfactory.

Cost studies find home care the least costly, hospice in-patient facility care somewhat more expensive, nursing home next, and hospital hospice unit care the most costly of all [11-14]. Kidder found that during the first three years of the hospice program Medicare saved $1.26 for every dollar spent on Part A—mostly hospital—expenditures. More recently, Kaiser Permanente reported an average cost savings of $1430 per patient in their patients who entered hospice, exclusive of the savings in mental health costs they would carry if there were no hospice bereavement care later [15]. Some voices disparage the savings from hospice (see discussion on pp. 300-301), but the authors believe that these findings should lead to greater use of hospice—particularly home-care hospice—and especially now, with clamor at fever pitch in our country to cut national and state budgets.

Patients' evaluation of hospice home care has been positive. When studied on admission and after three weeks of care, the majority in one study reported an improvement in the quality of their lives, while their caregivers reported an increase in the patients' quality of life in that period of time that was statistically significant [16]. Informal feedback to the authors and other hospice personnel with whom we have been in contact confirms this positive view.

A careful reading of this book is not needed to grasp the authors' position on this issue. We see the various kinds of in-patient hospice as being very valuable, even essential to some families when the time comes. We see them as being good answers to those patients who cannot be helped at home. But wherever the home-care model will work, we urge its use.

REFERENCES

1. A. Munley, *The Hospice Alternative*, Basic Books, New York, 1983.
2. D. Humphry, *Final Exit*, Hemlock Society, Eugene, Oregon, 1991.
3. B. C. Harper, Report for the National Task Force on Access to Hospice Care by Minority Groups, *The Hospice Journal*, *10*:2, pp. 1-9, 1995.
4. J. L. Bly and P. Kissick, Hospice Care for Patients Living Alone: Results of a Demonstration Program, *The Hospice Journal*, *9*:4, pp. 9-20, 1994.
5. S. R. Langner, Finding Meaning in Caring for Elderly Relatives: Loss and Personal Growth, *Holistic Nursing Practice*, *9*:30, pp. 75-84, 1995.
6. C. A. Corr and D. M. Corr, Adult Hospice Day Care, *Death Studies*, *16*:2, pp. 155-171, 1992.
7. W. R. Richards, D. E. Burgess, F. R. Petersen, and D. L. McCarthy, Genograms: A Psychosocial Assessment Tool for Hospice, *The Hospice Journal*, *9*:1, pp. 1-12, 1993.
8. D. L. Klingensmith and T. A. Novotny, Creating Primary Caregivers Where There are None, *American Journal of Hospice Care*, *5*:1, pp. 32-35, 1988.
9. D. MacDonald, Hospice Patients without Primary Caregivers, *Home Healthcare Nurse*, *10*:1, pp. 24-26, 1992.
10. L. Beresford, Home Alone, *Hospice*, *6*:1, pp. 21-24, 1995.
11. M. O. Amenta and C. A. Lippert, Hospice is a Concept, Not a Place, *Home Healthcare Nurse*, *12*:3, pp. 71-72, 1994.
12. D. Kidder, The Effects of Hospice Coverage on Medicare Expenditures, *Health Services Research*, *27*:2, pp. 195-217, 1992.
13. R. Latuchie and L. Sarafino, Hospice Away from Home, *Hospice*, *4*:4, pp. 18-19, 1993.

14. K. V. Mor, T. J. Wachtel, and D. Kidder, Patient Predictors of Hospice Choice: Hospital Versus Home Care Programs, *Medical Care, 23*:9, pp. 1115-1119, 1985.
15. T. Ryndes, New Beginnings in Hospice, *Healthcare Forum Journal, 38*:2, pp. 27-29, 1995.
16. S. C. McMillan and M. Mahon, The Impact of Hospice Services on the Quality of Life of Primary Caregivers, *Oncology Nursing Forum, 21*:7, pp. 1189-1195, 1994.

CHAPTER 3

Only God Knows When

Dying is never easy, and we in hospice cannot make it so. Suffering and grief are always part of dying. But closeness and warmth can be there too.

Grieving is hard but must be experienced for recovery to come. We don't try to stop it. On the contrary, we help our families grieve. We provide understanding and love, and we accept their feelings. We help them live with their grief and work it through so one day they can heal.

This is what our bereavement care is all about. It's about patience, and love, and faith in the remarkable capacity of human beings to heal. Even when hospice doesn't enter the scene until death approaches, this kind of care transforms the heart of grief.

HEATHER

December 2

"It's been a long, painful time for you both—are you holding up all right?" Dr. Grant, an intent woman in her early forties, addressed her question to the young parents seated before her. Karen, in her green warm-up suit and matching headband, could have graced a magazine cover were it not for the anguish in her face. Eric, although a few years older, looked as young and fit as his wife. He, too, had deep worry lines and fatigue etched on his face. Except for these expressions, the presence of these

slim, blond parents in the sober setting of an oncology office seemed a monstrous mistake.

"We're doing okay, Dr. Grant." Eric held his wife's hand, seeking strength as much as giving it.

Karen and Eric Brown were struggling through the final stages of their daughter, Heather's, leukemia. Heather wasn't yet seven years old.

"It's taken all the courage you could muster, I know—and I admire you," Dr. Grant said earnestly, without artifice. Then she paused for a moment. The next words would not be as easy.

"All we know to do has been done. We've given it everything we have, and after all that, it hurts bitterly to realize that Heather has very little time left." Her voice cracked, and she cleared her throat. "I know this is very hard, but have you thought about whether you want Heather to be at home or here at the hospital when the end comes?"

Two voices responded, together but totally out of synch.

"Oh, not at home," Eric gasped.

"At home. I think she'd want that." Karen's voice was so low she could barely be heard.

Dr. Grant got both messages. Clearly this grieving couple, devastated by what their little girl had suffered during the past twenty-seven months and by the loss they faced, differed in their ways of coping. Perhaps they differed in their views of dying as well. She hoped there would be enough time left for them to come to some agreement.

"Fortunately, you don't have to decide today. But you do need to talk about it. Try to arrive at a plan you can both accept. There's no right or wrong way. Whatever you decide, I'd like to see you have some help at home now. Heather's needs will only increase." Dr. Grant's voice softened. "It's hard enough to hurt inside; let's try to avoid your being exhausted as well." Karen's eyes filled with tears.

"There is a local hospice group that can send a home nurse and other members of their support team to give you a hand. They're familiar with children like Heather, and they can help you with what lies ahead. Shall I call and arrange that?"

"I suppose so," Karen responded. "Yes," her voice became stronger. "I think that's a good idea." Eric said nothing.

Earlier in the day he had gone out for a Christmas tree. The holiday was going to have to come early this year. Heather had watched the tree trimming from the sofa; then, with her pleading and that of Christine, her round-faced four-year-old sister, Eric and Karen had taken the girls to see Santa. Melanie, their eighteen-year-old daughter, stayed home.

The outing was a costly indulgence. The exertion proved too much for Heather. Frightened at how pale and exhausted she had become, they stopped at Doctors' Memorial Hospital to see Dr. Grant on their way home. Perhaps a transfusion of whole blood would help Heather hang on. At this stage they grasped for small reprieves, and on this occasion they were rewarded. The blood helped, and they left the hospital. Another week, another day, any postponement of the end was welcome.

December 9

A bittersweet week passed. Karen kept notes of every treasured incident. Heather slept a lot, looking tinier each day and exerting herself less and less. By the end of the week Eric panicked, becoming obsessed with her need for nutrition.

At his insistence, Karen called Dr. Grant. "She isn't eating anything," she said, her voice shaky. "What can we do?"

"There is hyperalimentation," Dr. Grant said, thinking out loud. "I don't really recommend it at this point, but it's possible to feed nutrients through a catheter into her veins, by IV. She would need nursing, Karen. Do you want her to be hospitalized?"

"No—We've decided we want her here at home. Can your hospice nurse who phoned me the other day handle it if she comes here?"

"I think so. I'll call her."

Karen waited impatiently that afternoon for Janice, the hospice nurse, and her nurse's aide colleague, Maya, to arrive. They would teach her what to do so she could care for Heather during the mornings, with some help from Melanie. Janice and Maya would manage the afternoon and night shifts, including handling Heather's frequent night-time toileting needs.

Bone-weary Karen welcomed the thought that she might get some rest. Hyperal, as the nurses called it when they arrived, would require round-the-clock monitoring of the IV.

Heather was once more connected to a tube, but this time it was in her own home. Janice and Maya then sat down to write Heather's history in the hospice chart, absorbing the story from Karen as she spoke:

It all began one day in September two years ago. I was planning to take Heather shopping for her first-day-in-kindergarten dress. "Hurry and finish your breakfast," I said, stifling some concern about how flushed she looked. I rinsed the yellow traces of egg from the other dishes before stacking them in the dishwasher. Heather, now alone at the round red-maple table, was toying with her food.

"I'm trying," she said, shifting in her seat. She was suspiciously restless and irritable, twisting one of her long blond curls between her fingers, her eyes red.

Approaching her fifth birthday, Heather was one of those rare children, considerate beyond her years and blessed with an uncanny wisdom. She seemed to have purpose about life. Her insight and choices often stunned us.

Her appearance set off an alarm in me. I dried my hands, found the thermometer and took her temperature. "One hundred two!" I gasped under my breath. "You're not feeling well, are you, Sweet?" I leaned over to kiss her on the forehead. The dry heat under my lips confirmed the fever.

"My stomach hurts," Heather complained.

"We'll have to postpone the shopping and put you back to bed for awhile. Come along." I scooped Heather off the chair and led her back to her bedroom. Tylenol® and a glass of water later, I tucked her in and encouraged her to sleep. Then I called Dr. Lawlor, Heather's pediatrician. He said she probably had the virus going around.

The fever came and went, changing with the level of Tylenol® in her system, and Heather missed her shopping trip and the first, second, and third days of kindergarten. She was finally better after the weekend and I gave her my blessing to go to school on Monday.

That morning Heather hopped from one foot to the other, unable to contain her eagerness as I cleared the breakfast mess and prepared to drive her to school. Her excitement spilled over to Christine, and the two of them skipped in a circle around the den, one with skill and the other tumbling like a puppy in her wake. They made quite a pair, quite close in height, Heather fair and sunny with her long almost yellow curls, and Christine a brown-haired butterball with bright laughing eyes.

The day that began so full of promise ended quite the opposite. By noon Heather was tired, and her fever returned in the evening. I called Dr. Lawlor, and he directed us to meet him at the emergency room at Doctors' Memorial Hospital. I fought a premonition of trouble as I drove there, praying silently that Heather would be well.

Dr. Lawlor and Dr. Rosewall, a children's cancer specialist, sat down with me after the physical exam and blood tests were completed. Heather remained in the emergency room with a nurse.

"Heather's white count is way up," Dr. Lawlor began. "She has far more white cells in her blood than we normally see, which tells us she is a very sick little girl."

"We won't know for sure until we examine Heather's bone marrow and spinal fluid, Mrs. Brown," Dr. Rosewall continued, "but you must be prepared for the possibility that she has leukemia. Are you familiar with the disease?"

"All I know is that children die fr . . ." I started to cry.

"Sometimes that's true. But more and more children survive now," Dr. Rosewall told me. "Please let me explain." He paused for a moment as I tried to collect myself, then began. "Leukemia is basically a disease of the bone marrow where too many white cells are produced, crowding out the normal red blood cells and platelets. Abnormal cells form in the bone marrow and sometimes move into the spinal fluid.

"We'll need to extract some marrow from Heather's pelvis and fluid from her spine this evening to see if the cells are normal or if leukemia is causing her illness. We'll have preliminary results from the tests in a few hours but we won't know for sure until morning. I suggest you plan to stay here tonight.

Heather may need you nearby." I held my breath, struggling for control.

"The bone marrow is drawn under a local anesthetic," Dr. Rosewall continued, "but in spite of that the procedure hurts. The spinal tap isn't as bad; it takes only a few minutes, and while it's no fun, children often tolerate it pretty well. The only thing is she mustn't move while we do it."

I kept myself together to ask some questions and then went to explain to Heather what was going to happen. "Sweet, the doctors won't know how to help you feel better unless they can do a couple more tests. They have to put in two more needles, and it's going to hurt. Can you try to be a big girl and hold very still while they do that?" Heather clung to me as I spoke.

"It's okay to cry as long as you don't move. I'll hold you close." Heather nodded her head, too frightened to speak.

I signed the permission papers and Dr. Rosewall led us to the examining room.

Heather was fearful but stoic through the spinal tap. However when they suctioned the marrow from deep within her pelvis she screamed, hanging on to me as if her life depended on it. She tried to be a big girl but she couldn't stop her screams. They exploded from her core, tearing at my insides. I must have hurt as much as she did.

Finally it was over, and I carried my limp little girl to the room assigned to us—the bed for Heather and the window seat mattress for me. "It's all over, Sweet. You can go to sleep now. Mommy will stay with you right here in this room. I'll be here when you wake up, you'll see." I reassured her the best I could. Sounding calm took all the control I could muster.

Heather slept, and before lying down I called Eric. We arranged to meet in Heather's room in the morning to hear the test results together. Neither of us slept that night, and it showed when Dr. Rosewall joined us the next morning. We walked three abreast to the parents' lounge, no one speaking.

The verdict, when we finally settled into our chairs, was bad. Heather was sick with acute lymphocytic leukemia. The only good news was that so far her disease was limited to her blood. Since it had not yet invaded her spinal fluid, it had a cure rate as high as 70 percent.

In shock, I asked my first question assuming the worst, deaf to the hope Dr. Rosewall had just held out to us. "How long do we have?" I heard my voice from a distance, feeling numb and separate from what was happening in the room.

"Perhaps you didn't hear me, Mrs. Brown. Heather has a very good chance. I'm optimistic that she's going to make it. But she will have to undergo treatment that should begin without delay—today."

I shook myself, trying to respond. "What will you do about her infection?"

"Leukemia is not an infection. She doesn't have an infection," Dr. Rosewall answered.

"But she never runs a temperature without having an infection. I know her." My objection sounded like a plea.

"The leukemia will make her very different, Mrs. Brown," Dr. Rosewall said as he got up to leave. "You may think you know her, but with this illness she'll be a different little girl. You may not recognize some of her reactions. You'll have to trust us to interpret what is going on." He stuck his hand out, first to me, then to Eric, looking at neither one of us. Then, his face like a mask, he left the room.

Panic gripped me. The news of Heather's illness was bad enough. In addition this unknown doctor had frightened me with his warning. How could anything change my beautiful little girl so only he and his colleagues could understand her? How dare he say I wouldn't know Heather? He was so cruel— stealing her away from me. In moments I was swept into the unfamiliar world of medicine where I couldn't possibly find my own way.

I was shaking; inside I felt a scream well up in my chest and throat. This awful man had to be wrong. She couldn't be that sick.

Once we were alone, Eric and I reached for each other. We were scared. We didn't know what to do. For starters, what could we tell Heather? We stood there for several minutes in the lounge, frozen in our embrace.

I suppose that somehow people find a way to adapt. Eventually I began to feel deep in my gut that the die was cast and I had to cope; we all had to. Despite my anger and fear, unconsciously I must have begun to organize myself, thinking of questions and preparing for the responsibilities I would have to assume.

At the same time, I saw that Eric's reactions, like his pain, were buried deeper. He seemed inaccessible. Instinctively I knew I would have to lead the way. I resolved to do whatever was needed to make Heather well. Anything.

I regrouped, took Eric's hand and headed back to Heather's room. In fact, by the time we reached her, Heather probably never noticed anything extraordinary. We sat down, and I explained that she had some sick cells in her blood which would require her to stay in the hospital for a few days. She would be given medicine to make the bad cells better. Heather accepted our explanation.

We decided I would stay on in Heather's hospital room while Eric went home to be with Christine and Melanie. A four-day regimen of IV medication began. The drug dripping into Heather's vein was powerful; it was intended to be lethal to the cancer cells without killing her. War had been declared against the leukemia. The drug would make her very sick.

Heather vomited the whole time, but her fever rapidly diminished. After four days of chemotherapy the IV was to be disconnected and she would be allowed to go home. So it was a shock on that fourth day when I saw the flush in her face return along with the fever—suddenly 103 degrees. An infection accompanied her leukemia after all. Dr. Rosewall had been wrong.

Antibiotics were added to her IV, and doctors and lab technicians came and went all day. The following morning, Dr. Rosewall and a surgeon arrived with news that Heather had an infection in her blood, or sepsis. It was caused by organisms in her bowel. That meant her bowel was infected, and worse still, the infection had gained some passageway to her bloodstream. The surgeon didn't hide the gravity of Heather's illness, now consisting of two deadly diseases. It was apparent by the look on his face.

"You need to know that Heather's chance of survival with this complication is about 50 percent, Mrs. Brown."

I felt my knees get weak. "Will you operate?"

"Only if we have to. Our first choice is to treat her medically. We need to continue the IV, and Heather will have to remain here as an inpatient until we can clear this up."

I felt a tight knot in my stomach, then conquered the sense that my knees were going to buckle. "I see."

Janice and Maya scribbled notes, watching Karen closely as she spoke. They took in the sudden trembling in her chin as she began the painful parts of her story, the frequent sweep of her long fingers from her brow down the sides of her face as she relived Heather's crises. She would sit silently then, with her chin supported by her clasped hands, until she could talk about what had come next. Occasionally Janice underlined something on her pad. Neither one interrupted Karen when she continued.

After three long weeks of treatment the infection finally cleared and Heather's fever left. Although pale, she once again bubbled with interest in her surroundings, shedding her sunny feelings on all of us around her. I allowed myself to look toward Heather's—and my own—homecoming. The house needed a thorough cleaning to be a safe, germ-free haven for her, so I left the hospital one Tuesday evening to get the work done.

I was overjoyed to get home to Christine, Melanie, and Eric, and there was a flavor of old times to the girls' bedtime ceremonies. Melanie wanted to know all about Heather, and little Christine kept asking, "Why didn't Heather come home with you, Mommy?" Eric and I explained, "She's getting better, girls, and she should be coming home soon," which reassured them. I couldn't wait either for her to be there with us, to round out the family.

Wednesday morning, before tackling the cleaning, I went to the phone and called Heather. After several rings the nurse at the station on her floor responded.

"Oh, I expected Heather."

"She's sleeping, Mrs. Brown. Why don't we let her sleep and we can call you when she wakes up?"

I agreed and threw myself into the work I had to do. About eleven o'clock, after a juice and cracker break with Christine, I went back to the phone, wondering why I hadn't heard from the hospital. When someone finally answered I could hear Heather crying out in the background—a cry of pain that took my breath away.

"What's wrong with her—why does she sound like that?"

"We were just going to call you, Mrs. Brown. Heather's had a stomach ache during the night and the doctor has been in to see her. He hasn't decided what to do yet, but we thought you might want to come back to be with her."

"Have you given her anything for the pain?"

"No. The doctor says that would mask the symptoms."

I hung up the phone and took Christine over to the neighbors. They called Eric for me, and I roared down the road to the hospital, thirty minutes away, my fatigue erased by the adrenalin pouring into my system.

The rest of the day I stood at Heather's side, rubbing her abdomen when she cried out. Eric ran in for a few minutes but had to get back to his insurance office, and I was alone when Heather's IV pulled out of her vein. I called out, and nurses came crowding around, each taking a turn trying to reinsert the needle. They poked and poked, finally getting the medicine to flow into a tiny vein in her foot after giving up on her arms. Through it all Heather didn't flinch or cry; the only sound from her was a weak "Mommy" from time to time.

It was hard to tell just when she slipped into a coma. I had her in my arms when she stopped responding. I thought she was dying. I panicked. I slapped her on the back—not knowing what to do. She just lay there in my lap like a doll with no stuffing. I called frantically for the nurse.

Dr. Rosewall came into the room with a nurse who lifted Heather out of my arms. "You look exhausted, Mrs. Brown," he said. "You can't help here. I want you to go down to the resident physicians' room and lie down. We'll call you if there is any change. This is best, please believe me. Now go." He turned to Heather, and the nurse guided me by the shoulder out of the room.

With no energy to resist, I found the room and collapsed onto a bed. I couldn't sleep, but I think I must have rested. I felt I was floating as a fog of images of Heather swam through my mind. Then the phone rang in the distance, and I realized a resident in the room had answered quietly, then left the room. The sound roused me. I got up quickly and returned to Heather's room.

With a crowd of white uniforms surrounding her, Heather lay silently on the bed, eyes wide open. "She has been seizing, Mrs. Brown," the surgeon said. "Her bowel has perforated, and we need to operate as soon as we can get her ready." He held my hand, looking directly into my eyes with an urgency I hadn't seen before. "We're going to the intensive care unit now."

I digested the fast-moving events and turned to Heather to explain.

"Sweet, the doctor has to put you to sleep so he can open your tummy and take the bad bugs out. Be my big girl and help them all you can. I'll go with you to your new room, and I'll be waiting there for you when you wake up." I choked down a cry with the last words, and Heather, watching me soberly, said in a small voice, "Mommy, don't worry. I'm not going to die."

Everyone froze, stunned mute by my child's eerie counsel. There wasn't a dry eye in the group.

True to her word, Heather survived the surgery. Four perforations were found; a section of her intestine was removed and an opening made to drain out the infected material. She came back to the intensive care unit on a respirator, hooked up to an IV and in restraints, looking tiny and helpless, but alive.

As I waited at Heather's side in the intensive care unit, searching her pale face for signs of waking up, I was reminded of something she had said to me several times in the past, first as a toddler and again at intervals since then. "I'm going to die before you, Mommy, but only God knows when." I didn't understand then and still can't believe she could have said this, but as I stood watching her I was overwhelmed by how close she had come. The events of the past weeks and her uncanny belief seemed connected. I shivered, although it wasn't cold.

When she regained consciousness I explained simply to her what had happened, and why the respirator and IV tubes were needed. Then I asked the nurse to remove the restraints.

"We can't do that with such a young child, Mrs. Brown. She'll pull out the IVs."

"She won't, I promise you. Don't keep her restrained."

Somehow I convinced the nurse, and Heather made good my promise. The nurses were amazed.

They shouldn't have been surprised. We had always given Heather honest answers about her illness. During the spinal taps and bone marrow tests she knew she had to lie still, and she did. With a mysterious sixth sense, she seemed to know what life was about, and frequently she seemed more adult than child.

As Heather recovered from the surgery, relatives and friends visited frequently. Melanie came almost daily to read to her. I prepared Christine for what she would see, explaining Heather's illness and surgery in the simplest terms, and one day brought her with me. After a few silent moments of staring wide-eyed at each other, they giggled, then played happily with a doll on Heather's bed. Being together again seemed to dissolve the moodiness I had seen recently in Christine.

Gifts quickly appeared around Heather's bed. She was delighted with each addition, selecting one and then another to play with or to give to Christine when she came to visit. She reserved one fuzzy toy monkey for a little boy she had heard crying frequently in the next room.

One of the residents who streamed in and out of her room took in the toy scene one morning. "You really shouldn't be spoiling her like this," he said.

I tried not to let my anger show. "It's natural for friends to send gifts when a child is in the hospital," I managed to get out. Then I turned away to face the window, biting my lips while I waited for him to leave.

Later I ran into him in the hall and exploded, "How dare you? How dare you?", my voice rising on each word. "You don't know what Heather's been through! You don't know what's been going on! All these gifts were from friends. We've bought ONE coloring book and a box of crayons! And even if all the toys were from us, we haven't spoiled her. I've forced her to walk when she was in pain because you people said she had to walk. I've told her she had to cooperate with all the pokes and sticks and treatment, and she's been wonderful. She's not spoiled! And even if she were, and even if I had," the words tumbled out like a waterfall, "what right do you have to say anything about it, especially right in front of her?"

I panted, out of breath and shocked at myself. The resident, his eyes wide, finally managed to stammer, "I'm really sorry, Mrs. Brown. I didn't realize. . . ." He and his voice faded back to the chart rack where he could take refuge in some paperwork. I felt distinctly better as I headed down the hall.

. Heather's recovery during the weeks following her surgery lulled everyone into a sense of optimism. But another crisis found her with a new pain in her stomach, one which no one but I believed was real. The surgeon thought it would pass, and he left town for a meeting. Dr. Rosewall suggested Heather get psychotherapy. The first words of a cynical surgical resident called to her room during the night were, "Are you going to cry now that I'm here?" I couldn't believe his sarcasm. I demanded that another surgeon be called and it was good that I did. A senior staff doctor came and listened. His examination found cellulitis, a fluid build-up in her abdomen that had to be lanced and packed before the pain would disappear.

After fifty-eight difficult days in the hospital, Heather was finally allowed to go home, eager but quite different from when she was admitted. She was skinny and unusually quiet—skinny because food by mouth had been withheld for weeks as a protective measure in case surgery had to be performed, and terribly quiet. The nurses said the prednisone she was taking could cause that. I missed my little chatterbox as we drove home together.

And I worried, too. Dr. Rosewall threatened readmission for Heather if she lost more weight at home. Her discharge was really just a pass; it would work only if she resumed eating.

That first night, Thanksgiving weekend, we all sat down together for dinner. Eric and I breathed a grateful prayer for being a whole family once more, and I brought meatloaf, buttered carrots, and mashed potatoes to the table. It was an appealing scene, green salads and eager faces at each place. Christine couldn't stop smiling at Heather, she was so happy to have her big sister home again. Melanie's pleasure seemed more constrained. We linked hands, and repeated together as we had so often before, "God is great and God is good, and we thank Him for our food. Amen." I glanced at Melanie as we prayed; a worry knot puckered her forehead, and her eyes were not closed. She was looking carefully at her little sister. I added my own prayer for an end to such worries.

"I don't want meatloaf," Heather announced imperiously, sensing her importance when the prayer concluded. "I want chicken."

I glanced at Eric, then reacted from instinct. "This is what I've cooked and served. You're back home now, Sweet, and you can either eat this or you'll have to go hungry." My throat was tight; I couldn't know whether it was the right thing to say.

Eric and I held our collective breath, trying very hard not to show our anxiety. Miracles! She ate! She not only ate, she translated the message into all of her behavior. There was no further testing; Heather had really come home.

Maya and Janice sat motionless, saying nothing lest they miss a single word. Heather, "hyperal" tube in place, slept on the hide-a-bed in the next room as Karen refilled the coffee cups at the kitchen table. Only the clicking of spoons against porcelain could be heard as Janice and Maya waited for her to resume the story.

During the next month Heather regained much of her former strength. Weekly visits to the outpatient clinic at the hospital confirmed how well she was doing. She won the hearts of everyone. She asked so many unusual questions, and she obviously cared about the other patients. In her special way, she tried to ease things for me, all without fuss or attention. Joyce, the gentle pediatric nurse practitioner who saw her at each visit, was entranced, as were the others on the clinic team. She and Joyce became fast friends, each regularly bringing little surprises for the other.

In December, we had to change doctors. Dr. Rosewall was leaving. That wasn't bad news; all along he had kept us in the dark too much, which is really hard when you're worried about your child. In the clinic, I asked other mothers about their experiences. They led me to Dr. Grant. She agreed to take over Heather's care and we liked her right from the start.

It was none too soon. Heather was ready for the reconstructive surgery which would remove and close off the drain from her intestine. The thought of readmission to the hospital seemed more palatable with a friendly doctor waiting for us.

On January 2, Heather celebrated a joyous birthday with all of us at home. It was a week before she was to have the surgery. She was five years old, a milestone we had not been certain she would reach. The party included cake and ice cream, friends and relatives—all in bounteous supply. Devoted volunteers from the outpatient clinic at the hospital delivered six helium-filled balloons for our celebration, five for her and, so she wouldn't feel left out, one for Christine. There was a self-conscious quality to the happiness we all felt; never again would we take such joy for granted.

The surgery on January 9 went well. After five days Heather had recovered sufficiently to be discharged.

January and the four months that followed were too good to be true. Heather's leukemia was in remission, and she had once more become our golden-haired angel. She threw herself into the activities of school, family, and neighborhood. She mothered Christine once more, and allowed Melanie to mother her. There were five-year-old type slumber parties, trips to museums, a Disney movie party followed by a group Big-Mac attack, and sledding and picnics in the mountain parks. With a vengeance, Eric and I made up for the earlier moratorium on fun. Being normal had an urgency about it now. Each week we celebrated the results of Heather's tests at the outpatient clinic. We simply didn't allow our sense of borrowed time to surface.

Spring was stirring. Birds returned, heralding each day with song; flowers bloomed and trees and shrubs sprouted leaves. The fragrance of apple blossoms hung lightly in the air. Burgeoning life stung the senses at every turn.

Spring, I reasoned, affects people differently, and I hoped that could explain the subtle changes I began to observe in Heather. She was becoming almost demanding, almost irritable, more in a hurry about everything. There were no clear signs of returning illness, no headaches, no bodily pain, no dizziness. But early in June, I asked for a spinal tap anyway, just to be sure, and was not surprised to learn a cancer cell was detected. Dr. Grant tried to be reassuring. Everyone knew, however, it was a bad sign.

We chose to make a long-talked-about trip to Disneyland with Heather and Christine immediately. Eric canceled his business schedule. Melanie, tied up with high school activities, moved in with the neighbors. We packed, and off we went. Eric and I made every effort to keep the trip carefree for the little girls, and we succeeded. For ourselves, borrowed time became the driving force.

We returned at the end of July, with Heather clearly unwell. We took her back to the clinic, and Dr. Grant delivered the sentence after the tests were completed. "I'm terribly sorry." She took my hands in hers and held them. "Heather has relapsed, and now her central nervous system (CNS) is involved. She has cancer cells in her spinal fluid, and she could begin to have some neurological problems. She should start another course of chemotherapy right away. If that fails to clear her spinal fluid by the end of August, she will need radiation therapy as well. This treatment will be aggressive; I'm hopeful it will do the job.

"I must also tell you that we'll be fighting to avoid a reappearance of cancer cells in her bone marrow. If she can clear her spinal fluid and then hold her own, with no CNS relapse for eight months, I believe we'll have it made."

Dr. Grant had always combined kindness with honesty, and these were the qualities that saved us from falling apart. She cared—about Heather, and about us. She stayed for our questions, then left us alone in the room together to collect ourselves. It was agreed that chemotherapy would begin on the first of August. Everyone was committed to the battle for her bone marrow, for that was where her leukemia would win or lose.

Karen's fingertips once more sought her brow. Janice rose from her chair and laid a hand on Karen's shoulder. "Could I interrupt your story just long enough to call the hospice office?

They're expecting me. But please don't stop. You and the family, and especially Heather, have been through so much. We must learn what you need now—what we can do to help you." She stayed until Karen nodded. Then Karen and Maya waited silently for Janice to complete her call. When she returned, Karen picked up her story once more.

Warned that the chemotherapy could cause Heather to lose her hair, Eric and I arranged to have her picture taken. We told each other any day is a good time for a new picture, but we both knew it was insurance.

Then we shopped with her for school clothes, a gesture for all of us to show we believed the outcome would be positive.

That completed, Heather started her outpatient treatment and soon thereafter, first grade. Twice-weekly spinal taps were done along with the chemotherapy, and remarkably, Heather never complained. Nor did she react badly when radiation therapy had to begin, as promised, because her spinal fluid didn't clear. The only thing that upset her was finding globs of hair in her bed in the mornings, and then facing children who laughed at her spotty, balding head. Heather's appearance disturbed Christine, too. She was baffled by the strange sight, and seemed to know something was wrong.

Joyce, Heather's nurse and good friend from the clinic, saw her plight and arranged to accompany her to school, armed with a Raggedy Ann doll and an IV needle. She explained to Heather's classmates what leukemia was, showed them how the medication was administered through the veins, and described the effects it had, particularly the loss of hair. Hers was a simple act, but it made all the difference to Heather who held the doll while Joyce demonstrated. It satisfied her classmates. They paid little attention to Heather's appearance after that. Later, she explained for herself when strangers stared or questioned why she had no hair. I heard her repeating the story to Christine that evening. Both children were remarkably matter-of-fact about it.

There were no cancer cells in her blood or spinal fluid after six weeks of treatment, but our worries didn't stop. Just before Heather's sixth birthday in January, the lab reported her hemoglobin was only 4.4, a terribly low measure of red cells in her blood. With each report, I watched her closely for any signs of change. In February I thought she seemed irritable again so I called Dr. Grant. "It's coming back, Dr. Grant. I can tell. She's not herself."

"Try not to borrow trouble, Karen. The tests don't show relapse. It may be she needs to see a psychologist for awhile. You know she's beginning to understand more about what's happening to her, and she may need to work some of these things through."

Heather began weekly sessions with a psychologist. Her irritability continued.

Chemotherapy had to be discontinued twice because of her low blood count. It was resumed again on April 1. Eric, Dr. Grant, the clinic staff, and I all pinned our hopes on it, for seven months had passed since her CNS relapse. Blood tests would show in one more month whether cancer had re-entered her bone marrow. Life or death likely awaited the outcome. All of us tiptoed around our feelings; it was an extremely critical time.

Resumption of chemotherapy this time, on April 1, left me with a cold chill I could not shake. It may have been the warning about eight months; it seemed more to be a change in Heather. Unlike her earlier acceptance of every procedure, now she lay in the induction room unmoved by Joyce's efforts to make her comfortable and to distract her. Her eyes died. "Nothing," she seemed to be saying, "will help anymore. What's the point?"

I watched her, a sense of doom enveloping me.

The blood tests a month later found bone marrow relapse, just eight months after her CNS relapse. The fight was lost.

Dr. Grant sat down in her office with Eric and me to talk about the only treatment option left to us—bone marrow transplant. It was a sad meeting, and a desperate one. We took comfort in the books and papers cluttering her desk and shelves, knowing she was someone who had the knowledge to save Heather if anyone could. We listened carefully. Dr. Grant explained that Heather's diseased bone marrow would be replaced in this procedure with healthy marrow from a donor, and, if the transplant were successful she could recover. Heather would have to be in remission for twenty-eight days to be accepted for transplant, and a donor would have to be found whose marrow matched hers. If both these conditions were met, we would go to one of several transplant centers in the country for treatments lasting from six to eight weeks. She would undergo high dosage chemotherapy and radiation to kill her own bone marrow. Then healthy bone marrow from the donor would be introduced into her veins. All the while she would have to be kept in isolation, not to protect others but to avoid infection from anyone else, until the donor immunity integrated as her own. Reverse isolation, they called it. It would be painful physically and emotionally—physically because the radiation turns mucous membrane raw, and emotionally because her contact with us could only be through a window and speaker system or with us hidden totally in protective gowns, gloves, masks, caps, and booties. After all of that, Dr. Grant said, the chance of success was a slim 15-20 percent. Even if it all succeeded, the marrow replacement could fight Heather's body later in what is called a graft-versus-host reaction, and she could die anyway. We were profoundly frightened by the proposal—a last resort, awful to accept, and awful to reject.

But Eric and I agreed to it. It was Heather's only chance, so what real choice did we have? We also approved placing a long-term catheter in a vein in her arm to save her being stuck over and over again during the IV chemotherapy. The needles could then pierce this broviac, as it was called, not her veins. A minor surgical procedure, it was done quickly so the new chemotherapy could begin.

Eric, Melanie, and I were first tested for the donor match, technically a minor procedure—but pretty painful. Eric and I were crushed to learn we could not provide her replacement marrow. Melanie, however, was identified as a potential donor.

"Heather's psychologist should see Melanie before we proceed," Dr. Grant explained. "While she may be very willing to be the donor, we must be sure she understands she's not responsible for failure if it doesn't work. We can have some bad repercussions if that isn't clear, so we want her to be prepared." Dr. Grant's care was apparent, but it loaded one more concern on us. Could we do this to Melanie?

An appointment was made for her. She was a very sober adolescent when she came out at the end of the interview to tell us she wanted to go ahead with the plan. We had to trust that she could handle it.

By the end of July, Heather was technically in remission. Her spinal fluid was clear and only 4 percent blasts were found in her bone marrow, a low level that would not rule out the transplant. I prepared for the trip. Heather, Christine, and I would fly to the Iowa transplant center, and after admitting Heather to the isolation unit, Christine and I would make our temporary home in a nearby motel. Eric would come as often as he could leave his business, and Melanie would arrive when Heather was ready for the transplant.

Lab tests would have to be repeated and remission confirmed at the center before the transplant could proceed. "Dear God," I prayed throughout the flight, "if Heather can recover from the transplant, let them find her in remission now. If she can't ever be well again, then let them say 'no' right now." It was a bargaining prayer, the kind offered by a child. Stripped of all my defenses, I guess that's what I had become.

The blood tests didn't take long the first day at the center. The answer came the next morning. I sat, tense and dry, as the report was given. Heather had relapsed. There would be no transplant. The elaborate plan was discarded, and with it all chance of a cure.

Dr. Grant called a conference when the girls and I returned. Clinic personnel, floor nurses, the social worker, and several of Heather's physicians at the hospital met with Eric and me to consider together what should follow. The room was heavy with sorrow over this latest, ultimate disappointment in the struggle for Heather's life.

The physicians were all for another course of chemotherapy, admitting it would not cure but might buy Heather more time. Eric and I listened intently. "How much time? What would it be like for Heather?" Eric asked. We shared our reactions to the answers with our eyes. Our decision came in unison. I spoke for both of us.

"You tell us chemotherapy won't cure Heather but could buy her some time; that she could be sick and require hospitalization a couple of days each week. That means we'd take what little time she has left and make her endure more sticks, more vomiting, more plugged up broviacs, more time at the hospital, until the time is gone and she is dead.

"No. We're not going to do it. We're just not going to do it! If she has three months left, as you suggest, we're going to let her be a little girl for a change. She's not going to spend what little time she has hooked up to a tube, or emptying her stomach into an emesis basin. She's going to play with her sisters and her friends as long as she's able, and we're going to be with her and love her like normal parents.

"And when it's over she will have had some happy times, and we will have given her some good family life!"

"You shouldn't say that," a surgeon across the table urged. He turned to Eric. "If you were the patient would you want people to give up on you?"

"If I had only three months to live, I would choose to stop treatment, yes." Eric spoke slowly, earnestly. "It's all so hard— such a grueling process. If it's all for nothing—and she's going to die anyway—why do it? Why? Why not take her three months and let her enjoy what she can? She's been such a good little girl, and she's had so little freedom from this tyranny." I nodded my head in agreement.

"That's not what you should say," the surgeon repeated. He was unable to find any way to stem this tide of rejection.

"Bull!" The vehemence of my reply surprised everyone in the room, including me.

Driving home later, Eric and I felt strangely relieved. For the moment we rode a crest of having made a decision, of saving Heather from further agony doomed to failure. We could hardly wait to tell her she had had her last stick, her last poke, that all of her remaining days could be free. At the same time, we wept.

That evening after Christine was tucked into bed, Eric and I gathered Heather between us on the sofa and explained to her what was happening. "You've been a wonderful girl in handling all this sickness so well, Heather. You've hurt many times, and we've hurt for you. It's been hard sometimes, hasn't it?"

She nodded her head. "I don't like needles."

"You've put up with a lot to cure those bad cells, Sweet. Mommy and Daddy have decided you should have some time free of all that. How would you like that?"

"D'you mean I don't have to have any more chemo or needles or spinals or anything?" Her voice rose in excited disbelief.

"That's what we mean, Heather. Does that make you happy?"

"Oh, yes." She squeezed her eyes shut and clasped her hands, then threw her arms first around Eric's neck and then around mine. "This is the BEST night!"

We held her close, grasping at the rare joy of bringing her happiness. Our own tears were saved for the privacy of our room, after Heather went to bed.

Heather started school in the fall, relishing being part of the group. I encouraged her to do all the things she had wanted to do, and we all entered into the spirit of her fun. We had cook-outs, and sing-along parties, an end-of-summer amusement park outing, library afternoons on the weekends and Sunday afternoon movie parties with her Sunday School class. It was a storybook time that went on for five weeks.

But we knew it couldn't last. The pain began in mid-October, and when morphine was required late that month, Heather had to leave school. A bleeder developed in her eye, and she went back to the outpatient clinic for platelets to promote better clotting. She began to sleep more, and each day she grew more thoughtful, greeting us in the morning and saying goodnight at bedtime with long hugs and "I love you."

One day, watching Heather try to relax with the pain, I told her of our naps curled up together like two nested bananas when I was pregnant with Christine. Heather visualized it and said shyly, "You can hold me that way again, Mommy." After that I would frequently lie down with her, to be close and to get a more sensitive reading of how she was feeling. It comforted both of us. Busy little Christine sometimes joined us, but she couldn't hold still long and usually crawled off the bed in a matter of minutes to play.

Heather talked in her sleep for a few nights. I asked one morning whether she was dreaming a lot. "Yes, Mommy. But it's all right."

"Can you remember what you dream, Sweet?"

"There's a light that keeps calling me. But I'm not ready yet. It's O.K., Mommy. It'll wait 'til I'm ready."

I steadied myself against the kitchen counter, then bent down to give Heather a kiss. The moment passed.

A couple of weeks later, Heather referred again in her child-serious voice to the light that beckoned her. "What's Mommy going to do without you when you go?" I asked her.

"Mom, you're just going to have to handle it. And you will."

"How like her," I thought. I took a deep breath. "Yes, Heather. Because I'll always have you in my heart where I can love you forever and ever."

"Right."

Heather could never know the tear in my heart. She seemed to view with a longer vision. With an innocent and gentle touch she led me to our inevitable separation.

The holiday season approached. Thanksgiving was always celebrated at Eric's parents' home, so despite how frail Heather had become, plans were laid to carry out the custom. When she became sick during Thanksgiving dinner, vomiting the little food she had eaten, and was unable to sit upright, we knew there was little time left.

December 9

"And here we are," Karen sighed. "It is very close to the end, and I don't know if I can handle it." Janice and Maya reached over to touch her hands, willing their contact to lend her support.

"You've found the strength so far, Karen," Janice said. "Have faith the same strength will continue to be there for you."

"I've never had anyone close to me die." Karen began to cry. "I don't even know what to say or do." Her words were lost in her

weeping. Maya continued to hold one hand while Janice moved her arm behind Karen, cradling her shoulders. Neither spoke for several minutes as Karen sobbed.

"We've traveled this road with lots of families," Janice said gently. "We'll help you; you'll find that you can do what needs to be done. Just try not to let it overwhelm you. Take one day at a time."

Karen blew her nose, took a deep breath, then thanked them. The only request she could think of was to help keep Heather at home. She could not see beyond that. Now that Eric had come around to this idea as well, she was afraid she couldn't handle what needed to be done.

The hospice task in general was clear: provide both physical and emotional support for the entire family; make it possible for Heather to remain in the loving surroundings of her home until she died and help the family to heal after it was over.

December 10

Christine left her play at Heather's side on the hide-a-bed to get a snack and soon returned with a chocolate doughnut. As was their custom, they split it and both girls began to eat. Christine enjoyed her half, but in just a few minutes Heather called for me and threw hers up onto the floor. After washing her face and letting her rinse her mouth, I sat down on the edge of the bed while she recovered. "Which do you hate worse, Mommy—throwing up or bloody noses?" It was a strange question.

"I'm not sure, Sweet, but I don't think bloody noses would be much fun."

"I don't either." Heather smiled uncertainly at me.

Maybe there was a message. Hemorrhaging was not a good way to die.

December 12

The hyperal, discontinued after the first three days because Heather was getting too much fluid, left her swollen with congestive heart failure. We gave her a diuretic to purge the excess fluid.

Tiny "petechiae," miniature bleeds under the skin, appeared on her arms and legs. The afternoon nurse noticed them just before she left, and when Maya arrived that evening she advised me to take Heather to the hospital for platelets before the bleeding became more widespread.

The platelets helped. Dr. Grant commented before they finished that Heather looked pretty good. I smiled gratefully and reported our plan for an early Christmas the next day and then maybe another celebration on December 25. Dr. Grant hugged me as we left.

December 13

As was our tradition on Christmas morning, I went downstairs early with a camera; the family was to wait until I called, "Ready, you can come down now." The tree lights were on, and brightly wrapped packages were piled beneath the tree. Christine didn't understand the delay, so she didn't get into the first picture. She was already down. Eric and Melanie, with Heather between them holding a hand of each, all still in their bathrobes, were framed at the turn of the stairway in my first picture. Fragile little Heather looked excited and happy.

The next pictures were candid—Heather and Christine knee deep in wrapping paper, Heather examining her new Cricket doll, Eric holding a ski sweater across his chest with a photogenic grin on his face, Melanie experimenting with the contents of a sophisticated new make-up kit, and Christine pushing a doll's baby carriage up and down the hall to the kitchen.

It was a happy morning, a morning to be treasured. Friends and relatives came by throughout the day, and Heather slept off and on. Maya didn't arrive until 10:30 that night, so she missed the festivities. More important, she was there through the night resting on a foam pad at the foot of Heather's bed to help with the hourly trek to the bathroom.

December 15

New petechiae appeared on Heather's arms and neck. My father discovered them when he made his weekly visit.

Platelets were needed again. By the time we got her to the hospital she was very close to death. The platelets brought her around, and when the procedure ended she climbed back onto her Grandpa's lap and asked to go home. He cradled her carefully in his arms all the way, the soft wide-waled corduroy of his parka keeping her warm. He kissed her forehead gently when we arrived home and laid her down in bed, fast asleep. She was not going to die that day; as she'd said, only God knew when.

December 16

"If you had two wishes, Sweet, what would you choose today?" I brushed Heather's hair back from her face and smiled into her eyes. Heather thought for a minute.

"I'd wish for Aunt Lou to come for a slumber party tonight, and I'd wish for a birthday party tomorrow." Her voice was certain.

"Well, we'll just have to do something about that," I promised.

Eric's sister, Louise, a much loved favorite of Heather's, came after work. The slumber party consisted of one game of Cootie and a communal retirement in the guest bedroom, with Heather in the middle of the bed, me on one side and Aunt Lou on the other. On the floor at the foot of the bed wrapped in a blanket was Maya. Heather was granted her first wish, and she fell asleep with a smile on her thin face.

December 17

Aunt Lou arose early to go to work, kissing Heather a happy birthday before she left. For the first time in her illness, Heather was too weak to go downstairs. Her antibiotic pill wouldn't go down. It was not a good start of the day.

"Heather, it's all right. You don't need to take the pill today," I reassured her.

She slept most of the day. When her quota of morphine pills ran out, I hooked up a morphine drip into her broviac to control the pain, as Janice had taught me, and friends and relatives came and went all day. When Maya arrived in the afternoon she checked Heather, then drew me out into the hall, taking my hands in her own.

"Karen, I believe the end is very close. I want you to be ready."

"Oh dear God, Maya, I can't stand it!" I buried my face in my hands. "Help me. Help me, please!"

"Easy, Karen. Easy." Maya reached for my shoulders and shook me gently. "You're doing fine. You're strong, and you'll do what is needed. Just love her, and be there. She may give you some warning in the way she breathes. Maybe there won't be much warning. You are going to manage." She leaned forward and squeezed me in a quick hug before we went back to Heather.

In the evening Heather roused and asked for her birthday party. I sent word downstairs for the group gathered there to come up to the bedroom, bringing the cake and Heather's presents. They paraded into the room in a long chain, singing happy birthday and creating a fuss that was appropriately festive. Heather loved it. She gave each one a kiss, and I will never forget her happy smile, her luminous presence in that room. Her second wish had come true.

The friends and relatives stood around, uncertain whether to stay or leave. I led them back downstairs, leaving Heather with Eric and a close neighbor. Maya went downstairs too, so they were without help when Heather called out suddenly, "Mommy!"

I heard her as I was returning from downstairs. I flew back up the steps and picked her up in my arms. Heart pounding, I tried to steady my voice. "What is it, Sweet?"

"There's the light, Mommy. I see the light!" Her voice sounded excited, awe-struck.

A steel belt clamped around my chest. I stifled the cry that filled me, "Don't leave me! Don't leave me, my darling child." Instead I managed, "If you're ready, go for it, Heather. We love you so much."

Heather's eyes opened wide; she gasped twice, then she was gone. I sat for many minutes rocking her, tears streaming down my face, knowing Heather, in her way, had said goodbye before going off into the light.

There seemed to be a golden aura in the room for some thirty minutes, spreading out in all directions from Heather's small form on the bed. Her expression was serene and beautiful. Eric tried to capture it in a photograph. I ministered to her, cleaning and dressing her in a fresh gown.

Neither of us was willing to leave, to call it over. How does one begin to live with such a loss?

EPILOGUE

There was never anything so hard to do as letting Heather go. During the months and years that followed, Karen, Eric, Melanie, Christine, and all of Heather's many friends ached for losing her, each in his or her own way, as they had ached for her pain and illness while she lived. For a long time Karen cried and talked voluminously about Heather, then cried some more. She felt there would be no end of crying. Eric cried and couldn't talk, then buried himself in his work. Melanie's life went on, with school and social activities, but the sadness of Heather's death touched her often, sometimes unpredictably, with moods and depression she could not easily shake. Christine felt lost and angry without her sister, hunting her disconsolately in all the rooms of the house until her mother reminded her that "Heather has gone to live with God."

Janice and Maya and a hospice social worker stayed in touch with Karen and Eric afterwards, knowing there would be no magic cure to the pain this family felt.

Janice held Karen's hand. She listened while Karen talked and cried with her when she wept. She invited Karen and Eric to join a group of parents who met at the hospice office once a month. Each parent had lived through a similar tragedy, and together, sharing their experiences, they were able to release some of the pain and start to heal.

Eric understood this purpose of the group, but after a couple of meetings he did not go back. Revealing his hurts was not his way, and he was uncomfortable listening to the stories of others. Now, almost four years later, he does not mention Heather's name and sometimes leaves the room when she is discussed. His pain continues unchanged deep down inside where he can no longer touch it.

Karen was uncertain whether she could handle her feelings in front of others. She didn't have to worry. The parents and the hospice leader understood and accepted her, and it helped to have a time when it was truly all right to talk and cry about Heather—to let it out. Her pain changed slowly, inch by inch. Sometimes it was fresh and acute, more often it seemed softer as the months went by. Each anniversary of a memorable event brought it back, a combined treasure and stab at her heart.

The group even helped Christine. Her unfocused anger worried Karen. During the parents' discussions the problems of other brothers and sisters came up, and Karen gained ideas for helping Christine deal with her anger. Physical outlets for her distress, special times with her father and mother, and a new doll house and doll family to help her act out her feelings all gradually made a difference.

Two years after Heather died, Karen invited Janice and Maya to lunch. They settled into their seats, and after orders were taken, Karen took a deep breath.

"I've never been able to tell you how much you two and hospice did for us, and how deeply I appreciate it." She began, swallowing hard.

"If you hadn't come to help us, Heather could never have stayed at home with us at the end." She stopped for a moment. "You didn't enter our lives until Heather's last week, but without you, I just don't know. . . . Remembering her happiness at being at home with us and all her friends . . . I can't thank you enough for that.

"Her being at home changed a lot of things for us. Melanie and Christine will always feel closer because they shared this time with Heather, I know. As hard as it was on them, it would have been much worse if they were kept separate from Heather, not really knowing how it was with her. They didn't have to imagine a lot of scary things, or feel left out . . . Heather was truly part of them, right to the end. That is such a gift!

"You know how different it would have been if she'd been away in the hospital."

Karen stopped, sipped from her water glass, then continued. "And there's more. I've thought a lot about it. . . . I realize that you were special. You gave from the heart, not because it was your job. You cared. You believed in us. We felt about you like you'd feel about family. We trusted you.

"I joined the parents' group because I trusted you." She turned to look at Janice. "I knew you believed it would help—so I made myself go. It was hard. . . ." She stopped to get a tissue from her purse. "The group is helping, Janice. I don't know if I can say this right, but it's beginning to help me understand something important."

Janice nodded, waiting quietly for Karen to find the words.

"At the start, every fiber in me hurt. I really didn't know how I could go on living. After a while, when I realized I not only could but would go on living, I think something in me wanted to keep on hurting. I believe I was afraid to feel better. It was almost like the pain was all I had left of Heather, and I couldn't let anyone take that from me too. That sounds silly, doesn't it? But if recovering meant she was completely and forever gone, I couldn't bear to recover. Do you understand?" Janice was listening intently. Without words, she nodded again.

"What I'm beginning to realize is that she's always here; that her goodness and love will always be with me. That nothing could possibly take her away, and I don't need the pain to keep her. It comes to me in flashes during the group meetings as I listen, and as I talk. Even though I miss her terribly, at times I know it's enough that I love her, and she loved me.

"It's taking time, and I'm not there yet. But the group is making it happen." She sat for a moment, looking at her hands. "I wish Eric could find this too. His hurt is so deep."

No one spoke for several moments.

"When I think of you two and hospice, and some of those good people at the hospital, I know I'm not alone. I know you understand. I know you have faith we'll survive and be whole again some day. With gifts like these, I know we'll make it."

Janice and Maya reached their arms out and hugged Karen. Hospice work was hard, but some days more than others the rewards were great.

NOTES:
Grieving; Bereavement

First, let's remind ourselves that grief is a privilege that comes with the capacity to give and receive love.

Allen D. Wolfelt[1] [1, p. 33].

How Karen and Eric could believe they were *privileged* when Heather died defies comprehension. At that point their total beings were bereft, wiped out by the force of loss so powerful it left them reeling. Yet Wolfelt is right. The richness of life that flows from loving is an unspeakable privilege. The deeper the love, the greater the suffering when the object of that love is lost. If one is blessed with knowing love, the other is inescapable. They are of a piece, a precious capacity that marks us as human.

Who would want to go through life without feeling keenly the joys, pains, challenges, and rewards of close human relationships? Who would want his time on this earth to go along on a level plane, never feeling up or, by contrast, down? No one, of course. A life that flat, that empty, would be half a life. The fulfillment of love and the devastation of loss both add to the magnitude of life.

We know that. Truly, it is a privilege to have to grieve, and to be able to grieve.

However, it would not have helped Karen and Eric much if a counselor had told them of their privilege after Heather died, any more than it helps a child for his parent to tell him, "This punishment is for your own good." The reality of the words has to come to them naturally, and it may take years. A suffering survivor will likely hate his pain, until one

---

[1] Reprinted with permission from Alan D. Wolfelt, Ph.D., Center for Loss and Life Transition, 3735 Broken Bow Road, Fort Collins, Colorado 80526, USA.

day after a long period of grieving it dawns on him that he has known the fullness of life because the lost relationship was so deep and special. Then, along with the pain of his loss (which we hope by then has mellowed), he will feel the blessing that is his.

We have found our patients' and families' adaptation to dying tends to move erratically through a number of stages, conceived differently by various people but, like the blind man and the elephant, all touching on the truth.

If the period of dying is long enough to permit it, families typically experience anticipatory grieving which may allow some adjustments ahead of time. Beginning when they learn of the diagnosis and prognosis, family members are struck with shock and pain. The characteristics of what they feel is the same for many (and may be familiar to our readers). Their physical reactions may include shortness of breath, fatigue, tightness in the chest and throat, difficulty sleeping, crying, dry mouth, empty feeling in the stomach, dizziness, nervousness, irritability, and oversensitivity to noise. Their psychological reactions can include numbness, guilt, longing, anger, sadness, despair, fear of going crazy, apathy or overactivity, depression, or ambivalence. Reactions of disbelief, disorganization, and confusion are common. Close survivors often also feel aimless, with a lack of interest and motivation, and may be unable to concentrate.

Some short time after this period of initial acute grief, rationality usually reappears. The family members realize that life is continuing for the present and there are things to be done [2]. Grieving begins to change character.

The thinking about grief has evolved over time, beginning with Freud's belief in 1917 that its essence was a withdrawal of emotional ties to the deceased, which he called *decathexis* [3]. Psychiatrist Eric Lindemann accepted Freud's definition, and in 1944 added as another stage the forming of new relationships [4]. They and others felt the grieving should be limited in time—four to six weeks in Lindemann's mind (which must come as a big shock to grieving loved ones struggling after months or even years), and up to three years in others'. Freud seemed to modify his position later, indicating that grief over the loss of a very close person could go on indefinitely [5]. The Committee for the Study of Health Consequences of the Stress of Bereavement of the Institute of Medicine concluded in 1984 that an end point of grieving cannot be identified, and for many people it can last a lifetime as a low-grade "shadow grief"—grieving which doesn't significantly inhibit daily functioning but persists to sadden them[2] [6]. Grieving survivors can at least now be relieved of the burden of considering themselves abnormal.

Kübler-Ross considered denial, anger, bargaining, depression, and finally acceptance to be the stages a dying person experienced, perhaps in erratic order, before death [7], a list considered by Corr to be incomplete[3] [8]. Similarly, the process of grieving is thought to have discernable steps that follow the initial shock: avoidance, confrontation, and accommodation [9], or in another array, acceptance of the reality of loss, working through to the pain of grief, adjustment to the environment in which the deceased is missing, emotionally relocating the deceased and moving on with life [10], and rebuilding faith and a philosophical system that had been challenged by the loss [11]. These steps are not necessarily—not often, would be more accurate—linear. As Rabbi Earl Grollman has said, no one follows a cookbook. We see our families moving back and forth, avoiding, then achieving some confrontation or acceptance, then avoiding the reality once more; they may reach some level of accommodation, then find it too hurtful and drop back for a time. These emotions often overlap; two or more can be present at the same time. The response we see to death is always more complicated than these descriptions imply, but for persons who suffer real loss, all stages must eventually be visited in some form and plumbed before health and a desire to live once again returns.

---

[2] Our families can feel relief to know this shadow grief is now considered normal, for it is very, very common.

[3] Although Corr criticizes Kübler-Ross's stages as being incomplete, he points out three often-neglected messages from her work which he considers to be important: dying persons are still alive; caretakers must listen to dying persons and let them define their own coping tasks; and caretakers have much to learn from dying persons and their coping.

Following Sigmund Freud's earlier discussion of the work of grief, in 1944 Eric Lindemann coined the phrase *grief work* to describe what survivors do as they attempt to cope with the loss of a loved one [4]. They must think through and face the reality of the loss, express their feelings and emotions and become reinvested in life, and that takes work. The term could not be more appropriate. It was adopted by professionals in the mental health field, and has been in use ever since.

The work, or tasks, we see our successful families assume include working through the anger or guilt some of them feel, and reviewing the relationship they had with the deceased in enough detail to result in a realistic view of the person—one which is neither idealized nor unfairly negative [6]. Either or both tasks may require the assistance of a therapist.

Keeping a journal has been suggested as a help to the survivor [12, 13], and a workbook approach is offered by Wolfelt [14]. Karen, in our story, kept a journal and found it helpful.

We should note that survivors are not isolated in doing their grief work. We have seen the family influence each member's grieving. Each one in the family together with his grief reaction has an effect on the others; the family unit, itself, also suffers grief which affects the individuals. Their grief can be seen in one or more changes: alteration of the amount and pattern of communication among them (a normally placid child may pound everyone's ears with anger, a husband may withdraw from all conversation); the reconnecting or cutting off of certain family members (one of the offspring may not have fulfilled her expected role in helping to care for the dying father, with resulting resentment from the others); confusion in the family hierarchy (none of the siblings steps into the now vacant head-of-the-family position); role confusion (who is going to be the family peacemaker and organizer); isolation of the family from outsiders and overprotection of family members (acquaintances don't know what to say to grief so they stay away or remain silent, and the family members circle their wagons as a protective act) [15]. Changes in family dynamics will either stymie or reinforce the grief work of the individuals in the family.

Families who had communication problems before the death and families who adhere to rigid roles for each member are apt to create or exacerbate problems in grieving. Their patterns do not help the individual members, who need particularly to be able to communicate openly, and who must function despite the death-created loss of family role-structure. Flexibility of roles—reorganizing so all of the roles are once more filled—would enhance everyone's adaptation.

Just as individuals must do their grief work, families have tasks ahead of them. They must share an acknowledgment of the death and loss (which can perhaps occur when the group takes time to look through old photos and records), reorganize the family system, and reinvest in new relationships and life pursuits. These are processes we take for granted, not recognizing their discrete elements until one of them breaks down or fails to happen.

The authors find with Moos [15] that rituals often help families and their members. Rituals mark the loss, affirm the life now gone and help family members express their grief. Rituals can illuminate the meaning of death and ongoing life, make sense of the loss and give the family a sense of continuity, all of which helps its individual members. Rituals can be as simple as remembering birthdays or anniversaries or as elaborate as planting roses or contributing something to the deceased person's synagogue or church or other organization, and many ideas in between.

Almost a truism, there is no shortcut for this process. The services and formal mourning period are over quickly; the time required to accept the absence of the loved one—to give him up—takes time, and it is painful. There can be no greater understatement.

The common first stage of grieving, avoidance, wears many faces. The behavior of avoidance is common and normal. We have all known the response of the widow who sets out on a never-ending round of travel, or the widower who buries himself in his work. We have all seen frantic activity in sports, social events, charitable endeavors, public service efforts, or any number of other arenas which protect the hurting survivor from coming to grips with the reality of the loss. He will deal with it "tomorrow," when he feels more ready—and meanwhile, he'll stay too busy to be able to think about it.

The problem, of course, is that until avoidance stops and confrontation begins, grief work is stalemated. In fact, it really hasn't begun.

The precurser of avoidance, denial, is known as the earliest defense to emerge in human psychic development. Avoidance, then, may also be a necessary psychological defense which will give way when the stress of the dying period is over, or when the survivor makes some physical recovery from too little sleep, abnormal eating patterns, etc., imposed during the illness and dying. Avoidance *which continues for a reasonable period of time* probably serves some good purpose for the person exhibiting it.

An often-heard comment is that "time heals all wounds." In time, one can presume from this saying, avoidance behavior will stop and the survivor will get on with his grieving. The problem with this theory is that time for time's sake is not apt to help when the survivor is avoiding, denying, or otherwise delaying working through his pain. Time likely is not what is healing wounds, rather the constructive efforts made during that time are responsible.

This is not to say that time is unimportant in eventual recovery. Recovery, as we've said, does not materialize overnight. According to Rando, typical, active grieving can go on for three or more years [9] even when the survivor is working very successfully at the task.

Confrontation or acceptance of the loss, as the words suggest, is looking the absence of the loved one squarely in the eye. It is admitting one's loneliness. It is giving up—truly letting go of old "together plans and rituals"—the Saturday night candlelight dinners, the annual hideaway vacation, the joint weekly grocery shopping trips. It is no longer looking for that familiar face; even more, it is knowing instantly that the similar face in the crowd is just a stranger.

Accommodation begins in inches—trying a new breakfast routine, inviting a friend to watch a video, beginning a redecorating or remodeling project, signing up for a class, joining a bird-watching group, anything that launches a new start as an individual. The former identity of the survivor was an integral part of the lost relationship, like the thumb to a hand; separation from that relationship takes courage. And just as the toddler discovers with his first tentative steps, small successes lead to larger ones, with eventual discovery of new strengths and capacities that make life vital, to be tried, to be lived.

One barrier to recovery, as Karen found out, is the reluctance to let go of sorrow, of pain. Mourning was the closest she could come to still being with Heather. As she said, to lose the pain was like giving up all she had left of Heather. She was nearing recovery, but could not yet allow herself. Along the path, as a survivor progresses through the process of grieving, he may at some point feel an urge, as Karen did, to resume the normal pulse of life. He may be ready to peel off the layers of weight in his heart, but out of fear of more loss or because it seems "wrong," he cannot.

Recovery is a choice. One must be willing. It can happen if we let it. As Karen was discovering, she still had her love for Heather, and always would; pain was not an obligation. Ultimate success is the realization that "the best testimonial we can give to our dead is to honor them by living great and fulfilling lives" [16, p. 19]. To choose to live is not to give up our love for the deceased. We can love them forever.

Because grieving has such a variety of profiles, it is difficult to know what is normal and what is not. Unresolved grief, we do know, is destructive. In a general way, it is safe to say that absence of normal grief, unusual prolongation of normal grief, and marked distortion of normal grief are signs of its being unresolved [9]. The first two signs are self-descriptive. The third, distorted grief, needs definition. Evidence of distorted grief can be seen in unreasonably angry behaviors, a persistent cloak of guilt, neurotic and recurring complaints of ill health or danger, chronic overactivity, or even destructive acts.

While generalizations cannot be applied to individuals, there appear to be some differences in grieving styles between mothers and fathers, between the elderly and the young, and between the sexes.

Mothers of children with cancer, even before the death, reported more engaged coping styles, more use of social support, and slightly more depression than did fathers [17]. This was certainly true with Karen and Eric.

Death of a spouse produced shock and disbelief initially, then sadness, in both elderly and young people studied by Anderson and Dimond, but the younger felt particular despair, disorganization and fear of breakdown [18]. While both groups had a constant awareness of loss and loneliness, the younger tended more often to feel guilt. Both the older and younger survivors found themselves conversing with the deceased at times, and both were helped by talking about their feelings with family members [18].

There is some agreement that men are less likely than women to reach out for help, even when their hurt is intense [9, 19]. Rando found it not uncommon for a bereaved woman to be "totally frustrated by her husband's not talking about a death, returning to normal routines of living sooner than she, and being uninterested in attending a grief support group." On the other hand, it was quite common for men "to feel that women react too intensely, need to talk about the loss too much, and rely on others too heavily to help them cope with their loss" [9, p. 64].

These sex differences may be cultural role products: males are expected to be self-sufficient and in control, not to cry or be emotional. Female traits, in contrast, include being expressive and vulnerable. With these differences, women may be better prepared to deal with grief since they can express their feelings and will use social support, while men are more apt to deny or repress their feelings and reject support from others [19]. Eric's handling of Heather's death certainly fit this norm. Somehow men need permission to "let it out," and that permission is very apt not to be accepted.

Observations support the notion that transition periods in both men's and women's lives (adolescence to young adulthood, early adulthood to middle adulthood, thence to late adulthood) are times of change and insecurity which make grief more acute and more difficult [20].

Another difficult terrain exists when society does not recognize the right to grieve. This can happen, for example, with unmarried couples, women who had abortions, friends of AIDS patients. Grieving in these cases endures without the usual social support and is made more difficult for these survivors, and has been referred to aptly by Kenneth Doka as "disenfranchised grief" [11].

Children's and adolescents' grieving are subjects deserving of separate space and discussion.

Because children have less emotional and intellectual maturity than adults, and because the relevant experiences they bring to a death are likely few if they exist at all, it is natural their response to the death of a friend or family member will be quite different from that of their elders. Because the death can have a profound impact on the child's further development, it is important to understand what the child is experiencing, and to respond to his need in an effective way.

Death means different things to children as they grow. For the youngster between two and seven years of age, death is seen as some temporary, reversible event, usually attributed to external causes. The person will come back; he simply went somewhere where a bad thing happened, but it will be over soon, and he'll come back. The child of seven to eleven years of age, on the other hand, grasps the permanence of death and is able to attribute it to some internal cause—some body function that has stopped. He recognizes that death is universal—that it can happen to anyone. By twelve years of age, children can deal in varying degree with abstractions; they begin to relate death to their own and others' religious and philosophical thoughts, often meditating about the nature of death and afterlife [21].

Deaths differ in their effects on a child, depending on the role of the person who died. Most devastating to his development is the loss of his parent. His ongoing growing-up process of separation, becoming an individual, is disrupted, often with little or confusing explanation. A young child is apt to think his parent still *is* somewhere, *doing* something, and be disturbed by the question of why he doesn't come back and do something for him. Eventually he will wonder *who* caused his parent's death. He may for a long time worry that death will come to him when he sleeps or gets sick, or through some accident. He may feel abandoned, or guilty. His ability to trust is harmed, maybe even shattered. He may fantasize his lost parent as perfect, making the job a nightmare for any eventual stepparent [22].

Children between four and sixteen years of age who had lost siblings were studied during the two-year period following the death. Rituals which support adult mourners (e.g., funerals, visitations, condolence calls) lacked relevance for these children, many of whom suffered school difficulties, stomach and head-aches, health fears, enuresis, sleep disturbances, jealousy and guilt, depression, and antisocial behavior [23]. Many of their problem behaviors fell into the category of aggression—arguing, demanding attention, disobedience, stubbornness, and sullen-ness—particularly among young children. Aggressive behaviors tended to decline with adolescence. Boys and girls differed, but all children had attention-seeking behaviors. If there is any single nugget of wisdom that comes from the studies of bereaved children, it is that they need caring attention.

The needs of children often conflicted with the needs of their parents, those devastated survivors who were suffering their own pain. The cross-current of need makes it very difficult for anyone to be consoled.

When asked what or who helped them through their griev-ing, children indicated first their mothers, then other family members and friends, support groups, adopting some of the deceased's belongings (a stuffed toy, a blanket, etc.), *not* remem-bering, or pretending their dead sibling was away, writing in a journal, and engaging in their old favorite activities. Describing the circumstances of the death, if the child witnessed it, can be a vital part of the grieving process [24].

When asked what did *not* help, these children reported failure of their friends to come around, being asked to talk when they didn't feel like it, and feelings of survivor guilt.

Predictably, the children's coping methods and communi-cation styles were the same ones they had used prior to the death. The investigators concluded that other people should not prescribe how a child should grieve [24].

Efforts should be made to help grieving children understand and make sense of what has happened and to express their emotions. They will benefit if they can commemorate in some manner the life of the person who has died—perhaps by plant-ing a tree, or making a photo album, or giving a book inscribed with the person's name and date of death to the library—with the ultimate goal of integrating the loss into their lives so they can go on with the everyday activities of living. For some children a formal therapy program can be useful.

Under the best of circumstances adolescents face the special stresses of their transitional age, with its fomenting hormones catapulting them along an emotional roller-coaster into physical adulthood, its peer pressures challenging their values and behavior, and its sudden thrust of their psyches into intermittent insecurity. The addition of loss of a parent, grandparent, sibling, or friend can cause immeasurable further disruption. Grieving is made especially difficult for teenagers by communication patterns that may not have been open before the death occurred, and by uncertainties that are an inherent part of the adolescent condition. In addition, as Earl Grollman points out in his useful self-help book, *Straight Talk About Death for Teenagers*, the death of a loved one may trigger other losses in adolescents such as trust, security, faith, opportunity, dreams, identity, and purpose [25].

Compounding all of these burdens of the age group is the drive toward independence which guides most adolescents. Many may find help from adults is difficult to accept.

Striking among adolescents is their inner spirit which propels them toward maturity. Growth and vitality beat in their loins, and death stands to contradict this message. For persons in this age group, death is unreal and cruel [20].

There is evidence from and beyond the authors' experience that hospice can help the bereaved, whatever the sex or age, through this difficult time. Survivors who had the help of hospice showed on survey fewer feelings of guilt, dependency, loss of control, despair, numbness, shock, and disbelief than were found in non-hospice survivors. This participation in hospice was not the only predictor of success in grieving; the death occurring at home, and resulting from an illness longer than six months were also correlated with successful resolution of grief [26].

Whether adult, child, or in between, grieving is hard. And because death must come to everyone, we will all have our times to grieve. It is part of the human condition.

The challenge is to grieve *well*. What we may not realize until experience teaches us is that in grieving we discover traits we never knew we had, strengths and capacities that make us more than the persons of our former self-images. Richard Dershimer, a long-time grief counselor, has observed that the survivor ". . . can emerge with greater confidence and deeper understanding of life in general, thereby better able to realize more of the potential he or she possesses." The alternative, he notes, is ". . . to let life's spirit ebb . . .", thus giving up what one might be [20, p. 1x]. He makes the very good point that bereavement care should be directed toward enhancing the survivor, not toward recovering per se.

When it is our time to grieve, we must live each day as it comes, dealing with both the mundane routine of living and our inner struggle. Grieving and living through the entire experience of bereavement will change us, and if we do it well, the change will be for the better. We know we are becoming whole when we can look to the future with some readiness to engage once more.

REFERENCES

1. A. D. Wolfelt, *Death and Grief: A Guide for Clergy,* Accelerated Development Company, Fort Collins, Colorado, 1988.
2. S. Huart and M. O'Donnell, The Road to Recovery from Grief and Bereavement, *Caring, 12*:11, pp. 71-75, 1993.
3. S. Freud, Mourning and Melancholia, in *The Standard Edition of the Complete Psychological Works of Sigmund Freud,* J. Strachey (ed. and trans.) *14,* pp. 237-258, Hogarth Press, London, 1957.
4. E. Lindemann, Symptomatology and Management of Acute Grief, *American Journal of Psychiatry, 101,* pp. 141-148, 1944.
5. S. Freud, Letter to Binswanger, in *Letters of Sigmund Freud 1873-1939,* E. Freud (ed.), Hogarth Press, London, 1961.
6. B. J. Horacek, Heuristic Model of Grieving after High-Grief Deaths, *Death Studies, 19*:1, pp. 21-31, 1995.
7. E. Kübler-Ross, *On Death and Dying,* Macmillan, New York, 1969.

8. C. A. Corr, Coping with Dying: Lessons that We Should and Should Not Learn from the Work of Elisabeth Kübler-Ross, *Death Studies, 17*:1, pp. 69-83, 1993.

9. T. A. Rando, *How To Go On Living When Someone You Love Dies,* Bantam Books, New York, 1991.

10. J. W. Worden, *Grief Counseling and Grief Therapy,* Springer Publishing Company, New York, 1992.

11. K. J. Doka and J. Nichols, No More Rosebuds: A Perspective in Perinatal Death, Funerals and Pastoral Care, in *Death and Spirituality,* K. J. Doka and J. D. Morgan (eds.), Baywood Publishing Company, Amityville, New York, 1993.

12. J. Tatelbaum, *The Courage to Grieve,* Harper and Row, New York, 1980.

13. E. A. Grollman, *A Time Remembered: A Journal for Survivors,* Beacon Press, Boston, Massachusetts, 1987.

14. A. D. Wolfelt, *Understanding Grief: Helping Yourself Heal,* Accelerated Development Company, Fort Collins, Colorado, 1992.

15. N. L. Moos, An Integrative Model of Grief, *Death Studies, 19*:4, pp. 337-364, 1995.

16. J. Tatelbaum, The Power of Saying Goodbye, *Hospice, 3*:2, pp. 18-19, 1992.

17. L. S. Larson, D. A. Wittrock, and A. K. Sandgren, When a Child is Diagnosed with Cancer: Sex Differences in Parental Adjustment, *Journal of Psychosocial Oncology, 12*:1-2, pp. 123-142, 1994.

18. K. L. Anderson and M. F. Dimond, Experience of Bereavement in Older Adults, *Journal of Advanced Nursing, 22*:2, pp. 308-315, 1995.

19. S. Brabant, C. J Forsyth, and C. Melancon, Grieving Men: Thoughts, Feelings and Behaviors following Deaths of Wives, *The Hospice Journal, 8*:4, pp. 33-47, 1992.

20. R. A. Dershimer, *Counseling the Bereaved,* Pergamon Press, now Simon and Schuster International, Heml Hempstead, England, 1990.

21. M. E. Tamm and A. Granqvist, Meaning of Death for Children and Adolescents, *Death Studies, 19*:3, pp. 203-222, 1995.

22. A. Bettie and M. L. Kemme, Bereavement in Childhood, *Journal of Child Psychology and Psychiatry, 5*, pp. 37-39, 1984.

23. D. E. McCown and B. Davies, Patterns of Grief in Young Children following Death of a Sibling, *Death Studies, 19*:1, pp. 41-53, 1995.

24. M. M. Mahon and M. L. Page, Childhood Bereavement after the Death of a Sibling, *Holistic Nursing Practice, 9*:3, pp. 15-26, 1995.

25. E. A. Grollman, *Straight Talk About Death for Teenagers,* Beacon Press, Boston, Massachusetts, 1980.
26. L. L. Steele, The Death Surround: Factors Influencing the Grief Experience of Survivors, *Oncology Nursing Forum, 17*:2, pp. 235-241, 1990.

CHAPTER 4

The Gift of Choice

Terminal illness can be very, very tough. After a long struggle, patients cannot be blamed for wanting sometimes to give up—for wishing that the whole process would end.

Suicide isn't common. In all these years, I can count on two hands the number of patients at Hospice of Metro Denver who have carried it out. Considering we have served some 8,000 patients, that is remarkably few suicides.

But a lot of my patients—maybe nine out of ten of them—speak of it at some time. Often quite seriously. Some have asked me to assist them. One even asked me to get a gun and "commit her suicide for her."

Most of the time these people just need to talk about it—to get the idea out in the light of day where they can look at it rationally. Some seem to be asking for approval—even permission.

Hospice neither promotes suicide nor helps people commit it. On the contrary, the hospice position is rejection of suicide as a solution. But when my patients talk suicide, I don't judge or condemn. I don't try to guide them. I just listen. I try to understand.

JOSEPH

Handsome and urbane even in his illness, Joseph moved with anticipation to answer the doorbell that cold November morning. He had returned home a week earlier from the hospital after twelve days of treatment for cancer of the pancreas.

Today he seemed more comfortable, able to put aside what he had been told by his doctors, that he would not recover. A visitor would be welcome.

The doorbell rang more insistently as he entered the front hallway. He bent his tall frame to peer through the peep-hole before disengaging the lock, and saw a slight, vital-looking woman whose youthful bearing belied her shock of white hair. He drew open the massive wooden door and pushed the storm door open, smiling expectantly at her.

Janice looked up at the barely graying gentleman in the doorway, noting how thin and wan he was, and yet how bright his eyes. She extended her hand and introduced herself.

"Good morning. You must be Joseph Sadler. I'm Janice Miller." A smile flooded her round face, the crinkle around her eyes deepening into well-worn creases. "I'll be your hospice nurse."

"Yes, of course," Joseph nodded, "They told me on the phone you'd come 'round today. How good of you!"

He leaned forward to open the storm door wide, welcoming Janice into his home. Once inside the vestibule, she slipped out of her coat and scarf and let him take them. In one courtly movement he laid them on a nearby armchair and guided her with his fingertips into the living room. His poise and posture were those of one whose fortunes were going full speed ahead rather than someone facing death.

Joseph's active treatment was over. Radiation therapy had stopped the acute pain consuming him during recent weeks, and today it was possible to feel that the doctors might have erred in the two- to three-month sentence they delivered when they discharged him.

He was sent home because there was nothing else to be done. Other than pain relief, there was no more treatment available to him. He did not fight back. Reacting to crises with anger or denial wasn't his way. He worked for solutions, and failing them, he accepted what had to be. This ultimate crisis in his life would be no exception. He knew he would die.

He was relieved to be at home. The hospital depressed him with its rules and uniforms, the constant blaring of the paging system, the lying on bedding that reflected body heat until he felt cooked. His illness was bad enough; the environment reduced him somehow. Hospital care might be necessary, but he much preferred to be in the familiar elegance of his turn-of-the-century Georgian-colonial house. There he could pad around in slippers and dressing gown, listen to his beloved Vivaldi and Mozart, rest in his study on the sofa or easy chair when he tired, and generally feel in charge. Even when the pain gripped him through the mid-section and radiated through his back and shoulders, somehow his place in life and all its familiar surroundings soothed him.

Over the past thirty-seven years Joseph had built a successful investment business, devoting endless hours and energy to the project, often at the expense of his wife. Gregarious by nature, he spent his spare time with other business and professional men. The men were drawn by his success and competence, their wives charmed by his savoir-faire and distinguished good looks. He moved through life with total assurance.

In contrast, Anne, his wife of nearly forty years, was uncertain and constrained. Nothing about her was strong or definite—not her manner, not her neutral-nothing hair color, not her nondescript face and figure. She was a tuft of pampas grass, always pushed upon and never pressing back. Her nature allowed her no internal ease. Her insecurity, if not genetic, certainly had begun early. She found her adjustments never ending and difficult. Unable to express warmth, she had adapted to Joseph's lack of attention by becoming a worker-bee in several charitable organizations in the community.

Anne fell into volunteer work quite naturally. As a peripheral part of Joseph's social contacts she was exposed to the movers and shakers who made the charities go. While these people first adopted Anne because of her husband, they eventually recognized her for her own capabilities and hard work. "The organization," regardless of which in the stream of her loyalties she identified with at any time, became her emotional home and source of rewards.

And so it was that Joseph and Anne found themselves, together but quite separate in the maturity of their lives. Equipped with all the comfort-providing things money could buy and admired by the society through which they moved, neither one reached out to nurture the other. They shared a house with no heart and soul when Joseph learned the pain in his gut was caused by cancer. The news did nothing to bring them closer.

Joseph led Janice to two facing loveseats in front of the fireplace, separated by a mahogany coffee table, where they settled in for their opening exploration of what was to come. It was a good arrangement; they could look directly at each other and say what needed to be said, a style that fit them both.

Janice began. "Before we get started, I need to know what you'd like me to call you." She gazed at him steadily, her expression alert.

"How about Joseph?" came back from his side with no hesitation. He heard himself and had to laugh, because throughout his stay in the hospital he had been annoyed every time someone he'd never met before first-named him. He objected to the pretense of familiarity when none existed. But Janice had asked. That made a difference.

"Fine. Please call me Janice." There was an ease about her as she reached for her pen. "Next . . . how may I help you?"

The question caught him off guard. He had expected to have to fit into whatever mold his physician and nurse set out for him. He wasn't prepared to suggest the course. "I don't know. I guess I hadn't thought about it that way. Won't you be like a visiting nurse or a private duty nurse? You know, giving medicine, following whatever the doctor orders, things like that?"

"Not exactly. Of course I'll provide your nursing care and do whatever I can to make you comfortable. I'll work with your doctor and stay in touch with him about how you're doing. He'll order any medications you need."

"But I'm also here to be your advocate. I'll try to find a way to guide your care in the way you want. If you'll say whatever is on your mind—ask questions—and react openly to things that happen—I'll be better able to do that. You see, Joseph, you really are in charge." Joseph's great shaggy eyebrows, strikingly gray next to his mostly dark hair, raised like a question mark as she spoke.

"That's the big difference between hospice and the traditional hospital or a nursing home," Janice nodded. "I'll share what I know, and tell you what I think, but your doctor and I are your resources and not your managers. This is your life, and you get to make the decisions."

Although he could not yet know what this would mean for him, Joseph was moved. He and Janice sat quietly for a moment, he absorbing what he heard, she waiting for his readiness to proceed.

Then Janice inserted a paper into her clipboard and began the routine initial assessment she had conducted so many times. Though many patients had similar diagnoses, each was different, and she wondered what lay ahead for Joseph. She hoped, as she always did at this point, that life would be kind to him during the time he had left, and that she would find the strength and wisdom to help him reap all the value he could from it.

For twenty minutes she was busy with the physical exam and history, noting his responses in a neat hand on the form clipped to her board. He tolerated the procedures well, although by the end he appeared tired. Janice closed her pen, finally, and placed it and the clipboard into her bag. "That's all for today," she smiled at him as she swung the straps of her bag over her shoulder.

"I want to come again in a few days to meet your wife, Joseph. I want to help her, too, you know. As time goes by I'll need to teach her what she can do, and she may have concerns and questions for me. I don't mean we expect her to handle everything alone; hospice has volunteers and home health aides who'll assist. But I do need to talk with her."

Joseph shifted in his seat and cleared his throat. "Yes . . . I'm sorry she couldn't be here this morning. Anne is so busy with the cerebral palsied children and her Animal League. . . . I don't really see a lot of her these days." He paused. "If she isn't going to be here much, can't we just hire someone?" He suddenly looked very tired.

"There are lots of ways to make this work, Joseph. Let's not worry about it now." She reached forward and touched his shoulder lightly. "We accomplished a lot for our first day. I'll call you in the morning. Tape my card near your phone, and if either you or Mrs. Sadler want to talk with me, feel free to call."

Joseph struggled to get to his feet as she prepared to leave, but Janice pressed her hand firmly on his shoulder. "I can let myself out." With that she turned and left the room, putting on her coat and scarf in the hallway and heading out the front door.

Anne flitted from the serving island to the kitchen window and back as she waited for Janice's arrival, the palms of her hands gliding continuously against each other in a habitual expression of anxiety. As if constantly overdosed on caffeine, she vibrated with the insecurity brought on by Joseph's illness and impending death. Although her life had long since become emotionally separate from his, their barren marriage had provided a needed structure in her life. Joseph's death would destroy her familiar world.

While Anne felt no particular warmth for Joseph, she wished him no harm. He was a gentleman, and he provided well for her. She simply could not respond to him with any emotion—even in his hour of need.

Of course she would do the things that needed to be done. She knew from visiting him in the hospital that he would require a lot of help. Dying was scary. She watched through the window with a tightness in her stomach as she waited for Janice, uncertain of what lay ahead.

A small green car rounded the corner into the driveway, and Anne leaned forward over the sink to examine its occupant. She saw a white-haired woman behind the wheel, and was surprised to see how quickly she moved as she picked something up from the passenger seat, locked the car and headed for the front door. Anne's face fell as she walked out of the kitchen. There was no way out anymore—no escape from what had to be done. It would start now, when she opened the door.

Quiet from the start as Janice talked with her in the den, Anne didn't respond to Janice's review of the needs Joseph would present as he weakened, and how each of them might fill those needs. Janice speculated silently about the reasons for her reserve. It could be a very real problem; home care had great value and Joseph seemed genuinely to want to be at home, but it would only work if someone could give that care.

"Anne," Janice said tentatively, "a serious illness like Joseph's is really a family affair, as I'm sure you know. It affects everyone, not just the person who is sick. Joseph's doctor called hospice so you'd have some support. That's why we're here, and we want to help both of you." She stopped. Anne said nothing.

"I'm not the only help, either," she continued. "We have home-health aides and volunteers and others we can call on to assist both of you. We expect you'll have needs before this is over—not just Joseph." Janice paused. Anne allowed a small smile that began and ended on her lips. Her grey eyes were wide, like a frightened doe. Her hands resumed their up and down stroking.

"You can call me for help or if you have questions. Don't hesitate; just let me know. Sometimes you may simply want to talk. That's okay too. Do you understand?"

Anne nodded her head without speaking. She appeared troubled. Janice watched her for a minute, then gathered her things and stood up to leave.

They looked in on Joseph before Janice left. He was resting on his side in bed, facing the far window, listening to some classical music Janice couldn't identify. His eyes were focused on some distant place, and he gave no sign he had heard them approach. Janice watched him silently, all the while aware of Anne shifting her weight from side to side as she waited, her hands in constant motion.

Janice tapped Anne on the arm, then led the way down the hall toward the stairs. "I'll be back next week—or earlier if you need me. Just call." With that she left.

On Janice's first regular visit she found Joseph awaiting her in the living room. He asked about his disease as she examined him, and she answered honestly.

"You've taken this pretty well, Joseph," Janice said at the end with a question in her voice. "Is there anything you don't understand?"

"I'm sure there's a lot I don't understand . . . What pleases me is that you'll tell me . . . So often in the past I've had superficial answers from medical people. I hate it. They treat me like a child when I want to know something about my own body. I've never had someone take the time you have, and tell me the plain truth, all of it.

"Sure, it's hard to deal with. It's devastating. I can hardly stand it. But thanks . . . I mean thanks for being straight with me." Joseph sank back in his seat, a sober expression on his face.

As she gathered her things that day Joseph was reluctant to let her leave. In his first show of uncertainty, he pointed toward the kitchen and opened his mouth to speak—only nothing came out. Janice turned to see what he was looking at, and felt the hesitation in his manner. Just a pause, then she heard a small voice sounding more like a plea than an invitation.

"Would you like to have tea with me? There is instant hot water in the side faucet at the sink, and tea bags are in a canister on the counter."

Janice smiled at this crack in his composure. "Why, yes, Joseph. I'd love to."

As she headed for the kitchen, she heard him call, "You could bring some cookies, too. They're next to the tea." She smiled again, then filled a tray which she brought into the living room for them.

A tea party became a regular part of Janice's care of Joseph, whether she saw him in the living room, the library, or as his condition deteriorated, in his bedroom.

For two weeks Joseph's health seemed no worse. He had very little energy, and he became thinner, but the days and nights went on pretty much without problems. He puttered, listened to music, and slept, complaining very little. He tried to focus for several hours each day on business matters that needed wrap-up, and there were visits from his assistants in the office as well as from his attorney and accountant.

Anne stayed home more, preparing meals and receiving his visitors at the door. She didn't shirk her responsibility. Joseph still managed his own dressing and bathing.

Janice came every few days to check his vital signs and general condition. Anne usually answered the door; however, after a limited conversation with Janice, she would lead her to Joseph, then disappear, heading for some other part of the spacious house.

On each visit Janice took Joseph's temperature, listened to his chest and abdomen, recorded his blood pressure, and questioned him about his complaints, noting his status in his chart. Sometimes she phoned his doctor before writing the chart notes. But always after her duties came the main event. Over tea and cookies or a cake they sat and talked.

He told her stories. She learned about investment maneuvers and golf feats, about family history and community legends. There seemed to be nothing he didn't know, nothing too sacred to tell. With relish he shared it all. Anne joined them occasionally; she would sit quietly, restrained, smiling politely at times, but never entering into the spirit of the stories. Usually Janice sat alone at his side, listening.

Joseph gradually lost his energy, and the pain returned. He began to spend most of the time in bed, moving only for short daily periods into a lounge chair close by. There was no question he was going downhill. Janice increased her visits and began a regimen of medication to control his pain. Her nursing became more active, managing the medication adjustments in conference with his doctor and teaching Joseph and Anne how to handle the pills, liquids, and record-keeping. One day he was too weak to bathe himself, and she called Anne into the bedroom.

"If you'll watch me today, you'll know how to handle Joseph's bath on those days he doesn't feel up to it. Then he won't have to wait for me."

Anne was once more rubbing her hands up and down nervously as she hung back in the doorway. "I'll try." She moved slowly toward Janice.

Janice led her through the bath preparations, filling a basin of water, setting out soap and linens and a bath sheet. Anne was stationed near Joseph's hips, Janice at his shoulders. Joseph turned his face away.

"Joseph, I'm going to wash the upper part of you, then you'll turn on your side so I can get your back. Here we go." She lowered his blanket to his waist, dipped the washcloth into the clear water and squeezed it out before turning his face back toward her and wiping it gently. He turned his face away again. She dipped the cloth into the water once more, then rubbed soap into the cloth and squeezed it again. "Best not to have it too wet; we'll drown him and his bed," she chuckled at Anne. Anne's expression didn't change.

Janice washed Joseph's chest and arms, then covered them with the dry bath sheet before rolling him onto his side, facing away from her. Next she swept the blanket down from his waist to his knees and tucked a towel under his back and hips, exposing his bony backside. Anne gasped involuntarily.

Janice shot a glance at her but said nothing. She proceeded to wash and towel down his shoulders and back, his buttocks and legs. At that point she rinsed, soaped and squeezed the cloth and turned him onto his back once more, pulling the sheet up to cover his genitals. "Joseph, take this cloth; you can wash your own private parts."

He took the cloth in one hand and reached under the sheet, stealing a glance at Anne. She had half-turned toward the window and was staring intently through the glass; as she turned back he dropped his eyes. Without looking up, he handed the washcloth back to Janice and once more turned his face away.

Janice finished the bath and put the basin away. "You'll warm up in a minute," she smiled at Joseph. Anne remained motionless. Neither Joseph nor Anne uttered a word as Janice replaced the bed linens with clean ones, covering him finally with the blanket. "We'll shave you tomorrow, Joseph. You look real good right now."

When the two women left the room, Janice said, "That was hard for you, wasn't it, Anne? Would it help to talk about it?"

Anne replied in a low, flat voice. "I haven't . . . We haven't slept together for thirty years." She stopped abruptly.

Janice was aware the two of them slept in separate bedrooms, but she had only suspected how isolated they were. Anne's help was going to require some big adjustments—for Joseph as well as for herself.

Many days during the next few weeks Janice perched on the ottoman beside Joseph's lounge or pulled up a chair to the side of his bed to listen to his stories. She became a trusted friend with whom he shared whatever was on his mind.

Joseph gradually unburdened himself to Janice. In serious moments he spoke of his marriage and how he had failed it, of his compulsion to pour his whole self into his business. He speculated about the difference it would have made if he and Anne had had children. He spoke of the importance of success as he had dreamed of it when he was young, and how casually he looked at it now. One day he wondered aloud whether his cancer was the ultimate punishment for extramarital affairs he had had. Another day he pondered, deep in thought, "What do you suppose it's like not to be?"

To all of this Janice listened carefully. She had no answers; she made no judgments. Sometimes they explored the issues he raised. Sometimes they sat quietly, just thinking about his questions. With increasing openness, he spilled out whatever was on his mind.

As he talked, Janice began to get a different view of her patient, a look at what was beneath the polished patina. Successful and bon vivant, yes. But also a human being who had made mistakes and failed. A person with doubts and weaknesses.

One day Janice asked as he mulled over one of his questions, "Have you ever shared this with Anne?"

"No. We've never been able to talk about anything important. We don't have that kind of marriage. Maybe years ago I wished for more; now it really doesn't matter."

A rueful smile on his lips, Joseph continued. "I guess nothing really matters any more. I've done my job; my estate will take good care of Anne. The business is in good hands. There's nothing more I know to do.

"I've lived an active life. I couldn't have done it any other way. I've worked hard, and I've accomplished a lot. I'm proud of that . . . I can't stand the thought of waiting around to die. When a person's finished, he should be able to go."

It fit Joseph, Janice thought when she left, to be so decisive. She understood how he felt. She also knew he might not be so sure when the time came.

It was a distraught Anne who met Janice at the door the next day. "What is it, Anne?" Janice asked.

"Joseph—I can't believe this—Joseph told me he wants to commit suicide. He stayed awake a long time last night and he decided!"

"And what did you say?"

"I told him 'Don't talk like that!' What could I say? I didn't know what to . . ." Anne's voice rasped. "What should I do? Oh, Janice, I am so glad you're here!" Her voice bordered on hysteria.

"Did he say why?"

"He just said it's all over, and there's nothing more he can do. He doesn't want to lie there waiting to die. You have to know him. He means it!" She covered her face and began to cry.

"Anne, I know how upsetting this is, but I want you to try to stay calm. Give this some time. Lots of patients I see talk about suicide, because they're facing a very difficult time. Very few actually do it. Let me talk with him and see what he's thinking."

Janice hurried to Joseph's room. She found him lying awake in bed, staring out the window. She stood for a minute in the doorway chewing her lip, uncertain how to proceed.

"Good morning, Joseph. How was your night?" In the end she didn't attack it head-on.

"Not the best. I couldn't sleep."

"More pain than usual?" Janice blew into her hands before touching him. It was snow-squeaky cold outside, and she had forgotten to wear her fleece lined gloves. Her hands ached. She knew better than to proceed until they warmed.

"No, about the same." Joseph seemed distant. He barely looked at her. Their conversations had recently required more effort on his part, but he had never before been unresponsive. It was a changed man she faced; something significant indeed had happened.

Janice moved about the room working quietly, waiting for some sign from him. Without it she couldn't be certain how to deal with the change.

The toileting, bathing, and bed-changing took half an hour during which Joseph said nothing. After writing her notes in the chart, it would be time to leave. Her opportunity was slipping away.

"Would you like some fruitcake with your tea, Joseph? I brought along a piece from home."

"No. Not today."

Technically he had rejected only the cake, so Janice headed for the kitchen anyway to fix the tea. That might get him to talk.

Once settled on the ottoman next to the bed, tea in hand, Janice began. "Something's different about you today, Joseph. What is it?"

Joseph's brow furrowed, his eyes barely visible beneath their toplining thatch. He said nothing.

"Is there anything I can do to help you?" she persisted.

He rubbed the border of the sheet between the thumb and fingers of each hand, looking all the time out the window. She waited silently.

"Yes," he said at last, meeting her eyes for the first time. "I need your help." He paused.

"In what way, Joseph? What's troubling you?"

"I've made a decision," he finally said. "I want to put an end to this. It's going nowhere, this lying here, waiting to die. I'm worth nothing this way, too sick to do anything. I'm tired of hurting, I'm tired of being waited on . . . I just want it to be over. I need some pills—enough pills—to end it."

"Have you felt this way long?"

"I thought it out last night when I couldn't sleep. Actually I've thought this way for a long time. But now it's real." He took a deep breath.

"I know my productive days are over. I've wrapped everything up. I'm ready. There's a limit to how much. . . ." He stopped, then began again. "Pills are the best way, I believe. That's where you come in." His words, in contrast to a voice that was weak and breaking, were as executive as ever.

"That's a terribly final step. How can you be sure you wouldn't want to change your mind?"

"I've made decisions all my life. That doesn't worry me. Enough is enough, and when I feel this way I can make the decision that goes with it." His chin sagged and grey circles underlined his eyes, but he forced himself to go on. "Will you help me with the pills?"

She set her cup down. "Getting pills for you is not the kind of help I can provide, Joseph. I'll tell you truthfully, I've been asked this before. It isn't new to me, and it doesn't shock me. We just believe that taking one's own life is a private act—a deeply personal one. It's not something other people should influence or make happen.

"I'll listen as long as you like if it helps to talk about it. And if you should decide to do it, I'll respect your decision. But I'm sorry; I can't get you the pills. I hope you understand."

Joseph's eyes closed, whether from exhaustion or disappointment wasn't clear. She rose from her seat and watched him for a minute, sorrow clouding her face. Then with a sigh she picked up the teacups, one empty and one still full, and carried them out of the room.

The days went by, each producing a change in Joseph. Frustrated by his inability to obtain the pills needed to carry out his suicide, he turned angry, then nasty. What had once been a cool but systematic household became a battlefield, with a tyrant on one side venting his spleen despite his weakened condition, and an ineffectual, put-upon and nearly hysterical wife on the other.

Hostile orders replaced his usual courteous requests. He barked his demands. "Get me fresh water, dammit—this is like dishwater." "Open the window." "Shut the window—now." "This bed's a goddamn mess—remake it." "Get in here and help me to the bathroom—d'you want a stall to clean out?" "You call Stanley and tell him he better get himself over here, and move." Whatever he wanted, he wanted immediately. Any delay in Anne's or Janice's response prompted a stream of curses. He was an executive gone berserk.

Anne was frantic. Joseph's illness, his dying at home and decision to do so by his own hand, and now his frightening behavior, combined to undo her completely. She alternated between crying and rubbing her hands, fleeing the sickroom in panic whenever she could escape. She became incapable of functioning.

For a week this went on. Anne's scanty reserves had long-since fled when a strange thing happened. One day her tears decreased, her walk became more determined, and Janice noted a grim look on her face.

On her arrival two days later, Janice heard a racket in the kitchen. She hurried in that direction. The formerly hesitant Anne stormed about, throwing pots and pans out of the cabinet onto the floor—aggressive, angry, and ready to do battle.

"Anne, whatever's happened to you?" Janice asked, thunderstruck.

"I've had it!" She slammed the cabinet door shut as hard as she could. "I've had it! That man who calls himself my husband has issued his last vacant threat of suicide! I won't listen to it any more! Before I go stark raving mad I'll get him the pills, and he can do it or not—I just don't care! I've put up with plenty of his junk in the past, believe me. But this—this is too much. I am not going to listen to him one more time!"

Janice and Anne stood staring at each other, rooted to the floor, Anne panting, Janice too stunned to respond. They remained so for some moments, then Janice turned and headed for the sickroom. She performed her duties quickly, her mind absorbed in the transformation in Anne.

Next day the first thing Janice noticed was a small unmarked jar full of white tablets on Joseph's night stand. A tall glass of water stood by its side. She examined the jar carefully before putting it down.

"My God, where did she get these—and NOW what do I do?" Janice's thoughts raced.

As calmly as she could, she lifted Joseph's pillow and roused him from his half-sleep. "Time for your bath, Joseph," she said.

A wan smile spread over his face as he realized who was there. He reached for her hand and looked up. "I have them."

She searched his face, then picked up the pills. "Now that you have them, what will you do?"

"I haven't decided yet," he said, gazing steadily at her. "But I have them."

She read the sigh of relief in his voice; it said it all. She squeezed his hand, then went ahead with the morning's procedures, listening with particular care to his heart and lungs and abdomen. He was declining rapidly, but it was never possible to predict with great accuracy how much longer a life would last.

He was changed; she moved about his room with the feel of their first weeks together. Once more courteous and kindly, he showed none of the harshness and cruelty of the past nine days. There was an ease that was new, something she could not define. The contrast was palpable, and comforting.

He was asleep by the time she drew the fresh sheet and blanket over him, so she left the room quietly.

The kitchen was empty. Janice went to the stairway. "Anne," she called.

Anne's face appeared briefly at the top of the stairs. "I'm on the phone, Janice. Is there anything urgent? Otherwise I'll see you tomorrow."

"He's sleeping now. I think he's okay. I'm leaving. Call if you need anything." It was pretty clear Anne had no intention of talking about the pills. Janice wondered if she ever would.

Days passed. The jar remained untouched at Joseph's bedside. No one mentioned the pills. It was an unspoken pact. Anne never volunteered to Janice where she had obtained them, or even what they were. Janice was not about to ask.

The tension dissolved. Joseph was calm, and Janice's presence resumed its reassuring comfort. Anne found an unaccustomed self-confidence in her step. Now when Joseph rang his little bell, she called back without hesitation, "In a few minutes, Joseph. I'm busy." She listened to his comments as before, but now also stated her own opinion. She was someone to be reckoned with, a person of stature. While they'd never been close, she and Joseph at last reached some level of peace with each other and with their waiting. Whether his death would be natural or self-induced no longer seemed to matter. They both knew it was going to happen. How it happened was up to him.

Exactly one week after the pills appeared Janice got the call from Anne. It was shortly after midnight, and she knew before Anne spoke that Joseph had died. Anne asked her to come, and Janice dressed quickly. The question prodded her—had he committed suicide? When she got into the car, she pressed the accelerator hard.

Anne opened the door, and briefly the two women hugged. Anne bared her anguish, her tension, her fatigue in that intimate, direct moment, and Janice gave her an extra squeeze, then led the way toward the room in which Joseph lay.

As she approached the bed the answer was apparent. There for anyone to see was the unmarked jar, still full of white tablets. Janice picked the jar up, shook it gently for a moment as she stared at it, then replaced it on the night stand. Without a word, she turned and put her arms around Anne.

Anne began to cry. The sobbing grew, then decreased and finally quieted. Janice stood back to look at her. Anne fished in her pockets for some tissues and blew her nose. She straightened her shoulders and smiled at Janice through the remaining tears.

Joseph was gone, his death, like his life, according to his own plan. Anne would be all right.

Janice led her away to the kitchen, then returned to the sickroom. She cleaned Joseph's body, preparing it for the mortician, then removed his bed- and bath-linens and started the laundry. After the mortician came and went, she joined Anne in the kitchen.

"You must be very tired, my dear. Why don't you go to bed and try to sleep? It's over now. You've earned a rest."

"Yes—suddenly I'm terribly tired. I think I will. . . . There's one thing, though . . ." Anne faltered. She blew her nose, then laid one hand on Janice's arm as she spoke again. "When this started I was so scared. I was afraid of Joseph's dying. . . . I didn't know what I'd do by myself. Even more I was afraid of his dying at home. I didn't think I could handle it—his care, and then his dying right here. I resented it, his wanting to do this at home.

"It's different now. I'm not sure I can tell you why."

"All my life I guess I was afraid . . . but, you know, I did all right. I took good care of him. It was hard, but I did it. I guess I'm going to miss him. . . . I'm not afraid any more, not like I was." She took a deep breath. "Thank you, Janice. Thanks for everything."

The two tired women embraced, then parted. One headed upstairs to bed, the other let herself out the door to her little green car. If Joseph were watching, he had to be smiling. Each of the women, in her own way, had given him the gift of choice.

NOTES:
Assisted Suicide; Withholding Treatment;
Advance Directives; Do Not Resuscitate Orders

Joseph's story raises the very complex issue of suicide, a subject bound in strong and often conflicting feelings.

Suicide has long been with our society. Despite the opposition organized religion has always directed toward this final act, some people have chosen to end their lives when suffering pain, disability, or failure and the despair those circumstances can create. Moral, religious, and other constraints have not always been strong enough to counteract the will to suicide. Furthermore, no state law makes suicide or attempted suicide illegal.

The American Hospital Association estimates that many of the 6,000 deaths in the United States per day are self-arranged, some with assistance [1]. Among the terminally ill, one or two out of 1000 cancer patients commit suicide, a rate about twice that of the general population [2].

In the first author's experience with hospice, a large majority of her patients talked about suicide, but during her nineteen years only three out of some 600 actually carried it out. A similar rate is reported by others [3]. It would appear that laying out one's thoughts in open discussion with a trusted person provides a release for a patient, a safety valve through which some of the intent can flow—leaving him feeling less boxed in, less compelled to choose this final answer to his problems.

The effects of a completed suicide on survivors can be devastating. Shock and pain often overlie the survivors' ordinary emotions triggered by death and loss, emotions which are hard enough to experience all by themselves. Along with their grieving, the suicide victims' loved ones bear the terrible burden of wondering and never knowing whether they might have made a difference—the "if only I had . . ." instinct. In addition, they must be acutely aware of the depths to which their loved one had fallen—the hurt he or she must have felt in order to make such a decision—and feel the pain even more deeply.

Occasionally there are exceptions. The family may know ahead of time what the decision is and why it is being made, even participate in the thinking, and share a sense that the time is right for the person to take this step. Designating this a "rational suicide," Siegel suggests this decision requires 1) that the person has made a realistic assessment of the situation (and can find no other satisfactory solution to the problems—authors' comment); 2) that his mental processes are unimpaired; and 3) that his motivation would be understood by a majority of uninvolved community members [4]. Werth adds two other requirements for a rational suicide: 1) that the decision be deliberate and reiterated over a period of time, and 2) if at all possible, the person's significant others be involved in the decision-making process [5].

Even when a so-called rational suicide is committed, the undocumented after-effects among the survivors may be difficult and long lasting.

Suicide has become a red-hot-button issue in our society in recent years with the introduction—more accurately, re-introduction—of the concept of physician assistance to accomplish its goal.

Debates about assisted suicide actually date back to ancient Greece and Rome [6]. Sir Thomas More (early 16th century) and Francis Bacon (17th century) favored a policy allowing euthanasia (from the Greek, "good death"), popularly known as "mercy killing." Later discussion in the 19th century specified the use of morphine and ether, then new agents of anesthesia and sedation, as the means of accomplishing euthanasia.

The debates today require some common understanding of the language that has grown up around these issues. Passive and active euthanasia, voluntary and involuntary assisted suicide and double-effect euthanasia are all terms basic to understanding and arguing the issues. The statements that follow, written by the Council on Ethical and Judicial Affairs of the American Medical Association are helpful:

> Life-sustaining treatment is any medical treatment that serves to prolong life without reversing the underlying medical condition. . . . At one time, the term "passive euthanasia" was commonly used to describe withholding or withdrawing life-sustaining treatment. However, many experts now refrain from using (that) term. . . .
>
> The provision of a palliative treatment that may have fatal side effects is also described as "double-effect euthanasia." The intent of the treatment is to relieve pain and suffering, not to end the patient's life, but the patient's death is a foreseeable potential effect of the treatment. An example is gradually increasing the morphine dosage for a patient to relieve severe cancer pain, realizing that large enough doses of morphine may depress respiration and cause death [7].

(Nursing experience leads us to believe that when the morphine given is titrated in 5 mg increments, decreased respiration is not observed appreciably. The effect of this increase in morphine more often is to help the body relax with relief from pain, permitting more comfort. Eventually the dying patient will die—but peacefully, and not from morphine-caused depressed respiration. Our observations are not unique) [8].

> "Euthanasia" is commonly defined as the act of bringing about the death of a hopelessly ill and suffering person in a relatively quick and painless way for reasons of mercy . . . the term euthanasia will signify the medical administration

of a lethal agent to a patient for the purpose of relieving the patient's intolerable and incurable suffering.

"Euthanasia" and "assisted suicide" differ in the degree of physician participation. "Euthanasia" entails a physician performing an immediate life-ending action (e.g., administering a lethal injection). "Assisted suicide" occurs when a physician facilitates a patient's death by providing the necessary means and/or information to enable the patient to perform the life-ending act (e.g., the physician provides sleeping pills and information about the lethal dose, while aware that the patient may commit suicide).[1]

(It should be noted that increasingly, physician-assisted suicide and voluntary active euthanasia, although different, are considered moral equivalents) [9].

The AMA's definitions should be used by the readers of this book when the terms appear.

The discussion of withholding or withdrawing life-sustaining treatment is best kept distinct from discussion of physician-assisted suicide, since they are quite separate practices, and their circumstances differ dramatically. In the former, death would occur *except* for the physician's intervention; in the latter death would occur only *with* the physician's intervention. We will discuss withholding or withdrawing life support last.

In the United States the first serious consideration of physician-assisted suicide began when legislation was introduced in Ohio in 1905 to legalize euthanasia. The bill failed to pass. Following this, there were no reports of any significant activity around the issue for many years.

The major argument raised against allowing euthanasia was the fear that it would pave the way to greater and greater use under circumstances not countenanced when the practice was first allowed. In 1958 Kamisar described this as the "slippery slope" notion [10], which still very much figures in the debate. His thinking was, if you allow A, then B will likely follow—but since B is not morally acceptable, we should not allow A. For example, society might begin with competent

[1] Source: Code of Medical Ethics Report of the Council on Ethical and Judicial Affairs of the American Medical Association, copyright July 1991.

patients approaching death who request physician assistance in dying. Then, since comatose or otherwise incompetent patients lacking the capacity to make the request should have the same rights, surrogates would be able to authorize the physician's role. Next steps might be to include patients not approaching death, with disabling chronic diseases; then persons with disabilities of one sort or another. The hypothesis can be carried as far as the debater likes, even to the extreme, justifying Nazi-type genocide. Along the line, each of us would find some next step unacceptable, until ultimately no one would approve.

To be valid, De Beaufort has since noted, the slippery slope argument requires that the consequences (B, C, etc.) be clear, negative and probable, that preventing them would be difficult if not impossible, and that there is an alternative less susceptible to the slippery slope [11]. In the main, however, the public debate today does not concern itself with the philosophical—and intellectual—niceties of De Beaufort's demand for validity. The "slippery slope" is rather a gut-level, generalized notion, argued in a more emotional way.

This argument has enjoyed increasing acceptance and may have delayed further developments of the aid-in-dying movement for a long time. But every movement has its triggers to jolt it out of lethargy. Derek Humphry provided a jump-start for the physician-assisted suicide movement in 1980.

Following his first wife's two-year struggle with acute leukemia and subsequent suicide, Humphry formed the Hemlock Society to promote a "Death With Dignity Act" permitting physician aid-in-dying. He saw the relief of suffering by self-inflicted suicide as desirable but unattainable by the terminally ill and hopelessly handicapped. Legalizing physician-assistance, he believed, would provide that relief. The Hemlock Society has grown since then, and at this writing has 40,000 members who take Humphry's same position [12].

Organized medicine early opposed the Hemlock Society and any physician role in aid-in-dying. Physicians looked at themselves as healers, not killers. The Hippocratic Oath to which they (still) swear includes the statement "I will give no deadly medicine to anyone if asked, nor suggest any such counsel."

Even if some physicians are willing to assist a patient in dying, they may believe they cannot; they believe that helping their patients to die is more than a personal decision. Because their training, oaths, licensure, and receipt of public money make what they do a societal matter as well as a personal one [13, 14], they believe being asked to help a patient die is forcing them into conflict [15]. Assisting with suicides, most physicians have in the past agreed, would be a breach of the public's faith.

Proponents argue that we must recognize the current medical reality that patients now live longer, some with problems physicians cannot cure; that legalizing assisted suicide will permit patients to retain control over their lives, allow dignity in dying, prevent unnecessary suffering and reduce the burden on the family, and promote accountability of the professionals involved, thus protecting them from criminal and/or civil prosecution. These arguments are wrapped in the belief that human beings can be faced with harms other than, perhaps worse than death, and the physician obligation to beneficence and non-maleficence may include assisting suicide.

Public opinion has gradually moved to favor allowing physician-assisted suicide [16], although some would deny that [17].

Public opinion polls on this, as on any issue, must be interpreted with the caveat that the people surveyed may not accurately reflect the total population; also the questions may be loaded, deliberately or inadvertently, to support one side or the other. Conclusions about public opinion can only be justified if those issues are addressed with appropriate rigor.

Support tends to rise with euphemisms like "dignified death" and to fall when more graphic terms like "lethal injection" are used. A study was made of the effects of using certain common terms in questioning persons about their approval or disapproval of physician-assisted suicide. It found that "some form of personal control over your own death" yielded the strongest approval, followed by "mercy killing" and "euthanasia," and last, "physician-assisted suicide" [18]. Clearly terminology makes a difference, and polls have some limitations.

A Roper poll conducted in May 1991, found 68 percent of 1500 people surveyed in Washington, Oregon, and California approved of allowing physician-assisted suicide, while 23 percent opposed [2]. Even among elderly respondents, a Gallup poll in 1992 measured 41 percent approving the legalization of assisted suicide [19]. These levels of support are surprising in view of the almost universal opposition of religious organizations: Catholic, Lutheran, Mennonite, Presbyterian, Mormon, Jehovah's Witness, Episcopalian, Christian Science, Baptist, Disciples of Christ, Islam, Jewish, Greek and Roman Orthodox, Hindu, and Buddhist. Unitarian-Universalist churches stood alone among religious groups in support of legalizing physician-assisted suicide from 1988 until 1991, when the United Church of Christ added its endorsement. Methodists now argue that compassion for the individual is above the law, so they also might find it permissible under some circumstances. The Episcopal Diocese of Newark adopted a resolution in 1996 calling suicide and assisted suicide a "moral choice" for the terminally ill or those living in persistent or progressive pain. Their resolution will be brought to the next national Episcopal Church convention, and it is possible that group may join the breakaway from religion's traditional position.

Despite the predominant religious opposition and the significant physician stand against it, an act of physician-assistance-in-dying occurred and was published anonymously in 1988 [20]. Subsequently ten American physicians said in a 1991 *New England Journal of Medicine* article, "It is not immoral for a physician to assist in the rational suicide of a terminally ill person" [21, p. 1532]. Seeds of disagreement among the medical community had begun to take root.

Later in 1991, of startling interest to the medical and general community, for the first time a physician, Timothy Quill, identified himself and put into writing in a prestigious medical journal his experience providing assistance-in-dying to a suffering leukemia patient [22]. A general understanding had existed for some time that these events did occur occasionally (how often we will never know), but always within the protective silence of a doctor/patient relationship—not with a public announcement. The issue became a flaming controversy overnight.

The 72nd Annual Meeting of the American College of Physicians called for a show of hands supporting this new role for its members, and 35 percent responded positively [23].

A survey of members of the American Society of Internal Medicine reported in 1992 found 20 percent of them had already at some time assisted a patient or patients in dying, and "many" of the 402 internists surveyed (how many the writer does not make clear) reported they might assist if requested, "depending on the situation" [24].

It seemed support for physician-assisted suicide was growing.

Meanwhile, in a move that shook the country, a pathologist in Michigan named Jack Kevorkian assisted an Alzheimer's victim to die in the back of a rusted 1968 VW bus, using a thiopental injection the patient controlled through a "jerry-rigged flea-market science project" [25, p. 46]. Subsequent repetitions occurred with other patients until the Michigan Supreme Court, in a 5-2 decision in December 1994, paved the way for Dr. Kevorkian to be prosecuted as a common-law felon. The first such prosecution in March 1996, resulted in an acquittal. A second acquittal has left Dr. Kevorkian relatively free to pursue his mission, and as of this writing he has assisted forty-three patients in dying.

By 1991, thirty-six states had bans on doctor-assisted suicide [26]. At that time, emerging from the growing support measured in the polls in Washington, Initiative 119 was drawn up as an amendment to that state's Living Will Law to legalize physician aid-in-dying via both voluntary active and voluntary passive euthanasia. The initiative was defeated 54 percent to 46 percent, despite the support suggested by the polls. The Washington State Medical Society and hospice groups waged a successful public education program against the measure, probably accounting for its defeat. The voters did approve the use of advance directives for terminal illness and permanent unconscious conditions, allowing the withholding or withdrawal of life-sustaining treatment under those circumstances, as long as an authorization had been written and signed, witnessed and dated by the patient at an earlier time.

The first postscript to the Washington story was an early 1996 reversal by the U.S. Ninth Court of Appeals of that state's existing ban on assisted suicide, upholding a lower court decision. Judge Stephen Reinhardt wrote for the majority in the 8-3 Appelate decision, saying there is a constitutionally protected liberty interest in determining the time and manner of one's own death that can outweigh the state's interest in preserving life. He found that Washington's law violates the right of mentally competent, terminally ill adults to choose a "dignified and humane death," an argument based on the due process clause of the Fourteenth Amendment. The second post-script on June 10, 1996, was the United States Supreme Court's ruling maintaining the ban, pending an appeal which was heard on January 8, 1997. The decision is expected in July 1997.

The next state to approach the voters was California, which, in 1992, placed Proposition 161 on the ballot to allow physician aid-in-dying when requested by the patient. Again, only 46 percent of the vote favored the measure, and it went down in defeat. Both the Washington and California initiatives were lost because of a perception that safeguards were inadequate, a concern arising from the slippery slope argument.

Meanwhile, in other parts of the world assistance-in-dying was becoming an issue. In Netherlands, where euthanasia had never been a legalized procedure, the practice had been occurring quietly and with acceptance for years without legal repercussions [27]. Efforts grew to change that country's laxness and require more accountability from physicians, resulting in a defacto decriminalization if official guidelins for euthanasia are followed. Overall incidence of active euthanasia in 1990 in the Netherlands was estimated at about 4,000 to 6,000. Ninety percent of these persons had a reported life expectancy of less than three months [28]. We should note that hospice care as it is known in England and the United States is not available in the Netherlands. Were that an option, we can safely assume fewer cases of euthanasia would have taken place.

Opponents to the practice in the Netherlands argue that physicians are sometimes making the decision for the patient, so assisted suicide may be changing into involuntary euthanasia. By one report, a number of Dutch people even carry "a passport to life" so they won't be euthanized in an emergency without their consent.

In 1993, The House of Lords Select Committee on Medical Ethics in Britain decided unanimously to oppose any change in the existing law of the United Kingdom which has held euthanasia illegal.

The Canadian Senate voted in 1995, after sixteen months of study, that assisted suicide should remain a criminal offense, and a full Parliament vote made that official.

Meanwhile, the only successful initiative in the United States (at the time of this writing) to permit physician-assistance in dying was Oregon Ballot Measure 16 which passed in November 1994 by a narrow margin. This measure allows such assistance only to competent adults with less than six months left to live, and it limits the assistance to the use of medication. The Oregon law requires that two physicians must determine that the patient has six months or less to live; it requires that the patient place his request three times for physician assistance, the last in writing with the statement signed and dated in the presence of two witnesses; and the physician must wait fifteen or more days after the first request and two or more days after the last written request to prescribe the needed drugs. Under the law, the patient's life insurance policies would not be nullified by the suicide, as is usually the case, and any failed assisted-suicide would be considered a complication of terminal illness, not an attempted suicide [29].

The scope of the Oregon ballot measure was narrower than either the Washington or California initiatives, with more safeguards built in, so the effectiveness of the education campaign waged by its opponents was somewhat mitigated and the measure was allowed to become law.

U.S. District Judge Michael Hogan first delayed implementation of the Oregon law pending hearings on a permanent injunction, then on August 3, 1995 ruled the law unconstitutional. That decision was appealed to the 9th Circuit Court five days later, and at this writing, a ruling has not been handed down.

In April 1996, the 2nd U.S. Circuit Court of Appeals in Manhattan struck down two New York state laws banning physician-assisted suicide. Judge Roger Miner's rationale differed from the earlier 9th U.S. Circuit Court ruling in the Washington case. Whereas the Washington decision held that a ban violated constitutional rights of individuals, the New York decision was based on the theory that the state had no interest and therefore no right to ban physician-assisted suicide, which was seen as no different from the already allowed withdrawal of life support, based on an argument of the equal protection clause of the Fourteenth Amendment. That decision was appealed to the Supreme Court, heard with the Washington appeal, and will be decided in the summer, 1997. Because the 2nd Circuit Court covers multiple states, many commentators expect there will be an increase in the number of ballot initiatives for allowing this assistance in dying. Some worry that insufficient safeguards are in place to protect people when this new freedom is acted upon, and many feel the courts are moving too fast—before the populace has truly thought through the matter.

Even without the sanction of the courts, movement toward acceptance of assisted suicide can be seen in the reports from the United States, Canada, England, and the Netherlands at the 11th International Conference on AIDS held in Vancouver in July 1996, in which suicide was found to be a common way out for patients with this disease. Over half of the AIDS specialists in San Francisco who responded to a survey indicated they had written prescriptions for overdoses rather than to allow botched "coat-hanger" suicides. (The issue of assisted suicide for AIDS patients may change substantially with the development of new medications—see Notes in Chapter 7).

Very large and profound legal decisions about physician-assisted suicide face the United States, and resolution of the disagreements around it will not come easily. First, the debate itself has inherent problems. Arguments pro and con grow out of theories of utility (or its close kin, clinical pragmatism), or deontology, knowingly or not. These theories conflict in a fundamental and crucial way.

Utility theory holds that moral decisions should be made by balancing the benefits against the disadvantages and obtaining the greatest net value for the patient, which is then expressed in terms of the quality of his life and justification for the dollars to be spent or not spent. Clinical pragmatism is the rigorous version of utility, refining the balancing equation with the scientific method. It requires observation of the problem(s), then hypothesis generation and validation with periodic review and hypothesis refinement, as a way of understanding and responding to ethical issues. It is a means of finding out what works, and is therefore best, or right, according to the theory.

Deontological theory holds that consequences of acts—benefits and disadvantages—do not make them right or wrong; rather, the act itself is either intrinsically right or wrong—moral or immoral. To the deontologist, it would not matter if the patient requesting assistance in suicide were receiving successful comfort care or suffering intractable pain with no one left to care about him—the deontological position is that assisting him in dying is *right* or *wrong,* in and of itself. The crux of this argument rests on whether physician-assisted suicide is believed to be right, regardless of its consequences. This theory is fundamental to the thinking of many religions.

Any debate is impeded inevitably by these differences in theory. The proponent guided by utility or clinical pragmatism does not follow the same thought process as one guided by deontology. Disagreement on what is believed to be right cannot be settled by vote or logic.

Confusion and disagreement about definitions underlying the debate also interfere with achieving consensus on physician-assisted suicide. Discussants need to be talking about the same things or resolution will never be achieved.

As for the central arguments of the issue, the bottom-line justification most often heard for physician-assisted suicide is that it will provide the patient a compassionate release from pain—a desperate and final solution, indeed. (The Dutch experience with euthanasia does not bear that reason out. Reportedly, pain was the sole basis for the request only 5% of the time) [3].

If pain is truly the justification for physician aid in dying, a better answer would seem to be a simple proposition: eliminate pain and you no longer need that way out. However, such a solution is anything but simple.

Opponents of physician-assisted suicide maintain the answer for pain-ridden patients is to provide them comfort care including palliation of pain [2, 15, 30-35]. Even those who support assisted suicide stress that improved pain control and comfort care at the end of life would reduce requests for such help [36-39].

The World Health Organization Expert Panel on Cancer Pain and Palliative Care recommended in 1990 that governments devote specific attention to the needs for cancer pain relief and palliative care prior to considering legalizing euthanasia [40]. That position is held by others [39, 41].

The American Geriatrics Society Ethics Committee recommends advising the patient that pain can be relieved, then carrying out aggressive palliation. Along with that recommendation, the Committee tells physicians to let patients know they may forego life-prolonging intervention, including nutrition and hydration [42].

But, say supporters of physician-assisted suicide, pain control sometimes doesn't work. Some patients are still left to suffer [43, 44].

True, the opponents respond—but while distress has not always been relieved, it is relievable [15]. Pain *can* be sufficiently reduced, if not eliminated, through modern technology and drugs, if health care professionals will but use what is available, they say. The World Health Organization reports that 50 percent of physicians do not give pain medication to relieve suffering, and a reported 81 percent of 1400 physicians and nurses recently surveyed in the United States agreed that the most common form of narcotic abuse in caring for dying patients is undertreatment of pain [45].

Ira Byock, past chairman of the ethics committee and 1996 President of the American Academy of Hospice and Palliative Care Medicine, describes a University of Wisconsin Medical School report "documenting that basic principles of pain management remain inadequately practiced—even within the nation's 'best' medical institutions" [14, p. 6]. He refers to a survey of American oncologists in which 86 percent felt most patients with cancer pain were undermedicated. In their own practices, nearly half of these oncologists believed pain control was insufficient [14].

A significant barrier to good palliative care in hospitals is administrative and financial. Dying has no diagnosis, or Diagnostic Related Group (DRG), a requirement for insurance billing, so another diagnosis must be found in order to insure third-party payment. Any other diagnosis requires active treatment, disallowing pure comfort care with good pain and symptom control. This amounts to a financial disincentive to palliative care [2]. Give dying a diagnosis and that problem is solved.

Other barriers include the skill mix of hospital staff which tends toward catheters, premature gastrostomy, use of restraints and sedation, and reluctance to control pain adequately. The end product is more pain, and more pressure for assisted suicide.

Hospice and some physicians are gradually overcoming the old negative myths and practices about using available agents of pain control, allowing greater success in ameliorating pain [8]. Especially in settings outside the hospital, true comfort care more and more often provides a good way to die. Do something to correct the pain control deficiencies; don't legalize physician-assisted suicide, the opponents say.

But, we repeat, the picture is not simple—nothing is ever black and white. Even when modern pain control technology is used to its fullest, pain has been found in some (perhaps few) patients to be recalcitrant [26, 43, 44, 46]. The first author's own very recent clinical experience with the most up-to-date pain control methods confirms this—fortunately only in rare cases. What, then, is to be done for them?

To complicate the issue more, there are those who argue that legal reform to allow physician-assisted suicide is not necessary since drugs at lethal strength can already be administered for the purpose of controlling pain [47].

The American Nurses' Association includes in its Position Statement on Promotion of Comfort and Relief of Pain in Dying Patients, 1995, the very clear line, ". . . the increasing titration of medication to achieve symptom control, even at the expense of life, thus hastening death secondarily, is ethically justified" [48]. To be held a crime, intent to murder is needed. The federal government simply requires that any controlled substance be issued for a legitimate medical purpose acting in the usual course of professional practice, thus spreading its protective cover over prescription of lethal-strength drugs for pain control purposes [49].

Interestingly, this argument has its flip-side. For a physician like Timothy Quill, (and we can presume there are more out there like him), who may, under special circumstances, feel the need to help a patient with suicide, the distinction over intent can only be damaging. He postulates that patients wanting to commit suicide must lie, requesting medication for pain in order to allow the physician to "stay legal." Lying not only jeopardizes the doctor/patient relationship and the medical service needed, but if the patient cannot openly request suicide help, Quill believes the physician is not apt to hear his call for help [50].

(A substantial discussion of pain control appears in the Chapter 6 Notes).

Less-often heard justifications for physician-assisted suicide revolve around the loss of quality of life. An artist, a writer, an attorney, a physician, a business-person whose illness has permanently cut off the part of his or her life that gave it value; the person who finds dependence intolerable; the victim of dementia whose vegetative functions continue without purpose; these are individuals who may consider (or in the case of dementia, may have considered) suicide the best resolution, with the need for physician assistance.

With some of these people, depression can and should be treated and the justification may disappear [51].

In the absence of clinical depression, these requests might be considered rational suicide—in which case the basic issue becomes patient autonomy. Judge Barbara Rothstein, of the U.S. District Court in Seattle, has argued that "there is no more profoundly personal decision, nor one which is closer to the heart of personal liberty, than the choice a terminally ill person makes to end his or her suffering and hasten an inevitable death," calling a ban on assisted suicide unconstitutional because of the 14th Amendment protection of liberty [52, p. A-1].

It was that decision that the 9th U.S. Circuit Court of Appeals upheld in March 1996, only to be stayed by the United States Supreme Court in June, 1996.

And so the debate goes, with the heat of each position steaming out in a different direction, like so many bubblings of a geyser. We are not even close to the final resolution.

We at hospice feel the most crucial factor is being left out of the discussion. That factor is the human value of the living-through-dying experience, the very reason Janice, in this story, and thousands of hospice workers like her, continue to give their time and energy—themselves—in hospice service. They have seen the reward a family reaps from the intimate experience of listening and talking, helping and caring and watching their loved one as he or she moves toward the end of life. Hospice people know from their ongoing work the positive value of a family living together through the time of dying, exploring every possible nuance of their relationships. The closure achieved by many of these families is deeply satisfying. Hartman put it into words: "As you walk people through their experience, you see them grow and you grow with them. It is a mind-expanding and priceless experience. It can even be beautiful, as families grow closer as death approaches"[2] [53, p. 332].

Ira Byock has said it eloquently: "The anticipated dying can represent an opportunity for inestimable growth for the patient as well as the family. This opportunity, which may be one of the most unique and precious features of the human condition, is obviated by choosing "The Final Exit"[3] [15, p. 60].

Are we as a society going to close that opportunity out for many people? Are we willing to rob patients and their families of this ultimate experience?

The National Hospice Organization says no. While not speaking for 100 percent of hospice proponents, in 1990 it adopted a resolution rejecting the practice of voluntary euthanasia and assisted suicide in the care of the terminally ill.

---

[2] Reprinted from Volume 153(3), 1995, by permission of the *Canadian Medical Association Journal.*

[3] Reprinted from Volume 7(4), 1991, by permission of *The Hospice Journal.*

On the reverse side of the coin, the other form of aid-in-dying, withholding or withdrawing life support, has the support of hospice and most of the rest of society [54]. Typically it involves patients who are in the process of dying—whose continued life functions require artificial support. Without that support, they would die. The decision to reject or discontinue life support is usually made by the physician and patient together or by the patient's legal surrogate, or by the physician in concert with the family. A hospital ethics committee may be involved; even the courts. The only circumstance under which it can be done on the independent choice of the physician is when further efforts are undeniably futile.

But here we have another problem. There is no clearly articulated threshold for futility. Decisions based on futility may be contested—although it is said that "like pornography, physicians know futility when they see it."

Tradition offers some support for the concept of discontinuing treatment that is futile. Hippocrates taught, "after relieving pain and reducing the violence of disease, a doctor's duty is to refrain from trying to cure those whom disease has conquered, acknowledging that in such cases medicine is powerless" [55, p. 15].

The advance directive can provide the basis for discontinuing treatment. This instrument was developed as an umbrella for a living will (a legal document stating one's desire not to be kept alive by artificial means if considered terminally ill) and a durable power of attorney (a legal document conferring decision-making power on another person who will represent a patient when that patient cannot make his own health decisions). It allows the individual to specify, to a greater or lesser degree depending on the limitations of the state in which the person has been residing, up to and including Do Not Resuscitate orders, what treatments he will accept and which he will not, under which specific circumstances of medical condition. It is the corollary of a signed informed consent form which one completes at the time of admission to the hospital, or prior to any of a variety of special medical treatments—only it is completed ahead of time. The individual signs an advance directive when he is both conscious and competent. The directive spells out the person's wish to be allowed to die if specific circumstances exist under which he would not want to be forced to live.

In 1990, a Patient Self-Determination Act was passed by Congress requiring that any living will or advance directive documenting the patient's wishes be placed in his health provider's and hospital's charts. (It is also helpful to complete and file with the health provider and hospital a Surrogate Power of Attorney, designating someone to speak with the patient's authority.) The Act also requires that any health-care organization into which a person enters give him information, in writing, about his right to participate in health-care decisions, including the right to refuse treatment. This legislation has helped to make it possible for individuals to maintain some control over their bodies, even when unconscious.

Unfortunately, the advance directive movement has not had great success. Estimates among the general population suggest only a very small percentage of patients in the general population have completed advance directives [56], and surprisingly, even among hospice patients that is true [57]. The most common barrier appears to be lack of prior discussion with the patient's physician.

Even with completed advance directives, breakdowns occur with alarming frequency in the chain of responsibility to observe them. Morrison et al. found that when patients were transferred from ambulatory to acute care settings, only 26 percent of patients who had executed the directives had them recognized by the admitting hospital [58]. Problems occurred when the illness was accompanied by delirium or dementia, or when admissions clerks hurried, giving all papers to the patient or his representative in a stack without explaining them. Inadequate education and this uncertain adherence to the law must be overcome [59].

A recent survey of a large number of patients, practicing physicians and physicians-in-training found that patients would like open discussion of advance directives earlier than physicians, and that they wish for physicians to initiate that discussion [56]. The professionals are often uncomfortable about bringing it up, so this may not happen [57, 61].

Lay people often do not understand the language in advance directives (e.g., *heroic measures*), and in many cases such words do not have legal definition or standing; another problem with advance directives lies in the failure of many persons to specify priorities to their directives.

Lest the picture we have drawn seem too gloomy, we hasten to point out that some progress has been made. Patient records from 1988 and from 1993, before and after passage of the Patient Self Determination Act, were reviewed, finding that Do Not Resuscitate orders were written by physicians, complying with patients' advance directives, within twenty-four hours of admission in 1993; in 1988 they were not written until the middle of the eighth day [62]. Thank goodness for small but positive steps; greased lightning is beyond any rational hopes.

The National Institute on Aging urges that advance directives be part of family and estate planning in order to avoid psychological and financial costs. Their study of 1,061 decedents found that 40 percent of them had had difficulty recognizing people in their final illnesses and would have required surrogate decision making [63]. The role of the surrogate, in the absence of an advance directive, is to decide as the patient would have decided, whether to withhold or withdraw treatment. A caution is seen in the findings of Zweibel and Cassel, who determined that younger surrogates tend to underestimate their seniors' quality of life, voting for discontinuance of life support or treatment where many seniors would have continued [64]. The moral to execute advance directives is clear. Then the surrogate has exact information on which to base his direction to the physician.

The remaining guiding principle for making decisions about an incompetent patient, failing the advance directive and the legal surrogate, is called "best interests" [65]. Presumably, whatever may promote the patient's best interests is done; if that fits with the patient's desire, all is well. There are no guarantees.

The need for advance directives will grow, in view of the estimates of a greater than 100,000 population in the United States by the year 2000 of persons living past 100 years of age [64].

Suppose the patient remains conscious but hopelessly ill, and is determined to die. He may decide that in the face of certain medical conditions he does not wish to be sustained with food and water, either by mouth or involuntarily through tubes, for death—probably a peaceful one—could be expected within three to fourteen days of their discontinuance [66]. Can an advance directive then instruct and achieve the withholding of nutrition and hydration as part of withholding or withdrawing life support? Or does "life support" refer only to medical technology like respirators?

The answers will depend upon what each state will allow, and what the hospital, nursing home, or practicing physician will countenance. Private institutions and persons, in particular, have every right to maintain their own philosophies, and quite legitimate refusal to comply may result [67]. Persons considering this particular directive may find it helpful to inquire at the time of executing the directive what position is held by each of these agents. Hospitals, hospices, and other health-care institutions have an obligation to spell out their policies regarding end-of-life decisions in their mission statements or other publication, so patients can know ahead of time what to expect [68].

The refusal of hydration and nutrition has also been suggested as an acceptable alternative to physician-assisted suicide for terminal patients still in control, as it relies on the patient's decision in order to die rather than on the act of someone else [69]. The common public and medical reaction is one of horror— my word, we cannot let you starve to death!

But studies of the effects of going without food or water (except for comfort-providing occasional ice-chips, etc.) while receiving good palliative care suggest there is nothing to be horrified about. Patients reveal only mild complaints of dry mucuous membrane and occasional and transient hunger, and that limited to the early period until ketonemia (the metabolizing of body proteins) occurs. Hunger and thirst may cause discomfort for as little as a day. In fact, for some people euphoria results [70-72].

As a matter of fact, the forcing of nutrition and hydration upon the person approaching death may have the effect of loading his body with fluids and protein he cannot handle. The excess fluid administered intravenously may not be absorbed by his body tissues and may fill the lungs instead; the protein given parenterally may not be processed by his digestive system, with resulting diarrhea and vomiting. Artificially providing hydration and nutrition may be a poor decision in any event.

In general, efforts to keep him or her alive may not be desired by the patient. Refusing any life-sustaining treatment, knowing death will be hastened, is the choice of some. This was found to be particularly true after long illness [73]. Few geriatric patients wanted cardio-pulmonary rescusitation (CPR) if they were to suffer cardiac or respiratory arrest, particularly when they learned how poor the odds are for survival. CPR produces only 10 to 17 percent survival after arrest during the acute illness of patients sixty years of age and older, and only 0 to 5 percent survival if the illness were chronic with no more than a one-year life expectancy [74].

When an emergency number (911) is called for a patient who does not want CPR, who may have specified a Do Not Rescusitate (DNR) order, there may be difficulties. Often medical technicians and aides staffing emergency vehicles are legally bound to carry out CPR. Several states now have laws or regulations allowing DNR rights, at least for home-bound patients. A common practice among hospices is to register their patients with the county emergency service. A DNR bracelet worn by the patient is a helpful device [75].

Of special and haunting consideration in a discussion of assisted suicide is the persistent vegetative state in which all function of the upper part of the patient's brain is lost, a condition that describes some 35,000 Americans each year [55]. Such a patient cannot control conscious actions, think, speak, or eat. Only the primitive brain remains functional, a fact that can be verified by brain scan. The patient is unconscious but not in a coma; his eyes may open and close, he may appear to sleep and awaken, his breathing and heartbeat may continue unassisted. This vegetative state is considered "persistent" if it lasts more than a month. (Care must be taken in the diagnosis, for recent reports from England indicate some patients identified by non-technical, clinical evaluation as being in a persistent vegetative state later became alert and aware.) A naive observer finds it difficult to believe this patient in a true persistent vegetative state is so damaged as not to be salvageable. Our society has struggled with the issues these patients present.

The widely known case of Karen Ann Quinlan, who existed in a long-term persistent vegetative state, made news when a judge finally ruled in 1976 that she could be taken off the ventilator to which she was attached. She continued to live in a vegetative state for almost ten more years, sustained by artificial feeding and hydration, before she finally died.

The point at which the patient is dead and artificial life support should be discontinued has always been controversial. The 22nd World Medical Assembly held in Sydney, Australia, in 1968 concluded that the point of death of the different cells and organs is not as important as the certainty that the process has become irreversible, evidenced by a persistent, deep coma, absence of attempts to breathe when ventilators are removed, no pupillary response to light or blinking to touch on the eye or grimace to pain.

An ad hoc committee of Harvard Medical School recommended in 1968 that death be defined as cessation of brain activity, and in 1981 the Uniform Determination of Death Act was formulated with that definition by a President's Commission. All states now accept this, although, since mechanical ventilation can continue vital functions, critics continue to raise the question of when the signs of life no longer represent the life of a human being [76].

More physicians are accepting the futility of life support in these extreme cases. The majority of a large sample interviewed recently have changed their attitudes since beginning their practices, and now will accept the non-treatment option. The investigators feel certain requirements should be met, including optimal palliative care, good prognostic knowledge, consultation of other specialists, absence of defensive motives, and patient involvement in the decision by way of advance directives or surrogate, if possible[4] [77].

---

[4] Copyright 1995, American Medical Association.

Another guideline which has been proposed is to have the direct or reported experience of at least 100 similar patients whose treatment turned out to be futile; with this knowledge a physician can regard further support of his patient as futile. Continuing unconsciousness and failure to end dependence on intensive care mark futility [78].

Efforts are being made to establish a reasonable policy for these tragic patients in a vegetative state. Three recommendations have been made: enlarge the definition of death to include the persistent vegetative state; establish criteria for treatment based on the extent and duration of the patient's neurological damage; or assume that the person in a persistent vegetative state would not want to be kept alive, so after a certain time life support would be turned off. This last alternative reverses the current policy in which an argument must win to discontinue life support. With the last recommendation, it would become necessary for someone to argue and justify why life support should continue [79].

Another special situation is the patient with severe dementia. Are continued nutrition, hydration, and treatment for infection or cardiopulmonary arrest appropriate for him? The success rate for resuscitation in these persons is exceedingly low, and worse, often leads to more dementia. Tube feeding may require restraints or even surgery, and their infections often return. The withholding of life support, including nutrition and hydration, is being accepted increasingly in these cases [80]. Comfort care would seem to be the treatment of choice.

While the debate about assisted suicide is heated, the supporters and opponents do profess a common ground. They agree that patients should always be managed with compassion; that decisions must be made with the patient or his surrogate, and be patient centered; that treatment and life support must always be effective or potentially so, and be of net potential benefit to the patient. They agree that physician input to decisions should be exclusive of considerations of age, disease, social merit or ability to pay, and that pain and suffering should be avoided even if measures shorten life. They agree that when conflict exists, mechanisms should be utilized for conflict resolution[5] [38].

From this common ground, given the rising frustration with current treatment of the dying and the likelihood that will increase because of population and resource pressures, some planning and decisions will surely take place.

We hope the decisions will increase the hospice option for more people. It is the positive solution.

In the meanwhile, and as an abiding principle, hospice will respect the decision of the patient, even if his considered choice is suicide. We will not abandon him or his loved ones. We will strive to help them live fully and richly in the time they have together and achieve the closure that will bring comfort and acceptance to the survivors.

REFERENCES

1. R. Weir, The Morality of Physician-Assisted Suicide, *Law, Medicine and Health Care, 20*:1-2, pp. 116-126, 1992.
2. D. Cundiff, *Euthanasia is Not the Answer,* Humana Press, Totowa, New Jersey, 1992.
3. P. J. Van der Maas, J. J. M. van Delden, L. Piunenborg, and C. W. N. Looman, Euthanasia and Other Medical Decisions Concerning the End of Life, *Lancet, 338*:8768, pp. 669-674, 1991.
4. K. Siegel, Psychosocial Aspects of Rational Suicide, *American Journal of Psychotherapy, 40,* pp. 405-418, 1986.
5. J. L. Werth, Rational Suicide Reconsidered: AIDS as an Impetus for Change, *Death Studies, 19*:1, pp. 65-80, 1995.
6. E. J. Emanuel, History of Euthanasia Debates in the United States and Britain, *Annals of Internal Medicine, 121*:10, pp. 793-802, 1994.
7. Council on Ethical and Judicial Affairs, American Medical Association, Decisions Near the End of Life, *Journal of the American Medical Association, 267*:16, pp. 2229-2233, 1992.
8. S. Aranda and M. O'Conner, Euthanasia, Nursing and Care of the Dying, *Australian Nursing Journal, 3*:2, pp. 18-21, 1995.

---

[5] Drawn from *Archives of Family Medicine*, Vol. 2(10), pp. 1078-1080, copyright 1993. Used with permission of the American Medical Association.

9. J. J. Fins and M. D. Bachetta, Framing the Physician-Assisted Suicide and Voluntary Active Euthanasia Debate: The Role of Deontology, Consequentialism and Clinical Pragmatism, *Journal of the American Geriatrics Society, 43*:5, pp. 563-568, 579-580, 1995.
10. Y. Kamisar, Some Non-Religious Views against Proposed Mercy Killing Legislation, *Minnesota Law Review, 42*, 1958.
11. W. van der Burg, The Slippery-Slope Argument, *The Journal of Clinical Ethics, 3*:4, pp. 256-268, 1992.
12. Hemlock Society, personal communication, September 1995.
13. I. R. Byock, The Hospice Clinician's Response to Euthanasia/ Physician-Assisted Suicide, *The Hospice Journal, 9*:4, pp. 1-8, 1994.
14. I. R. Byock, The Art of Dying in America, *The American Journal of Hospice and Palliative Care, 12*:2, pp. 6-7, 1995.
15. I. R. Byock, Final Exit: A Wake-Up Call to Hospice, *The Hospice Journal, 7*:4, pp. 51-66, 1991.
16. R. J. Blendon, U. S. Szalay, and R. A. Knox, Should Physicians Aid Their Patients in Dying? A Public Perspective, *Journal of the American Medical Association, 267*:19, pp. 2658-2662, 1992.
17. K. A. Feucht, D. R. King, and R. C. Wright, Response to Miller et al., *New England Journal of Medicine, 331*:24, pp. 1656-1657, 1994.
18. R. Huber, V. M. Cox, and W. B. Edelen, Right to Die Responses from a Random Sample of 200, *The Hospice Journal, 8*:3, pp. 1-19, 1992.
19. L. Seidlitz, P. R. Duberstein, and P. D. Cox, Attitudes of Older People toward Suicide and Assisted Suicide, *Journal of the American Geriatric Society, 43*:9, pp. 993-998, 1995.
20. Anonymous, It's Over, Debbie, *Journal of the American Medical Association, 259*:2, p. 272, 1988.
21. N. Spritz, Gatekeeping, *New England Journal of Medicine, 327*:21, p. 1532, 1991.
22. T. E. Quill, Death and Dignity: A Case of Individualized Decision-Making, *New England Journal of Medicine, 324*:10, pp. 691-694, 1991.
23. N. Spritz, Speeding the Dying, *The Hastings Center Report, 21*:4, p. 4, 1991.
24. C. Crosby, What's the Physician's Role? *Internist, 33*:3, p. 10, 1992.
25. M. Betzold, *Appointment with Doctor Death*, Momentum Books, Ltd., Troy, Michigan, 1993.

26. T. E. Quill, C. K. Cassel, and D. E. Meier, Care of the Hopelessly Ill: Proposed Criteria for Physician-Assisted Suicide, *New England Journal of Medicine, 327*:19, pp. 1380-1384, 1992.
27. R. Fenigson, A Case against Dutch Euthanasia, *Hastings Center Report, 19*:1, pp. 22-30, 1989.
28. H. ten Have and J. V. M. Welie, Euthanasia: Normal Medical Practice? *Hastings Center Report, 22*:2, pp. 34-38, 1992.
29. A. Alpers and B. Lo, Physician-Assisted Suicide in Oregon, *Journal of the American Medical Association, 274*:6, pp. 483-487, 1995.
30. G. A. Sachs, J. C. Ahronheim, J. A. Rhmes, L. Volicer, and J. Lynn, Good Care of Dying Patients: The Alternative to Physician-Assisted Suicide and Euthanasia, *Journal of the American Geriatric Society, 43*:5, pp. 553-562, 1995.
31. C. Tehan, Victory's Paling Light, *Hospice, 4*:2, pp. 11-13, 1993.
32. H. D. Koenig, Legalizing Physician-Assisted Suicide: Some Thoughts and Concerns, *Journal of Family Practice, 37*:2, pp. 171-179, 1993.
33. Catholic Health Association, Care of the Dying: A Catholic Perspective. Part III: Clinical Context—Good Palliative Care Eases the Dying Process, *Health Programs, 74*:4, pp. 22-26, 1993.
34. E. S. Ringerman and D. Koniak-Griffin, A Reexamination of Euthanasia: Issues Raised by Final Exit, *Nursing Forum, 27*:4, pp. 5-8, 1992.
35. S. Kowalski, Assisted Suicide: Where do Nurses Draw the Line? *Nursing and Health Care, 14*:2, pp. 70-76, 1993.
36. C. K. Cassel, Caring for Dying Patients: Physicians and Assisted Suicide, *Cleveland Clinic Journal of Medicine, 62*:4, pp. 259-260, 1995.
37. H. Brody, Assisted Suicide: A Challenge for Family Physicians, *The Journal of Family Practice, 37*:2, pp. 123-125, 1993.
38. J. M. Freeman and E. D. Pellegrino, Management at the End of Life, *Archives of Family Medicine, 2*:10, pp. 1078-1080, 1993.
39. F. G. Miller, T. E. Quill, H. Brody, J. C. Flecher, L. O. Gostin, and D. E. Meier, Regulating Physician-Assisted Suicide, *New England Journal of Medicine, 331*:2, pp. 119-123, 1994.
40. R. J. Miller, Hospice Care as an Alternative to Euthanasia, *Law, Medicine, Health Care, 20*:1-2, pp. 127-132, 1992.
41. J. Lynn, Response to Miller et al., *New England Journal of Medicine, 331*:24, p. 1657, 1994.

42. American Geriatrics Society, Care of Dying Patients: A Position Statement, *Journal of the American Geriatric Society, 43*:5, pp. 577-580, 1995.
43. G. A. Kasting, The Nonnecessity of Euthanasia, *Physician-Assisted Death*, J. M. Humber, R. F. Almeder, G. A. Kasting (eds.), Humana Press, Totowa, New Jersey, pp. 24-45, 1994.
44. D. C. Turk and C. S. Feldman, Facilitating the Use of Non-Invasive Pain Management Strategies with the Terminally Ill, *The Hospice Journal, 8*:1-2, pp. 193-214, 1992.
45. M. Solomon et al., Decision Near the End of Life: Professional Views on Life-Sustaining Treatments, *The American Journal of Public Health, 83*:1, pp. 14-22, 1993.
46. H. Brody, Assisted Death—A Compassionate Response to a Medical Failure, *New England Journal of Medicine, 327*:19, pp. 1384-1388, 1992.
47. G. J. Annas, Reply to Quill, *New England Journal of Medicine, 332*:17, p. 1175, 1995.
48. American Nurses' Association, *Position Statement on the Promotion of Comfort and relief of Pain in Dying Patients,* Washington, D.C., 1995.
49. G. J. Annas, Death by Prescripion—The Oregon Initiative, *New England Journal of Medicine, 331*:18, pp. 1240-1243, 1994.
50. T. E. Quill, The Ambiguity of Clinical Intentions, *New England Journal of Medicine, 329*:14, pp. 1039-1040, 1993.
51. J. A. Billings and S. D. Block, Response to Miller et al., *New England Journal of Medicine, 331*:24, p. 1657, 1994.
52. T. Egan, Federal Judge Says Ban on Suicide is Unconstitutional, *New York Times,* p. A1, May 5, 1994.
53. S. Hartman, in B. Gibson, Volunteers, Doctors take Palliative Care into the Community, *Canadian Medical Association Journal, 153*:3, p. 332, 1995.
54. S. H. Wanzer, D. D. Federman, S. J. Adelstein, C. K. Cassel, E. H. Cassem, R. E. Cranford, E. W. Hook, B. Lo, C. G. Moertel, P. Safar, A. Stone, and J. Van Eys, The Physician's Responsibility toward Hopelessly Ill Patients: A Second Look, *New England Journal of Medicine, 320*:13, pp. 844-849, 1989.
55. D. O. Weber, Deathcare: Exploring the Troubled Frontier between Medical Technology and Human Mortality, *Healthcare Forum Journal, 38*:2, p. 15, 1995.
56. M. K. Robinson, M. J. DeHaven, and K. A. Koch, Effects of the Patient Self-Determination Act on Patient Knowledge and Behavior, *Journal of Family Practice, 37*:4, pp. 363-368, 1993.

57. R. S. Schonwetter, R. M. Walker, and B. E. Robinson, Lack of Advance Directives among Hospice Patients, *The Hospice Journal, 10*:3, pp. 1-11, 1995.

58. R. S. Morrison, E. Olson, K. R. Mertz, and D. E. Meier, The Inaccessibility of Advance Directives on Transfer from Ambulatory to Acute Care Settings, *Journal of the American Medical Association, 274*:6, pp. 478-482, 1995.

59. J. M. Teno, T. P. Hill, and M. A. O'Connor, Advance Care Planning, *Hastings Center Report, 24*:6, p. S1, 1994.

60. S. C. Johnston, M. P. Pfeifer, and R. McNutt, for the End of Life Study Group, Discussion about Advance Directives, *Archives of Internal Medicine, 155*:10, pp. 1025-1030, 1995.

61. T. Wetl, Individual Preferences and Advance Directives, *Hastings Center Report, 24*:6, pp. S5-S8, 1994.

62. K. A. Hesse, Terminal Care of the Very Old, *Archives of Internal Medicine, 155*:14, pp. 1513-1518, 1995.

63. D. J. Foley, T. P. Miles, D. B. Brock, and C. Phillips, Recounts of Elderly Deaths: Endorsements for the Patient Self-Determination Act, *The Gerontologist, 35*:1, pp. 119-121, 1995.

64. N. R. Zweibel and C. K. Cassel, Treatment Choices at the End of Life: A Comparison of Decisions by Older Patients and Their Physician-Selected Proxies, *The Gerontologist, 29*:5, pp. 615-621, 1989.

65. D. W. Brock, Good Decision-Making for Incompetent Patients, *Hastings Center Report, 24*:6, pp. S8-S11, 1994.

66. R. S. Morrison and J. Morris, When There is No Cure: Palliative Care for the Dying Patient, *Geriatrics, 50*:7, pp. 45-51, 1995.

67. S. H. Miles, P. A. Singer, and M. Siegler, Conflicts between Patients' Wishes to Forego Treatment and the Policies of Health Care Facilities, *New England Journal of Medicine, 321*:1, pp. 418-450, 1989.

68. I. R. Byock, Rights of Patients to Forego Treatment, *American Journal of Hospice and Palliative Care, 7*:5, pp. 16-17, 1990.

69. J. L. Bernat, B. Gert, and R. P. Mogielnicki, Patient Refusal of Hydration and Nutrition: An Alternative to Physician-Assisted Suicide or Voluntary Active Euthanasia, *Archives of Internal Medicine, 153*:24, pp. 2723-2728, 1993.

70. R. J. Sullivan, Accepting Death without Artificial Nutrition and Hydration, *Journal of General Internal Medicine, 8*:4, pp. 220-224, 1993.

71. R. M. McCann, W. J. Hall, and A. Groth-Juncker, Comfort Care for Terminally Ill Patients: The Appropriate Use of Nutrition and

Hydration, *Journal of the American Medical Association, 272*:16, pp. 1263-1266, 1994.

72. J. E. Ellershaw, J. M. Sutcliffe, and C. M. Saunders, Dehydration and the Dying Patient, *Journal of Pain and Symptom Management, 10*:3, pp. 192-197, 1995.

73. M. Danis, J. Garrett, R. Harris, and D. L. Patrick, Stability of Choices about Life-Sustaining Treatments, *Annals of Internal Medicine, 120*:7, pp. 567-573, 1994.

74. D. J. Murphy, D. Burrows, S. Santilli, A. W. Kemp, S. Tenner, B. Kreling, and J. Teno, Influence of the Probability of Survival on Patients' Preferences Regarding Cardiopulmonary Rescusitation, *New England Journal of Medicine, 330*:8, pp. 545-549, 1994.

75. R. J. Miller, Hospice and the Do-Not-Rescusitate Order, *The Hospice Journal, 7*:4, pp. 67-77, 1991.

76. S. J. Youngner and E. O'Toole, Withdrawing Treatment in the Persistent Vegetative State, *New England Journal of Medicine, 331*:20, p. 1382, 1994.

77. L. Pijnenborg, P. J. Van der Maas, J. W. P. F. Kardaun, J. J. Glerum, J. J. M. Van Delden, and C. W. N. Looman, Withdrawal or Withholding of Treatment at the End of Life, *Archives of Internal Medicine, 155*:3, pp. 286-292, 1995.

78. L. J. Schneiderman, K. Faber-Langendoen, and N. S. Jecker, Beyond Futility to an Ethic of Care, *American Journal of Medicine, 96*:2, pp. 110-114, 1994.

79. M. Angell, After Quinlan; The Dilemma of the Persistent Vegetative State, *New England Journal of Medicine, 330*:14, pp. 1524-1525, 1994.

80. L. Volicer, B. Volicer, and A. C. Hurley, Is Hospice Care Appropriate for Alzheimer's Patients? *Caring, 12*:11, pp. 50-55, 1993.

CHAPTER 5

What's Best For Me

Members of the family of a dying patient cannot be expected to agree and feel close to each other all of the time. Conflicts arise. Conflicts are part of life.

Some differences are small, some are real battles. Under the stress that has drawn them together, people can sometimes react very badly. Especially when relationships are unhealthy to begin with, conflicts can be very destructive. When there is love, however, disagreements can be productive.

My role in the family is to help each person understand what is really going on, because ignorance or misunderstanding may be the cause of conflict. Beyond that, I try to accept the feelings of each one, and get counselors involved if they might help.

I don't expect to make everything go right, to solve all problems. I can't play God. I'm just there to help, and when I'm lucky my help gets something moving so people find a way to work out their own fights.

Unfortunately, not all problems are resolved . . .

HENRIETTA

"We're going to try something different, Henrietta. Your lymph glands are more involved, and now your skin is, too. This calls for strong medicine. I want you to begin a course of treatment we call hyperthermia. It's a brand new treatment using heat."

Dr. Pemberton sat behind his desk shifting the papers spread out before him. The woman listening to him leaned forward on the edge of the chair across the desk. She watched him uncertainly, fear in her eyes, as she twisted and untwisted a handkerchief in her hands.

The new treatment would be a last ditch effort to stop the cancer for which his patient had already undergone a mastectomy, two courses of chemotherapy, and radiation treatment. Dr. Pemberton moved nervously as he waited for her response.

Henrietta could have been pretty, and probably had been a decade earlier. A light ash-blonde, she had deep circles under her eyes. These and the deep vertical anxiety grooves between her eyebrows provided the only accents to her pasty-colored face, marring her once-doll-like image and making her appear very old. Nearing fifty, this somber lady wasn't sure how to take his news.

"I've never heard of hyper—whatever you said, Doctor. Will it stop the cancer?" she asked, wishing Jim, her husband, were with her.

"There are no promises, of course. It's so new, it's still something of an experiment. Some reports have been encouraging. The thing is, there really is nothing else to try at this point. I've talked with Jim and he wants us to go ahead."

"Will it hurt? I can't take it if it's going to make me so sick again. That chemotherapy. . . ." Her words faded into tears.

"I can't say it won't hurt, Henrietta." Dr. Pemberton looked at his hands, then out the window at the side of his desk. "You see, the heat is delivered to the tissue through needles we put into your skin, and we try to control it so it will stop the cancer without burning you. But it's touchy; to be honest, we don't know precisely how much heat you should have. We'll see as we go along. You may have some burns."

She lowered her head and was quiet for a moment. She tucked the worried hanky into her purse which she continued to finger, opening and closing its latch. Finally she looked up at him. "Do I have to?" she asked, her face sagging.

"It's either this or give up, Henrietta. You know we can't do that—you and Jim aren't quitters. This offers you some hope, and we have to give it a try. You should go along with it." He got up and came around the desk. "You can handle it." He patted her on the arm, then turned and left the room. The stress in his face was shielded from her view.

Henrietta dressed slowly after Dr. Pemberton left. She was profoundly frightened and depressed. She had been through so much since her diagnosis two years ago—the panic and fear, and the mastectomy and chemotherapy that followed—then the high, thinking she might be cured, and finally the dashing of her hopes when cancer recurred in her lymph system. She had suffered through four more months of chemotherapy, this time with radiation; it made her so ill the memory itself brought back nausea. At the end of the series everyone was jubilant over the report of success. The scans were negative once more. Her husband, their two grown children and Dr. Pemberton all celebrated the news.

But a month ago she'd begun to feel discomfort under her arm, and her fears returned. The fears were justified; Henrietta's malignancy was growing again. It grew with renewed vigor; during the past week she had developed an open sore on her chest over the growth, and raw ugly tissue appeared in fissures on the sore. It was painful; her prosthesis irritated it and even when she didn't wear clothing, any movement of her arm hurt. On top of all that, worse to her than anything else, the sore smelled bad. The odor made her sick to her stomach, as apparently it had her children when they paid their last visit. Distaste on their faces, they had withdrawn involuntarily after placing greeting kisses on her cheek. She buried her face in her hands and shuddered as she thought of them.

Her plight overwhelmed her. She stayed another five minutes in the dressing room, too low to mobilize herself to get up and leave. A youthful nurse popped her head into the room, a fixed smile on her face. "Are we ready to go, Henrietta?"

Henrietta sighed, forced a polite expression on her face and moved apologetically to the door.

At the insistence of her husband, Jim, and Dr. Pemberton, Henrietta began a weekly trek to the hospital for hyperthermia. Each treatment would last thirty seconds. Needle-nosed electrodes would be inserted into the affected area to burn away the diseased matter.

She would require constant nursing care to keep the treated area sterile. Dr. Pemberton called the local hospice group, which sent Janice, an experienced registered nurse, and Marilyn, a licensed practical nurse, to provide her care at home.

Janice arrived just as Jim brought Henrietta home from her first treatment. Together they eased her into bed. Then Janice sat down to explain what she and Marilyn would be doing to help them.

"Marilyn will come in to handle the dressings during the daytime. If we show you how, can you change the dressings at night, Mr. Kirstin?" Janice knew from the referral papers in her chart that Jim's life as comptroller of a large industrial plant was not a likely starting point for taking on nursing duties like changing dressings, but she kept her fingers crossed as she asked.

Jim's expression was guarded. "Yes," he said. His salt and pepper crew-cut hair matched his steel grey eyes, and he looked as crisp as his response. Janice struggled to interpret him. He had to support and assume some of Henrietta's care.

"I'll stop in every day," Janice said. They discussed the arrangements as Henrietta lay pale and passive, pain distorting her face. For the most part Jim spoke for her.

Janice continued. "Are there other things you need now? Someone to talk with? Household help? We have a variety of people at hospice who could assist."

Jim's response was prompt and restrained. "No. I just want Henrietta to be at home. Your care of her will make that possible. I guess if you see that Dr. Pemberton's wishes are carried out, that's all we can ask."

Despite Jim's short, round build, something about him created the image of an angular, sharp edged man. Perhaps it was only the way he set his square jaw; it seemed to color his entire being. Whatever it was, it gave Jim's words a second, hidden meaning, and Janice's attention to him held for some moments before finally turning to Henrietta.

"Please tell me—whatever your feelings and needs are," she said to her patient. "We will be guided by them, Mrs. Kirstin, so be open with us. You can call me anytime." Smiling warmly, Janice reached over and took the tense woman's hand. "Oh, another thing. Please call me Janice. What would you like me to call you?"

"I suppose we may as well all use first names," Jim interceded. "You're going to be around, and you'll help Henrietta get well. That should put us on a first-name basis." He stared fixedly as he spoke, no softness in his face.

Janice turned, then tried to ease him. "We'll be here for you . . . A home-health aide can come if you need help with shopping, or laundry, or cooking. We have a family counselor and a chaplain, therapists and a nutritionist—all to help." She smiled. "Besides all of that, there are trained volunteers who'll be happy to do whatever they can." He said nothing in response.

Janice waited, then got up to leave. "I'll stop in tomorrow," she said, leaning over to touch Henrietta. Jim walked her to the door.

"I want to make something clear right from the start," he said brusquely, his hand on the doorknob. "I want this treatment to proceed, and it won't do to encourage Henrietta's objections. It's her only chance to get well; she has to go through with it."

Janice swallowed hard. Moments passed before she spoke.

"I appreciate your letting me know, Jim. I need to understand how both you and Henrietta feel about her illness and her care. I'll do my best to meet her needs; that's what I am here to do." She extended her hand to say goodbye. She'd have to deal with him another day.

Henrietta's chest and underarm soon looked like they had been barbecued. Hyperthermia was burning her. Seared and angry, the tissue began to ooze and slough off, requiring constant renewal of the dressings. The smell of burnt and putrid flesh pervaded her room.

One day Janice arrived to find Henrietta propped up in bed, weeping, a dull, despairing moan accompanying each sob. Janice hurried to her side and reached out to stroke her forehead. "What can I do for you, my dear? Are you having more pain?

Can I get you some Tylenol®?" She sat down and took one of Henrietta's hands in hers.

Henrietta shook her head wordlessly, tears sliding in two streams down the sides of her face. Janice blotted the wetness with a tissue and waited, smoothing Henrietta's hair back from her face. Henrietta slowly calmed, finally taking some jerking gasps of air that concluded the tears.

"Janice, what am I going to do? I can't bear . . . this is so awful . . . is there no way to make this torture end? I'm not getting better . . . I'm going to die, I just know I'm going to die. . . ." She covered her face with her hands as a new wave of weeping overcame her.

Janice made no effort to answer. Instead she reached out, cradling Henrietta's shoulders in her hands, waiting as Henrietta wept out her pain. After several minutes, Janice disengaged one hand and curved an arm around Henrietta's far side, rocking her gently until the sounds began to quiet.

"Are you frightened, Henrietta?" Janice spoke softly. Fear struck at some time with all of her patients.

Henrietta nodded silently.

Janice took Henrietta's hand in hers. "I'm sure you are. It is fearsome. Have you felt this way long?"

Again Henrietta nodded, looking miserable. "I can tell this hyperthermia isn't doing any good, and there isn't anything else. I'm scared. I'm so scared, Janice! And I can't tell Jim. He won't hear of it!"

"When you feel like this, Henrietta, you let us know— Marilyn or me," Janice urged. "You know, fear is like steam. If you can't let it out, it builds up. We understand, and maybe we can help."

Janice said no more, waiting for Henrietta to continue.

"But it's not just that. I HATE the treatments." The cords in her neck tightened as she spoke. "I can't get either Jim or Dr. Pemberton to talk about them. They must see I'm not getting any better, but they won't even talk about it. I feel trapped. It's hopeless!" She stopped talking and her eyes closed. Janice squeezed her hand, then rose to check the medication log lying on the bureau.

Janice left Henrietta's home that day with a surprising spring in her step. Henrietta's outburst was a breakthrough. With the release of her feelings, Janice had reason to hope for her patient. Not hope for recovery, but optimism that Henrietta's remaining days could have some good in them. If she would only keep talking.

When Jim came home from work each day, his first stop was to see Henrietta. One day, like all the others, he braced himself before walking through the bedroom doorway, putting on a face of confidence.

"Hi, dear. How did it go today?" he asked.

Henrietta recited what she knew he wanted to hear. "Pretty well." She tried to hearten her voice and expression, to be more convincing.

"That's great!" Jim could easily sound like a football coach during half-time, and Henrietta stifled a giggle as she experienced the sudden, unexpected image of him in that position. She could just see him, pot-belly and all, projecting his strength into the players so they would "Get out there and fight!" It amused her for a moment, then reality set in once more. She sighed.

Jim related a couple of successes from his day at the office, then with some bluster about the things he wanted to do around the house, turned and left the room.

The charade was over.

Jim walked into the family room with its mirrored bar. It was becoming a nightly habit, this urgent anointment of bourbon and soda upon his return home. He poured his drink and walked over to the fireplace where he rested one arm on the mantel, his back to the room. Unseen from the doorway, Janice eyed him for some minutes, debating with herself how to approach him. Finally, she squared her shoulders and started across the twelve feet of carpet that separated them.

"Jim," she began. "I need to ask you something. How are you feeling about these hyperthermia treatments for Henrietta? Do you still think the experiment is worth her suffering?"

Jim stared at the drink in his hand, his back hunched against the intrusion. He finally turned to face Janice, his expression wiped clean of any sign of emotion. "It will get rid of the cancer." The words came out flat and even, like the output of a robot.

"Perhaps it will. The reports have shown a few successes. But we both know her chances aren't good. I believe the treatment has to be weighed against Henrietta's feeling about it. She dreads it so; you must consider that as you watch what it's doing to her."

"You stay out of it," he flared. "It isn't up to you! I know what's best." In a minute his control returned. "I must remind you—I warned you right from the start not to encourage Henrietta in her objections." With that he slammed his drink down on the mantel and left the room. Immobile, Janice watched him leave. He disappeared from sight. She threw her hands up in silence, then walked out the way she had come in.

Henrietta's treatment was becoming excruciating. Her pain, first managed by non-prescription drugs, now required much more. Janice talked with Dr. Pemberton about medication. That evening she received a call at home from Jim.

"Janice, I have learned that you want to keep Henrietta doped up. Please understand that I do not approve, and she is not to have drugs. You are not to discuss this further with Dr. Pemberton. Do you understand?"

"But Jim, she is suffering. You can't mean you want her to be in constant pain!"

"I know it looks like that to you, but I don't believe the pain is that great, and I simply will not have her doped up," he said in increasingly precise syllables. "She is going to live, and when this is over my wife is not going to be an addict!" His final sentence was punctuated with brittle authority.

"Jim, I wish you'd talk this over with Dr. Pemberton. You have a fixed view of medication, and it really isn't like that. And Henrietta is truly suffering. We must give her some relief."

"You heard what I said. I won't discuss—this is the last I want to hear about it." A loud click followed—then silence . . .

Janice stared, unbelieving, at the dead phone in her hand for some seconds before jamming it into its cradle. Then she stormed into the kitchen. She picked up a dirty fry-pan still greasy from the morning's bacon and eggs and banged it as hard as she could on the counter. Grease spattered all over the cabinets and floor. She groaned, "My God! What other crimes can be perpetrated in the name of love?"

Late the next day when Janice stopped in to see Henrietta, she found her in tears once more. Marilyn was there, for by now she was spending nearly eight hours a day at Henrietta's side. "She's in great pain, Janice, and she knows Jim won't hear of medication for her."

"Henrietta, have you told Jim how bad it is for you? Do you think he really understands how much you hurt?"

The words opened a sluice. Henrietta sobbed out her despair over the disastrous hyperthermia. "They're torturing me! It's so awful, and they keep making me go back for more. No one ever asks me what I want; I could die with all this pain and nobody listens. No one cares. Aspirin, Tylenol® . . . they're no good. God . . . that's not all." A curdling sound came from her throat. "I've become a horror. My own kids can't stand the sight and smell of me! They don't even come over! Please, please, stop it, somebody! Let it be over." Her outburst ended in a wail that could be heard throughout the house.

Janice and Marilyn stared at Henrietta as she released her torrent, then seated themselves on opposite sides of her bed and waited for the outcry to end. Finally Janice asked, "What would you like us to do?"

The weeping continued, more calmly now, and shortly Henrietta took a long staccato breath and whispered. "I have to keep up the treatments; Jim won't allow them to stop. But please, please let me take something to stop the pain. I'm going to lose my mind. Can't you get something to me without Jim knowing?"

Janice and Marilyn exchanged glances. Janice straightened up and breathed deeply, then squeezed Henrietta's hand. "I'll call Dr. Pemberton again, my dear. Let's see what he can do."

She walked into the kitchen to phone him. "Henrietta is suffering terribly, Dr. Pemberton," she said after their greetings. "This is so unnecessary. Won't you please prescribe some meds for her?"

"I'd like to say yes, Janice. Jim is adamant, you know. He's afraid of addiction."

"We both know that's not an issue here. It's not addiction when you're in great pain and dying. Can't you get him to see that? She needs help—and she's becoming desperate."

"I understand."

"After all, the drugs aren't for kicks," Janice added.

"You're right, of course. I'll call the pharmacy and I'll deal with Jim. Maybe I can get him to understand."

"Thanks." Janice came back to Henrietta's room triumphant. "We did it, Henrietta. You're going to get some help. Dr. Pemberton is ordering something right now. It should be here soon."

Henrietta's eyes bored into Janice as she listened; at the end she turned her face to the pillow and wept.

During the next few weeks the atmosphere changed. Although Jim never acknowledged what was going on, Henrietta was given the much-needed pain medication. She became calmer, more thoughtful. Janice, again despite Jim's instructions, began to respond to Henrietta's hesitant references to dying.

"I wonder what it's like, dying?" she said one day.

"Does the thought scare you?"

"No . . . well, I'm not sure. You've watched them . . . Do they seem like it's hard? The people who are dying, I mean."

"No. Not really. In fact, most of the time I get the feeling it's almost lovely. That sounds strange, but if they've suffered a long time . . . it's like closing the door on all that, and moving into something serene. I often get the feeling they're happy."

Henrietta watched Janice carefully for a long time. Finally she confessed, "I've never talked to anyone about this. Does it seem like a weird question, what I asked you?"

"Henrietta, it's the most natural question in the world! All of my patients wonder about dying, and many of them talk about it. And those who don't probably want to. If it's on your mind, you should ask." Janice reached over to fluff the pillow. Henrietta lifted her hand and caught Janice's wrist near her neck and held it there. Janice returned the pressure before she turned to go.

Another day the subject arose again. "I wonder who will take care of my plants when I die."

"You love those plants, don't you?" Janice said. "They'll remind someone of you. I know they will."

Henrietta's expression had the barest suggestion of a smile, more in her eyes than on her lips.

Their conversations revealed her awareness that life was approaching an end for her—some days reflecting fear and some days acceptance, sometimes even wonder at the mystery that lay ahead. On other days she refused to acknowledge what was happening.

"Jim should be working the garden. We need to get the beans in early next spring, and the soil will be too hard if he doesn't break it up now." She and her husband could both play the game of make-believe.

Without reaction, Janice followed in whatever direction Henrietta's thoughts led. They moved with the normal, irregular adjustments any dying person would make if allowed.

She was not surprised one day to hear Henrietta ask in a low, intense voice, "You'll stop them, won't you? I don't want machines."

Janice had a bottle of warmed oil in her hands, pouring from it to massage Henrietta after her bath. She set the bottle down on the night stand and turned to study Henrietta's face. Deep creases furrowed her brow. A plea was in her eyes. "You don't want heroic measures to keep you alive, is that it, Henrietta?"

Henrietta's head moved weakly from side to side, her eyelids closing momentarily in dramatic and utter rejection of the idea. Then she fixed on Janice once more, waiting for her answer.

"I understand. You have my word. I will do all I can to carry out your wishes." The worry lines softened in Henrietta's face. "But you really need to tell Jim and Dr. Pemberton," Janice continued. "They are the ones whose decisions will count if you're not able to speak for yourself." She continued to stand for several minutes, looking at her patient.

Distress filled Henrietta's face, then she turned her head to the wall.

Janice phoned Jim the next day at work.

"Jim, Henrietta needs your support. Something's troubling her. She told us she doesn't want heroic measures if things start to go bad for her—if she loses consciousness. It's worrying her. I know that's a scary thought for you, but could you reassure her?"

"Oh-forgodsake, are you crazy?" Jim's voice bellowed into her ear. "I couldn't go along with that! Just stop it!"

"Please, don't shut the door on it so fast. Look, how about if you meet with our family counselor and talk it through? It helps when you're making a big decision—'specially such an important one. Can I have her call you?"

"Don't you dare. That's the last thing I need. I have to go now—work to do." With that he hung up.

Though Henrietta's downhill course continued unabated, she seemed generally composed. Medication kept the pain tolerable. With the release of her questions and concerns, she appeared more peaceful, more accepting. The tumor had grown larger and the erosion of her chest wall was spreading. The end could be predicted.

One day Janice arranged to discuss the inevitable with Jim. So far he had shown no visible sign that his expectations for Henrietta's recovery had changed. She met him in the family room as he was pouring his bourbon.

"Jim, the treatment isn't reducing the growth, and Henrietta is fading. We need to look realistically at what may happen. I believe she can't hang on a great deal longer. Do you see this too?"

Jim rotated the glass in his hands, biting his lips as he prepared his response. "I will not give up. I've never been a quitter, and I won't start now."

"You've tried so hard, Jim; that's plain for all to see. I know you love Henrietta, and you don't want to lose her. Sometimes," she added gently, "no matter what we do, we can't make it turn out the way we want."

Jim stared at the floor.

"It's quite likely," she continued, "the end will come soon. You need to be ready when that happens, and we must talk about it.

I know you said earlier that you would choose heroic measures. But let me ask you, if you walked into her room now and saw that she wasn't breathing, what would you do?"

Instant panic replaced the control in Jim's face. "I'd call Emergency," he blurted out. Fear laced his voice.

"Why?"

"I don't want her to die!"

"But Jim, do you realize what resuscitation means at this point? Bear in mind that Henrietta has been able to stay here with you, surrounded by the familiar things she loves, knowing the comfort of privacy in her illness. Why would you want to call in a group of strangers now to do a lot of awful things to her? They'd stick tubes down her throat, shock her heart and rush her to the hospital—all for what?" Janice stopped for a moment, watching him. "Do you really want her to continue like this?"

Janice let that sink in before completing the familiar picture for him.

"If she were put through resuscitation and breathing is restored, she'd be taken to the hospital, probably to intensive care. She'd be put on a respirator. In a short time, most likely you'd be called to decide whether you want the respirator turned off. Believe me, nothing is more agonizing than having to make that decision."

Janice moved a step closer. "Henrietta doesn't want this, Jim. She's told me so. You should ask her yourself." Jim's expression remained closed. There was no sign the description had changed his view. Janice persisted. "You know, if the time comes, you'll be the one to decide because you're her husband. I would strongly urge you to call hospice rather than the emergency service. We can help in kinder ways."

Janice was familiar with the Emergency procedure. A phone call would bring the paramedics, the police department, and the fire department, all seeming ten feet tall, some armed with guns. Lights would flash and sirens would pierce the air. The whole scenario would be a glaring blasphemy to the effort of hospice, the "caring host" over the past three months. No longer a way to support her with love and quality during her remaining days, her care would become a violent fight to keep her heart beating no matter the odds. That, after all, was the work of the emergency team. If they are called, their job is to carry out the resuscitation. The only way to avoid this and keep her promise to Henrietta to allow a peaceful end was to make Jim understand.

Gritting his teeth, Jim just shook his head. He refused to respond.

Janice made several more efforts to change Jim's mind during the days that followed. Finally, she drew Marilyn away from the others, into the kitchen where a radio could be turned up to cover her voice.

"Marilyn, I'm not getting anywhere with Jim. He's determined to call Emergency if Henrietta shows signs of dying."

"Did you expect anything different from him?"

"No, I guess not. He's immovable, as always."

"Yeah. He wouldn't let her have anything for her pain, and he wouldn't let her admit her fears—and now this," Marilyn added.

"I know." Janice shot a quick glance back through the doorway before continuing. "As long as he insists, you know you are duty bound to call Emergency if Henrietta stops breathing. We have to follow the rules."

Marilyn groaned, put her elbows on the kitchen counter and lowered her head onto her hands.

Janice wasn't finished. She turned Marilyn to face her once more. "Call them, Marilyn, but then I want you to do something else. Just before the team arrives, I want you to remove Henrietta's dressings as if to change them." Marilyn's eyes widened. "No one in the human race will do CPR on her if he has to push his hand through that hole in her chest. We'll see that Henrietta's wishes are honored!"

The two women stared intently at each other as they agreed on this last strategy available to them to prevent the use of the machines Henrietta abhorred. The rest was up to Jim.

Ten days later Jim faced exactly what Janice had described. He entered Henrietta's room to do his usual pep-talk, and found her unresponsive in bed. "Henny," he called out his old pet name for her, patting at her cheek. "Henny!" he yelled louder, now slapping harder. "Oh, dear God . . ." Marilyn, his first source of help, had left for the day. He ran for the phone.

"Operator, operator, get me Emergency. QUICK, . . . it's my wife . . . I can't wake her up. QUICK, GET SOMEONE HERE . . . What? Oh, yes . . . we're at 439. . . ." He finished giving directions, his heart pounding and mouth suddenly dry.

He hung up and raced back to Henrietta's side, leaning over in front of her face to determine whether she was breathing. He couldn't tell. He put his hand on her chest to feel for a heartbeat, then quickly withdrew it as he remembered she had no chest wall over where he thought her heart should be. Panic overcame him.

The image of testing someone's breathing with a mirror came to him. He raced into the bathroom to find the hand mirror. It wasn't on the counter top. He threw the drawers open one after the other, at last finding the mirror in the bottom drawer. He ran back to Henrietta, nearly tripping on the bedroom rocker on the way. Just as he stood before her, trying to steady the mirror under her nostrils, he heard the siren. Then the doorbell rang. The emergency unit had arrived.

"COME ON IN, COME IN," he yelled at the top of his lungs, running at the same time to admit the uniformed man and woman who stood on the front porch. Door open, he motioned them to follow, turned and half-ran back to Henrietta's bedroom.

"What happened?" the leader started his question as they hurried down the hall.

"She's not breathing," Jim yelled without looking back.

"Has she been sick?"

"Yes. Cancer. Breast cancer." Jim croaked out the words, barely missing the rocker for the second time as he entered the room. He ran to the side of the bed and stopped, appearing uncertain what to do.

The leader grasped Jim's arms from behind and said firmly, "Stand back; we need to work on her." Jim jumped convulsively and mumbled his compliance, moving back so the team could begin. The leader laid a pack on the end of the bed and reached to search for a pulse in Henrietta's neck.

The woman pulled an oxygen tank behind her. She set the tank upright against the wall, then ran back outside, returning quickly with a bed board. A policeman had arrived; he followed her into the house.

The leader placed a mask over Henrietta's nose and mouth, not quite covering the blue spreading from her lips. A tube ran from the mask to the oxygen tank, and a steady hiss emerged from the tank. "Pull the rocker back out of the way," he instructed Jim.

The two paramedics shifted Henrietta from her bed to the bed board and lowered her to the newly created space on the floor to begin CPR. The woman then reached for the lifepack on the bed, opened it and removed wires and electrodes they would attach to Henrietta's chest to monitor her heart. As she worked, the leader cut open Henrietta's gown. He paused momentarily, taking in the dressings covering her chest from side to side and from the top of her breastbone to her navel. Slipping the flat tip of his scissors under the dressing at one side, he jerked the dressing off. Neither he nor the silent policeman in the doorway was prepared for what they saw.

Instead of the flat, scar-outlined chest the paramedic expected to see where Henrietta's breast had been removed, he stared at a hole extending from the center toward the left side of her chest, a hole as big as a tennis ball through which he could see her lung. It lay wet and still in the cavity framed by pointed, white remains of ribs.

"JESUS!" escaped his lips. The woman, working to separate the wires in the lifepack, turned to see what had happened. She sucked in her breath.

Recovering, the leader reached forward, tentatively testing the borders of the hole for some resistance to allow CPR. Until he reached the far left side of her chest or the very top of the breastbone, there was no resistance. Henrietta's disease had not left enough bony structure over her heart to permit the pressure of CPR.

"Bag her." He shot his message to the woman. She was ready. Her hand was on the airway kit in the open pack on the bed, and with his words she pulled it out. Holding Henrietta's tongue down with a blade, she focused a scope down her throat to see that it was clear.

While the woman held Henrietta's tongue down, the leader swiftly inserted a curved hard tube deep into her throat, connecting it through a ball-shaped bag to the oxygen tank. The hard tube in her mouth was taped into place, and he began to squeeze the bag at regular intervals, forcing oxygen into her lungs.

"Monitor." His rapid-fire direction was not needed. His partner was already squirting electrode jelly onto each of Henrietta's shoulders, then a spot on her abdomen. She fastened the electrodes to each place with tape. With one hand still squeezing the bag, he stood at the machine and turned dials, watching the trace of her heart function for ten seconds. "V-fib; full arrest," he reported tersely. Henrietta's heart was fluttering or fibrillating, not beating, and her lungs had apparently shut down. He called out to the policeman, "Radio for fire backup; we have a Core Zero on Ambulance 23. Then get a doc at our control center on the line." The policeman spoke into his radio.

Jim stood rooted to his place in the corner, open-mouthed, watching the controlled frenzy before him.

"Go for shock," the paramedic telegraphed to his partner. Jim saw the woman take out two wired paddles, squirt more gel on one side of each, and place them gel-side down—one on the upper remaining breastbone, the other at Henrietta's side, level with the top of her heart. Her partner stood ready at the machine housed inside the pack. He adjusted a dial, called "All clear," then hit the fire button. A jolt of 200 joules of electricity hit Henrietta's chest, and her frail body jerked, her chest rising off the bed board and her left arm flying up. The jolt released both bladder and bowel, but her heart action did not change. The monitor continued to show only shallow fibrillation, no true beats.

"Here's your doc," the fireman handed the radio to the paramedic.

"We've got full arrest. Can't do CPR 'cause the ribs are gone. We're bagging, and 200 joules didn't start the heart."

He listened for seconds, then signed off.

"We'll try once more," he said to the woman. "I'm upping to 360." He rolled the intensity up.

Once more the woman placed the paddles; once more he called "All clear," and once more he fired a jolt through Henrietta's body. This time she jerked higher, and a smell of burning skin joined the foul odors already strong in the room. The trace on the heart monitor did not change. Jim blanched. He moved over to lean against the wall.

"What's her rhythm now?" the woman asked.

"Still v-fib. Start a line and spike a bag. I'll begin epi down the ET." The male paramedic's code told his partner the heart was still fibrillating. She was to insert an IV tube into a vein and begin dripping sugar water into it while he squirted epinephrine into the hard tube down Henrietta's throat. The woman found, after sticking her needle over and over into Henrietta's arms, that her veins were all collapsed. She succeeded finally, inserting the needle downward into the external jugular vein in her neck. Her partner was "spiking the bag" with epinephrine, removing the squeeze-bag from the tube to provide access for the drug, then reattaching it and squeezing rapidly to hyperventilate Henrietta.

"Any response?" the woman asked.

From his post at the machine, the man reported in three words. "Now it's flat."

Neither worker moved. Suddenly everything was quiet. Both exhaled deeply. In the dead silence that followed, a siren could be heard approaching.

Her face was unlined and serene; her struggle was finally over. There would be no more denials, no more decisions made for her, no more subterfuges to meet her needs. For over two years she had lost her self. In death she was free. The unwritten but fitting epitaph for this woman who was unable to say no is "Here lies a lady who submitted and suffered. May she now, at last, rest in peace."

Jim was devastated by her death. He had commanded that she live, and she could not. He was left to try to come to grips with his defeat and his loss, and with the memory of how he had waged his battle.

Janice and Marilyn spoke little as they worked together, cleaning the sickroom. Inevitably each one reviewed her care of Henrietta. They had failed to help her stop the hyperthermia treatment. They had succeeded in arranging to ease her pain. They had made it possible for her to talk through her feelings about dying when no one else would listen. And they had planned a way to avoid resuscitation—a plan not implemented, but a way to keep faith with Henrietta. They had managed to give her a degree of comfort through the last weeks. They had affirmed her dignity and worth.

Janice reported on Henrietta in the next hospice case conference. When she finished, she put her notes down on the table. "I had to pull my car to the side of the road on my way home that last day," she said in a low voice. "I was crying. I couldn't stop . . . the tears just kept coming. I sat there for quite a while, letting it pour out." She shook her head. "Even now, I swear I don't know which one I was crying for—Henrietta, poor misguided Jim, or maybe for myself."

NOTES:
Dignity in Dying; Patient Control

Death with dignity. The words appear in every discussion of death and dying. Anyone you ask says he wants death with dignity for himself and his loved ones when the time comes—of course. We in hospice espouse the patient's right to death with dignity. The mantra of the supporters of assisted suicide is *death with dignity.* There may be no phrase more frequently heard today in these discussions—unless it's *quality of life.* That's another one. The two phrases are thought of in the same breath, two tap roots of the same trunk.

The problem with words and phrases that are used with such frequency is that they begin to lose their meaning. The reader and listener become inured to their implications. It is time to look carefully at these overused expressions—to rediscover their original intent.

Webster defines *dignity* in several ways that bear on the dying patient: worthiness, nobility, stateliness, and last, calm self-possession and self-respect. He defines *quality* as the degree of excellence which a thing (life, in this case) possesses. We can consider the patient and decide what promotes or allows, and what destroys, these elements of his nature and life as he moves through the dying process.

Most observers would agree that there is indignity—perhaps great indignity—and loss of quality in the life of someone seriously ill and dying. Modesty is violated again and again, dependence is forced on the patient, pain can reduce him to crying for help, skills and competence are lost, bodily changes can be unpleasant—even offensive, and we could go on.

What incontinent patient can feel stately as someone else cleans his bottom and changes soiled bed linens—or worse yet, digs out an impaction? What bedfast patient can feel self-possessed when someone else must retrieve his pills or whatever else has rolled out of reach for the 'teenth time? What pain-ridden patient can feel noble as he cries out his agony? If these things are happening to him, we can understand his feeling less worthy, less stately, and less noble than he would like. It would take great strength of character to avoid feeling diminished in this condition. It would take remarkable spirit to accept these changes in one's life willingly, on an irretrievable basis.

Yet some patients suffer all of these things *with dignity*, without breathing, or more to the point, feeling a complaint about their quality of life. What is it that makes the difference?

The authors submit that being included—both in information sharing and in decision making—is the crucial factor in an ill and dying patient's feelings of dignity. This is true even if the patient's illness is not life-threatening. It is true for the "simply" sick patient, although the problem for him is not acute. He can look forward to a future when the indignities will stop and his health is restored. But it is particularly true for the dying patient; he no longer can regard the indignities he suffers as temporary. He can no longer tell himself he'll put up with the hard parts for a while, after which things will get back to normal. He knows he must accept the hard things *for the rest of his life*.

For the dying patient, being respected enough to be given the information that is available, and being part of the decision making, having some control, can allow him to feel self-respect and an inner worthiness. It can permit him to tolerate what is happening to him, keep it in perspective as the unfortunate but peripheral-to-his-personhood kind of thing it is. It can preserve the essential being inside him.

That is dignity.

Henrietta suffered many things. She fell ill with a disease that eventually killed her, but which first carried her on an enervating bungee-ride of peaks and depths. She dealt with unbearable pain for a long time. She lost the companionship of her children. She suffered mutilation of her body. The blows to her psyche were profound and repeated.

With all she suffered, the worst was the loss of her own integrity, of the control of her life. In being told she had no choice but to accept hyperthermia, in being denied any expression of her fears, and in being given no prescription medication for which she begged in order to relieve her pain, she was made a non-person. She was made a nobody, an object to be acted upon. Her dignity took a never-ending series of body blows that all but destroyed her.

Our effort in hospice was to restore Henrietta's control of her life to the extent we could under the difficult circumstances imposed by her husband. We recognized and accepted her as a person—her fears, her needs, her questions, her weakness. We built one arena around her in which she could be herself, and express herself. We acted on her desperate efforts for control, arranging the pain medication she requested, and promising to keep faith with her, doing what we could to avoid the use of life-support technology for her. She had us in her court.

Henrietta needed more than we could do, but we contributed something good, something positive that she would not otherwise have had, that protected her psyche from total obliteration. We like to think that when she finally died she was wrapped in some semblance, if not a full blanket, of dignity. Her comfort care was a gift of respect from hospice.

The issue of control is bandied about loosely in the literature. It is often joked about—controlling parents, controlling women, controlling bosses, even controlling children. We assume this much-used word of only seven letters is broadly understood and that we all mean the same thing when it is discussed. Not so. Take the area of health care.

Traditional medicine and many consumers have opined that when seriously ill, most people prefer to be in the hands of those who know—the experts. They argue that control is not desired by these sick people. They say informing these patients and letting them decide things is not necessary, because they don't want to know; they don't want to decide.

Traditional medicine and others who join in this position miss the point. To put oneself in the experts' hands is a choice; to make that choice is exercising one's control—the same as choosing not to turn the decisions over to the experts. The point is to have the choice. Control means choice.

Each hospice patient is given that choice. A fundamental sphere of negotiation takes place early, and also in a continuing way, in the patient/hospice relationship. In this negotiation, the hospice team seeks definition of the patient's choices, always feeling out which decisions the patient would make himself and which he chooses to give to others. Within the mandates of the particular hospice organization, the hospice team attempts to follow the patient's wishes.

Henrietta was not unlike some other patients we have seen. Perhaps from early-formed personality, perhaps from suffering one disappointment after another, and perhaps from fear of or a habit of deference to her mate, she had little will in her when hospice was called to her home. By default, it seemed, not by choice, she accepted the direction of her husband and her physician. She accommodated to the plan to try experimental hyperthermia. She went along with the introduction of hospice. She left up to her husband the discussion of arrangements for her care. In short, she was passive and did what was expected of her.

Then, when others' decisions made her life unbearable, Henrietta sought changes. Hospice was there to hear her need and to support her emerging self—in short, to give her some control. The first time she heard the words, "What would you like us to do?" must have been like bugles heralding the opening gates. She surely had a sense of being freed.

Control is also the central issue, we believe, in the many patients who threaten suicide. Stories abound which demonstrate the relief such patients feel when they can discuss it openly and the means to commit suicide are made available to them. Andrew Solomon, author of the book about his mother, *A Stone Boat,* says it vividly, "Everything that had been intolerable to my mother was made tolerable when she got those pills, by the sure knowledge that when life became unliveable, it would (could) stop. . . . Once we all settled the future, we could live fully in the present. . . . The excruciating business seemed suddenly unimportant, because the symptoms were permanent only until she decided she could take no more, and so the disease was no longer in control of her"[1] [1, p. 58].

Control was the crucial core of the matter for Andrew Solomon's mother. Many persons contemplating suicide, once equipped as she was, never carry out their threats. Having control often gives them a different perspective, a different tolerance for their suffering. Even being respected enough to feel they can talk through their wishes about suicide can create for the burdened patients a sense of control. In either event, very often the suicide does not take place [2]. We have seen this among our patients, and know it to be true.

Although the subject of advance directives is treated more fully in the Chapter 4 Notes, a discussion of patient control would not be complete without mentioning this helpful tool that became a legally-protected reality in 1990, with some extension of the protections in 1991. Persons can control their future treatment in the event of incompetence while ill by spelling out what they would accept and what they would reject, subject to limitations imposed by state law. It is a blessing all adults should use while they are able, for the future is unknown for all of us. Advance directives are future controls we can put in the bank, providing asssurance we will have the dignity we choose.

Another element of Henrietta's story bears some updating. It is the then-experimental treatment she was given called *hyperthermia.* At the time of her experience not much was known

---

[1] Copyright 1995 by Andrew Solomon, reprinted by permission of Wylie, Aitken and Stone, Inc.

about it—particularly the degree and timing of heat needed to kill mammalian cells. But there was evidence that the procedure offered great hope. In those beginning years, heat was delivered in the form of electrical energy.

Since then much has been learned. Today heat is produced from radio frequencies, microwave or ultrasound, all more precise and less prone to unwanted damage than electrical energy through electrodes. It is known now that a temperature of 42 degrees centigrade or higher can kill the offending cells, and together with radiation, the heat can effect palliation and even cure local recurrence of breast cancer on the chest wall after mastectomy. Since recurrence happens in 3 to 22 percent of patients who have undergone mastectomy, this treatment can be useful for significant numbers of patients [3]. Protocols are most frequently tied to a schedule of a one-hour treatment given twice weekly. The safety and effectiveness of using hyperthermia on these patients was rated in 1994 by a panel of AMA physician experts in the field as midway between promising and established [3]. The adverse effects they note include surface burns and blistering, pain, ulceration and infection, all now reversible.

Hyperthermia alone has not been as effective as when combined with radiation [4, 5]. Conversely, in women with recurrence, radiation alone has not been as effective as when combined with hyperthermia [6], even when mitoxantrone chemotherapy was added to the radiation [7]. The addition of Cisplatin® to the radiation/hyperthermia protocol may offer further benefits [8]. The smaller the tumor and higher the thermal dose, the more favorable the tumor response was found to be [9].

Henrietta would have suffered much less had her care been provided today when hyperthermia treatment is better understood, when treatment criteria are defined, and when helpful chemotherapy has been identified and can be added. It is even possible the treatment might have been successful. The destructive problem for her, however, was not the hyperthermia alone. It was in large part the failure of those in her environment to accord her respect, to allow her to choose her own way.

REFERENCES

1. A. Solomon, A Death of One's Own, *New Yorker,* pp. 54-69, May 22, 1995.
2. A. Mullens, The Real Value of Euthanasia Comes Not From the Act Itself but From the Ability to Speak Openly About It, *Canadian Medical Association Journal, 152*:11, pp. 1848-1849, 1995.
3. R. Miller-Catchpole, Hyperthermia as Adjuvant Treatment for Recurrent Breast Cancer and Primary Malignant Glioma, *Journal of the American Medical Association, 271*:10, pp. 797-802, 1994.
4. J. B. DuBois, M. Hay, and G. Bordure, Superficial Microwave-Induced Hyperthermia in the Treatment of Chest Wall Recurrences in Breast Cancer, *Cancer, 66*:5, pp. 848-852, 1990.
5. M. Amicheti, R. Valdagni, C. Graiff, and A. Valentini, Local-Regional Recurrences of Breast Cancer: Treatment with Radiation Therapy and Local Microwave Hyperthermia, *American Journal of Clinical Oncology, 14*:1, pp. 60-65, 1991.
6. C. K. Lee, C. W. Song, and S. H. Levitt, Large Field Hyperthermia Using Thermotron RF-8 for Extensive Chest Wall Recurrences of Breast Cancer, *Meeting Abstract of Thirty-Eighth Annual Meeting of the Radiation Research Society and Tenth Annual Meeting of the North American Hyperthermia Group,* April 7-12, 1990, New Orleans, Louisiana, No. 39, 1990.
7. C. Kolotas, N. Zamboglou, W. Audretsch, K. Muskalla, M. Rezai, and T. Schnabel, Primary Interstitial Thermoradiotherapy and Simultaneous Chemotherapy with Mitoxantrone followed by Salvage Surgery in Locally Advanced Breast Cancer (Meeting Abstract), *4th International Congress on Anti-Cancer Chemotherapy,* February 2-5, 1993, Paris, France, No. 130, 1993.
8. T. S. Herman, B. A. Teicher, M. S. Jochelson, P. J. Scott, S. M. Fraser, J. Hansen et al., Treatment of Recurrent Breast Cancer with Cisplatin/Hyperthermia/Radiation, (Meeting Abstract), *38th Annual Meeting of Radiation Society and 10th Annual Meeting of North American Hyperthermia Group,* April 7-12, 1990.
9. R. A. Steeves, P. Phromratanapongse, S. B. Severson, and B. R. Paliwal, Hyperthermia and Re-Irradiation for Recurrent Breast Cancer (Meeting Abstract), *38th Annual Meeting of the Radiation Research Society and 10th Annual Meeting of the North American Hyperthermia Group,* April 7-12, 1990, New Orleans, Louisiana, 1990, No. 38, 1990.

CHAPTER 6

Cocktails and Images

The early hospice movement came to be known by its attempts to control pain, and to do so while maintaining alertness. In fact, for many years, the "hospice cocktail," the early pain control medication, was synonymous with hospice—when little else about hospice was understood. The cocktail was adapted from a morphine-cocaine elixer developed in a vehicle of alcohol, syrup, and chloroform water in England in 1926. That "Brompton Cocktail," named after the hospital in which it was developed, was finally published in 1952, and the pioneering British hospice at St. Christopher's Hospital adopted and modified it in 1967. The hospice mix was first a heroin-cocaine mix, then a heroin mix in various liquids (chloroform water instead of alcohol; gin, whisky, or brandy instead of ethyl alcohol; honey or juices or soft drinks to make the elixer palatable, etc.) The hospice mix was revolutionary, both in content and in the way it was administered.

The medication was very powerful. More surprising, this medicine was given at regular and frequent intervals, i.e., every four hours—not following the patient's complaint after pain had built up. This new schedule built up a satisfactory, steady level of the drug in the patient's blood, thereby avoiding the usual cycle of pain, then stupor from drugs, then more pain and again stupor.

Dr. Robert Twycross, St. Christopher's Chief of Clinical Pharmacology, felt strongly enough about this approach to pain control that he drew up a list of ten commandments for physicians, including some beginning with "Thou shalt not." In this list he proscribed: "give PRN orders (medicate only in response to complaint); underprescribe analgesics; fear narcotics; start out with simple analgesics; assume pain is from malignancy; limit approach to pain control only to drugs" [1, p. 183]. His work in pain control set the stage for one of the most important strengths of hospice.

Laws in the United States barred the use of heroin and cocaine, so neither the Brompton Cocktail nor St. Christopher's hospice cocktail could be used here. Hospice of Marin County in California adapted the cocktail, giving a "Hospice Mix,"— morphine, alcohol, and phenothiazine in a sweetened water solution—every three or four hours. For a decade or more this mix continued to be used for many patients, with the addition of an anti-emetic separately for the first week to control transient nausea when necessary. Patients were advised that they might experience drowsiness for a few days while adjusting to the medication. The mix has for the most part been discontinued in favor of straight morphine, although some think the mix or some morphine elixer can still be helpful at the start of pain control measures because the short interval of administration permits flexibility of titration to an appropriate level, at which time slow release morphine tablets can be given.

Unfortunately, no pain control measure works for everyone. New drugs and new methods of administering them, along with new approaches beyond drugs, have been developed, and we are always on the search for another idea when pain appears to be intractable. Pain control continues to be an absolutely essential part of hospice care.

An open mind is the cornerstone to pain control. Reducing or eliminating pain demands a willingness to look at every available option—even creating one where none exists. That is where hospice shines. Being flexible and creative—that is the key.

WILLIAM

"Hypnosis! You have to be kidding! They do hypnosis in side shows! It's a big fake." William's face fell, his hopes deflated. In disgust, he reached for a magazine on the bedside table.

William's reaction was just one more unpredicted step in Janice's long struggle to do her job. The story began much earlier in the hospital on a rainy spring day.

"We took the entire prostate," Dr. Paulson said when William returned from the recovery room. Eva caught her breath and reached for William's hand. "It was best. We found malignant cells throughout the gland." His mouth pursed as he selected his next words. "The good news is that I think we got it all, and with chemotherapy, I believe you should be all right. Keep that in mind as you try to deal with this."

"Oh God." William closed his eyes. Eva sagged, standing at the side of William's bed, then gripped William's hand tighter in hers. Adrenalin raced in both as though it coursed between them.

Neither William, an attorney in his early forties, nor Eva, his wife of six years, had prepared for this outcome. Still newlyweds in spirit if not in the length of their marriage, they had been too buoyant, too young, a week earlier to take seriously the threat of William's upcoming prostate surgery.

His spirits had not always been so high. Before Eva, he was a very different man.

A workaholic most of his life, William had destroyed his earlier marriage and very nearly himself. He had become a dry lonely man.

The seeds of change came one day when Eva appeared at his office to propose a pre-trial mediation service her firm was offering. She was articulate and logical, and the more he listened the more intrigued he became. He felt his pulse quicken as his response formed and he arranged a second meeting. That evening he thought about her as much as her proposal, wondering how he might lead this business relationship into something more personal.

It wasn't that she was beautiful; her face was too interesting for that. Freckles sprinkled across her cheeks and nose, framing her steady green eyes with flaws that left her looking unfinished—slightly ragged. Her jaw was too narrow, especially for the full lips that dominated it. It wasn't her body, either. She was clearly female, but there were plenty of shapely women in his world. It was her intensity and self-assurance, he decided. She exuded a sense of something important, something exciting, which pervaded her whole being. She caught his imagination and made him feel alive. He was determined not to let loose until he found out why.

William's determination paid off. He approached Eva and found, to his wonder and delight, that he was woman-worthy and capable of loving. He was not a business machine. Indeed, within weeks he and Eva were deeply in love. It transformed their lives.

William and Eva nurtured their love. They invested in each other. He limited his work time, and she delegated some of her duties to a younger associate so they would have time together.

Backpacking in the Tetons on their honeymoon, William reveled in Eva's capacity for fun. She challenged—"Come on, I'll race you to that next big rock," and they waddled with their unaccustomed loads to the targeted boulder and collapsed against it, laughing. She adapted—a sudden rainstorm caught them unprepared, ponchos packed tightly in their packs. Eva, drenched to the skin, raised her arms to the sky and smiled. "Rain your blessings on us, dear Lord," she sang out. That was the time they set up camp early, laid out the new double sleeping bag on the tent floor, and undressed each other—casting the sopping clothes outside the flap before burrowing down together in the bag.

The adventure exhilarated them, so each year they packed into another wilderness. They learned fly-fishing, then fly-tying, sitting shoulder to shoulder on winter evenings tying royal coachmans, blue duns, black gnats, and wooly worms. "This is great," William would say to Eva with a straight face. "A family that ties together, sties together." She'd groan, leaning into his sturdy warmth.

They were an appealing couple, neither very tall, with William as square-built as Eva was slim. He had brown wavy hair touched with prematurely grey wisps at his temples, and one eyelid that drooped slightly, giving him a serious, thoughtful expression. Frequently when they walked or sat together his arm rested lightly around her shoulders in a protective posture, her auburn page-boy shining beneath.

By choice, they were often together. They cooked together. They joined a local book club. She laughed at his jokes and he at hers. They learned each other's foibles, and how to accommodate. They found ways to resolve their disagreements. They had fun together.

This surgery was the first threat to their union.

After his discharge from the hospital, William began a three-month treatment program. Each week he returned for chemotherapy aimed at killing any remaining cancer cells. Eva went along for moral support. They lay side-by-side in two recliner chairs lined up against the wall of the treatment room. A tube connected his arm to a clear plastic bag hanging above him. She spoke intermittently to him.

"Perlman will play in the winter concert series," Eva offered tentatively. "Let's get season tickets."

"I'd like that."

Both were silent.

"I just know you're going to be okay," Eva smiled at him, reaching for his hand but withdrawing as she remembered his tubes.

"Of course, my love. Being young and strong has to have some benefits." He grinned. "We have an endless agenda to complete together, you know."

She leaned over and buried her face in his shoulder.

The chemotherapy was followed every other week by a check-up at Dr. Paulson's office. The visits began well, but in spite of freedom from the nausea usually produced by chemotherapy, the examinations revealed his growing illness. Within a month he began to lose weight, and two weeks later he was complaining mildly of pain in his lower abdomen. Eva stood by, sharing his disappointments and lending her courage wherever she could. The two of them snatched all the good moments they could find to pretend everything was normal, knowing nothing would ever be normal again.

They found distraction and comfort in light moments. She watched him grow thinner. "I know what you're doing," she teased one day. "You're making room in your pajamas for both of us, you dirty old man."

He obliged by pinching her as she passed the big leather contour chair in which he spent more and more hours. She curled up on his lap, resting her weight on the chair's arms, and they both giggled.

But the days grew more difficult. He could no longer go to the office, and Eva often stayed at home with him. One day almost three months after his surgery, while William slept, Eva phoned Dr. Paulson.

"It's getting very hard, Doctor," she said quickly, swallowing with effort to keep control. "I have to help him now when he gets up from bed or from his chair, or when he gets into or out of the car. I can manage, but he's in pain more of the time, and that's the worst. It's so awful, watching him. Do you have anything . . . can you help?"

"Bring him in, Eva. Let me look at him. I'll find something."

The worry line in Eva's forehead eased as she put the phone down.

Later that day she took William to Dr. Paulson's office.

"Eva tells me you're having a good deal of pain, William." Dr. Paulson leaned over the table as he palpated William's abdomen. "How bad is it?"

"Not good. Actually, it's mostly the nights. They're wicked . . . The pain keeps me awake, and just when I finally doze off, a stab in my gut wakes me up."

"Show me where it is."

William swept his hand from the center of his pubic bone to the left, then up and down from his waist to the inside of his leg.

Dr. Paulson nodded.

"Besides," William added, "I keep Eva from getting her rest." He reached his hand out to Eva, smiling his apology as he spoke.

"Well, that won't do." Dr. Paulson responded. "I'll start you on some Darvon® now, and if that doesn't help, we can find something better. But there's another thing." He swung around to face Eva.

"I think the time has come to ease your load, particularly since you both seem to want to keep William at home. I'm going to give you a phone number. I want you to call these people. They're a hospice organization, and I think you should hook up with them. Do you know anything about hospice?"

"I know the name," Eva said. "And I guess I know the general idea. But I've never paid any attention. I don't actually know any specifics . . . "

Dr. Paulson explained hospice to them. He told them hospice was there to help patients like William who had life-threatening illness, and he talked about the hospice team, and what each member does, particularly in the home-care hospice program he was recommending. "You'll find," he concluded, "that they'll be a great help to the two of you. I've watched them. They'll give you support and strength."

"Would you still be our doctor?" Eva asked, uncertain.

"Yes. That's one of the beauties about it." He looked at William. "The nurse will be there with you as much as you need. You have another month of chemotherapy, so she'll see your reactions to that, and to the Darvon. She'll know your needs. And she'll tell me. We'll work together." Dr. Paulson's kindness flooded his face. Eva looked at William; wordlessly they agreed.

"We'll do it," she said for both of them.

Eva's worry line returned as they drove home. "I'll take a leave of absence, my love. I want to be with you, not away at the office when you're feeling bad." Hearing no response, she glanced sideways at him. He was pale and half-asleep. She looked again at the road, pressed the accelerator down and headed for home.

Within a day of Eva's phone call to the hospice program, William's nurse arrived.

Short, topped with white curly hair and laden with a leather case and large purse, she smiled at Eva in the doorway. "Hi. I'm Janice Miller, from hospice. I'm here to help."

With no more fuss or ceremony than that, Janice entered their home and became part of their lives. She stayed nearly two hours that day, examining William and responding to their questions.

When she left, Eva kneeled and laid her head in William's lap. He stroked her hair gently, then asked, "What do you think?"

Eva looked up and took his hands in hers. "I like her."

"So do I."

She tipped her head, kissing the palms of each of his hands before resting her head once more in his lap.

William's pain escalated over the next four weeks. The last two scheduled trips to the hospital for chemotherapy were very difficult. Janice reported almost daily to Dr. Paulson that the Darvon wasn't adequate. He gradually increased the dosage. When that failed to relieve William's pain, he switched to morphine.

By the time the course of chemotherapy ended, neither Eva nor William was sleeping much. While the medication sometimes took the edge off of his pain, it could not seem to stop the compelling pressure low in his gut or the pulling, electric shock-like sensations that radiated in waves upward through his hips from there. Eva, on the other side of their king bed, lived each cycle of pain with him, and when he cried out she clenched her jaw so she, too, wouldn't scream.

The morphine wasn't enough. Neither massage nor heating pad helped. William could find no relief. In desperation, Eva phoned Janice about 4:30 one morning.

"It's ghastly, Janice. He can't stand the pain, and neither can I, watching him. I've given him all the medicine I'm supposed to. Nothing does any good. Help us, please!"

Janice dressed quickly and drove to their home. The horizon was beginning to lighten as she pulled up to their front door.

Eva admitted Janice and led her without ceremony to William in the bedroom. He moaned, turning from side to side as if to escape the grinding pain that bound him. Janice moved quickly to the dresser, picked up the chart she had taught Eva to keep, and reviewed the medication schedule. Then she turned back to William.

"William," she touched his arm, momentarily stopping his motion. "Tell me, does this go on constantly or does it come and go?"

"Comes and goes," William expelled, then gulped another breath.

"Do you have any warning? Does anything in particular bring it on?"

Eva intervened. "No, not that we can tell." She described his feelings of pressure and electric shock-like pain, tracing them on her own trunk as she spoke. "They get stronger . . . really settle in. They always come in waves."

"How often is this happening?"

"Off and on all day and night. Probably a dozen times, I would guess." Her eyes pleaded. "Can't you do something to help him?"

"I'll call Dr. Paulson—we'll try." Janice's voice held a commitment, but it did not promise miracles. She had seen patients like this before, when there seemed to be no answer to the pain.

Dawn had arrived when she walked into the kitchen to use the phone. "Janice here, Dr. Paulson. I'm with William and Eva. His medication isn't covering his pain. He's suffering."

Dr. Paulson's sleep-laden voice quickly shed its fuzziness, and he was fully alert as he reviewed with her the drugs they had tried. No other alternatives seemed suitable. "We'll up the morphine," he decided. "Let's see . . . he's taking 4 mg tablets now, isn't he? Inject it, and titrate up to 15 mg and we'll see how that goes."

"Okay . . . He's tight as baling wire with each wave of pain," Janice observed, "and that's bad. We can't get his body to respond in a helpful way. He fights the pain." She thought for a minute, then brightened. "I want to suggest something, Dr. Paulson. I've seen it work before."

"Fire away, Jan. Anything that will help."

"Good. At the office I've read reports of success using mental imagery and autohypnosis along with medication to control pain. Dr. Lamay over at the medical school has been teaching hemophiliac patients to use the techniques to control blood pressure and reduce bleeding. A year ago he agreed to teach autohypnosis to one of our patients who had intractable pain. It was an enormous help.

"I believe William's pain is emotional as well as physical, Dr. Paulson. Maybe hypnosis and imagery reach emotional pain. I don't know."

Eva waited for a response, but there was none. She continued.

"There are a couple of other psychiatrists in town who work with hypnosis too, and if you would agree we could get one of them involved."

"Oh, I don't know," Dr. Paulson balked when he finally spoke. "that kind of thing has never impressed me much. Maybe blood pressure can be lowered with hypnosis. But pain like his? I don't think so . . . No, that's another matter."

Janice took a deep breath and gripped the telephone tight in her hand. "But what harm would it do? Shouldn't we try every possibility?"

His voice was kind but firm. "No, Janice, hypnosis is not a solution. I'm inclined to think it's one of those psychiatric fads. I doubt it would help. Go ahead with the shot of morphine, and call me tomorrow."

Janice hung up the phone. "Damn, **damn**, *damn*!" she uttered under her breath, shaking her head. She stood for several minutes, hands on hips, before turning back toward the bedroom.

When she returned to William to give him the ordered morphine injection Janice appeared calm and collected. Neither Eva nor William seemed to sense her disappointment.

At the end of the day Janice went back to her office. She searched through a file of journal articles, seeking ammunition to educate Dr. Paulson.

She worked late into the evening. Before going home she laid a small stack of articles on the desk of the volunteer clerk who would photocopy them in the morning. Each described a different study showing the success of hypnosis and imagery in easing pain.

The next day Janice labored over a cover letter to Dr. Paulson, composing with great care the case for trying this approach with William. Writing was not her particular skill, but she kept at it. Finally, the effort complete, she pounded the stamp onto the envelope with her fist before dropping it into the mail tray. "Do it, do it," she implored as she walked away.

Very few days later William was again overwhelmed with pain despite the increase in medication he was now receiving. Janice phoned Dr. Paulson, then drummed her nails on the kitchen counter while she waited for his response. The conversation would be their first since his rejection of her proposal. She shifted her weight from one foot to the other. Had he read the material she had sent? Did it change his mind?

Dr. Paulson finally came to the phone. There was no warning for his first words. "Which psychiatrist should I call?"

Janice's heart missed a beat. She had been prepared to do battle, not to assist in the decision she had hoped he would make. "Uhh . . . Vince Lamay or Gordon Johnston would be good. They trained together at the med school." She recovered quickly, hiding the triumph that surged in her breast.

Dr. Paulson's change of mind would allow Janice to discuss hypnosis with William, and with his approval she could proceed. She was by then convinced that they had found an answer to his pain. As soon as he awakened, she would approach him about it.

"We've had some success with other ways to control pain when medication alone won't do the job, William. Let's try one, what do you say?"

William looked up, new hope in his eyes.

"I'd like you to learn to use a technique called imagery and hypnosis to allow . . . "

This was when William stunned Janice with his response. She expected an eager approval, not his scathing rejection, his irreverent castigation of hypnosis as fakery. Her face matched his in disappointment, then when he turned from her to get the magazine on the table, she set herself to convince him. Side shows, indeed!

"Hey—Hold it!" Janice laughed. "You sound like the world's original skeptic! Now just wait a little minute and hear what I have to say." As she spoke, she bumped his shoulder lightly with the palm of her hand.

She described a patient who had lived with a feeding tube down his throat for eleven months. When the tube was removed he couldn't swallow. He flat-out refused to put food or water into his mouth. A psychiatrist induced a hypnotic trance in the patient, and in that state the patient finally swallowed solid food. Over the next week the trance was lightened until he accepted swallowing while he was fully conscious. Dramatic evidence, she thought.

William was not convinced. The situation seemed so different. Interesting, but it didn't apply to him.

Janice tried again. This time the story followed a patient who couldn't tolerate chemotherapy. While many people begin to have nausea and vomiting the day after they receive chemotherapy, his started during the treatment, before the tubes were disconnected. His vomiting was violent and continued almost a week, finally subsiding the day before he was hooked up for the next treatment. The vomiting left his abdominal muscles badly bruised, and he was discouraged to the point of considering suicide. When the course of treatment was only one-third completed, he announced he would never go back. Since chemotherapy was essential, a psychiatrist was called in to train this patient to hypnotize himself.

Seven daily sessions and guided hypnosis through the next chemotherapy treatment produced a dramatic change. This time the patient did not become nauseous. During the following week he and the psychiatrist prepared tape recordings for him to use to induce his own state of hypnosis. After that he coped successfully with his treatments all by himself.

Janice told William her stories and Eva urged him to try. He was opposed, but with his increasing bouts of pain his arguments grew weaker. Two weeks into their campaign, his resistance withered. He greeted Janice one morning with his new decision.

"You win, Janice. I've decided to buy."

"William, you mean you will . . . you mean we can try the hypnosis?"

"Yup." William had a resigned look on his face.

Janice glowed with pleasure, then took his hand and said softly, "I'm so pleased . . . and I promise, if it is too difficult—or it doesn't help, we'll try something else." William's face crinkled into a half smile.

Janice went to the phone and called Dr. Paulson. "He said yes! William's going to try hypnosis!"

"Good. I'll call Vince Lamay. Keep me posted, Janice. Thanks for your call." Dr. Paulson was too busy to talk.

A boyish-looking resident psychiatrist from Dr. Lamay's clinic appeared at the house the next day. "Please call me Carl. Let's see whether I can help."

"I hope so," Eva sighed. "It's been so bad."

Carl was shy. William found himself reaching out to help him. When Carl asked William to pick a scene of calm and beauty around which they could build his self-hypnosis, William searched his memory with more concentration than he expected to give.

Arriving at an image of a favorite meadow through which he had often hiked as a child, picnic lunch under his arm, William began to develop a scenario with Carl. They used his memory of stretching out on the grass on summer afternoons to watch the clouds move across the sky, and Carl encouraged him to describe the shape and color of the clouds and the fresh gentle warmth of the air. As William talked, Carl recorded his description, jubilantly noting a change in his voice from an early crisp raspiness to a steady quiet calm.

That was enough for the first session. Carl promised to return the next day.

Carl sensed William's emerging investment in their effort when he started work the next day. It was a bad day, and William had difficulty recalling the image he had selected because the searing pain in his gut intervened.

"Settle back on the bed, William, and feel it hold you up," Carl instructed him calmly. "Just sink in, and feel the bed support you." He waited.

"Okay," Carl continued after several minutes, "breathe easily and a little more deeply, nice and regular . . . now I want you to think of your body in stages. Start with your toes, and we're going to move up slowly 'til we reach the top of your head. Consciously, deliberately, make your toes relax. Let them feel heavy on the bed.

"Now relax your feet . . . Your heels . . . Let your whole feet sag into the bed . . . Now your calves and knees; let them go limp and heavy into the bed." In quiet, unhurried steps he continued to talk William through each part of his body, until William felt like a leaden sack—dead weight on the bed.

Then, with William totally relaxed, Carl turned on the tape recording they had made just the day before. William closed his eyes and listened. Unknowingly, he began to allow the pain to recede in favor of the image deep in his memory.

It was a process he would repeat many times, each time with more proficiency. The meadow became his retreat, more instantly accessible with each exercise of his new skill.

"I can't believe the power I have," William exulted to Eva one day. "You know, I'm not the victim any more!" He flexed what was left of his biceps, flashing the old smile weakly at her. "You can't imagine how great it is to make the pain go just by thinking it away! ZAP!" His voice gained strength.

"You feel like superman, don't you? God, I'm glad to see you like this!" Eva reached out impulsively and hugged him. They kissed, and suddenly the old, sweet passion returned.

Wasted and dying, William seemed more a man than he had for many weeks.

Janice reported William's success to Dr. Paulson. They both rejoiced. It would not cure him; it would not even slow his dying. But it brought an end to the shared nightmare William and Eva were living.

"I treasure these days, my love," William whispered to Eva in the king bed one night. "We don't have many left, and being able to keep the pain away is such a gift. You must remember. . . ."

As his time grew shorter, Eva and William took to holding hands when the pains began. She knew his recording by heart and joined in, so their two voices blended to lead him in his relaxation and imaging. Each step in his withdrawal from pain was familiar to her; his victory became hers as well. The total relaxation at the end often brought sleep to William. She rested alongside him, and when he roused they would talk quietly.

One day when the pain pounded in, he asked Eva to turn on the recorder. She lay down beside him, took his hand, and began the slow, quiet litany of grass and clouds and air and sun that had become the music of their recent life. She felt him grow still and heavy, becoming so herself. They lay together as they slept. An hour later she awakened, then discovered he had died.

Eva grieved as a new widow might, feeling numb and exhausted at first, then hurting as the loss, the missing of her partner and lover became more real.

Two weeks after the funeral, Janice visited Eva. "How are you, my dear?"

Tears filled Eva's eyes. "I miss him so."

"Of course you do," Janice responded, reaching for her hand.

Neither one spoke for a minute. Then Eva brightened. "His victory over the pain helps. When I feel low, I remember it. It slips in to comfort me, the power he had to overcome the pain, and his pride—his pleasure. He asked me to remember. . . . It's like a gift he left to help me now."

A bird sang outside the kitchen window. The sun shone on the shiny counter-top. The grandfather clock in the dining room chimed, and the two women talked on.

"You may not realize it, Janice, but I was aware of what happened with you and Dr. Paulson. I know you fought for us."

Janice interrupted. "He wanted what was best for you, too, Eva. He just had trouble getting over some biases he had."

"I know."

Several months later Eva phoned Janice. "I want to do something," Eva struggled to find the right words. "I must find a way to thank you. What can I do? What will give you some notion of how grateful I feel?"

"You've done it. You just told me. . . . I don't need anything more."

"Come on, Janice—you can think of something!"

"Well," Janice pondered. "I don't know what you had in mind. But we sometimes have families without insurance who can't handle the costs of hospice service, and we arrange it anyway. You could maybe help with some of their needs."

"Can you give me a for-instance?"

"Great Scott, yes!" Janice laughed. "There are so many things. Sometimes renting a hospital bed will make the difference between managing home care and not being able to stay at home. Supplies for a patient can mount up—things like dressings, drugs, water mattress pads, oxygen—all kinds of things. Nursing visits are a big item. Some patients run a large tab—others have smaller bills.

"Sometimes there's no way home care can be managed. Maybe the spouse is sick. Maybe there's no one at home with the patient—or maybe he just doesn't want to be at home. Then the person would go to the inpatient hospice, or a hospice nursing home. That costs a lot more."

"Could I take on a family, Janice? I mean pay the bills for some family?" Eva asked with eagerness, then sobered quickly. "I'm not ready to help in a more personal way, but this is something I can do. I'm serious . . . it would feel so good. Can you pick someone out for me?"

"Eva, of course I can. What an offer!" Janice blinked. "But you'd better set some kind of cap on how far you will go," she added with a grin. "To leave it open-ended could spell trouble for your pocketbook. Tell you what—I can put you in touch with our director. Then you can work it out together."

Eva's pleasure lit up her face.

That evening before retiring, she wrote her plan in her diary, adding at the end, "This one's for you, too, dearest William. We'll do it together." She reread her entry several times and finally, reluctantly, closed the book. Slipping under the covers, she seemed more complete and less alone in the king bed than she had since William died. The tears that spilled onto her pillow were strangely sweet.

NOTES:
Pain Control

Modern medicine has tackled and made enormous strides in conquering disease of many kinds. But pain, like some bacteria and viruses, while much reined in, remains a challenge—one that must be met if the human condition is to be improved, and if we are to be able to achieve a "good death." A fifteenth-century adage set the priorities for health-care providers of that day: to cure sometimes, to relieve often, to comfort always. The seventeenth-century poet and essayist, Alexander Pope, said it so well, "No greater good can man attain than to alleviate another's pain."

Dr. Charles Moertel, once president of the American Society of Clinical Oncology, was convinced that relief of pain is the single and most overriding responsibility of the physician caring for the cancer patient who cannot be cured. Cancer has no exclusive rights to this benefit; the obligation holds for any patients with pain.

Fear of pain is compelling by itself; it also stokes the fires of fear of dying. Universally, where pain threatens or exists, it can loom enormous as a problem. Beyond its psychological power, evidence exists that pain and stress can inhibit immune function and may actually promote cancer [2]. The consequences of unrelieved pain can include muscle tension, a stress hormone response (increased metabolic rate and blood clotting, tissue breakdown, water retention, and impaired immune function), decreased mobility, shallow breathing and cough suppression, retention of pulmonary secretions, pneumonia, and poor gastric and bowel function [3].

The control of pain has always been an integral and crucial part of the hospice effort. William and Eva were the fortunate recipients of a history of hospice determination to eliminate or greatly ameliorate pain. That will has been played out in the movement's work of studying pain, self-educating about pain, and being open-minded and creative in the selection of methods to control pain. While hospice has not functioned alone in this arena, it has played a substantial, leadership role. It has provided the itch that medical education has now begun to scratch; it has pushed and prodded research by others to raise the level of knowledge; it has engaged outside professionals in its dedication to the task of relieving pain. Much has been accomplished; there is still more to do.

From the beginning of the modern hospice movement in England, care of the dying aimed to provide physical and emotional comfort for its patients. St. Christopher's Hospital's hospice cocktail, which was effective in keeping many dying patients free of pain while still lucid, provided a quantum leap forward in the effort to bring comfort to the dying. Major continuing efforts of hospice are focused on improving the control of pain.

Analyzing and discussing a human being's pain has a quality of disjointedness about it, because doing so is intellectual; human pain is anything but intellectual. We are talking about something personal, subjective, and so deeply felt it can tear the will out of someone—yet to make progress in the efforts to conquer it, we must dissect it objectively.

With that in mind, never forgetting the human experience we are talking about, we can identify four components of pain [4]. The first of these is physical—from stretching, compressing or otherwise irritating nerve endings. With cancer patients, physical pain is the result of either direct tumor involvement, comprising three-quarters of pain problems in those patients, or from their treatment—chemotherapy, surgery or radiation therapy—the remaining one-fourth.

The second component of pain is psychological—the fear, anxiety and depression caused by having disease and physical pain. Life-threatening illness often brings an expectance of pain, and any symptoms can lead to preoccupation with it. While this focused worry and stress do not cause pain, they can surely exacerbate it. In the first author's work in hospice, fear, anxiety, and depression have often appeared to be the greatest burdens the patients carry.

Then there is social pain. When the patient feels his attention is always riveted on his illness and fighting his physical pain, he becomes isolated from family and friends who cannot truly know what he is feeling. He finds it difficult to share their lives and happenings because he is consumed with his own, a script limited to pain. The setting in which he is treated may add more isolation. The effect is to heighten his sense of suffering.

And last, when life has lost its meaning and living has become deprived of purpose or value, the patient experiences the worst—a deep, spiritual pain.

Each aspect of pain suggests its own treatment—or at least its own approaches to treatment. Physical pain requires medical attack aimed at reducing the cause or blocking the pain—keeping it from being felt. Psychological pain requires rooting out the object of the patient's anxiety and providing effective support to help him cope with it. Social pain must have social solutions coming from persons relating to the patient. And spiritual pain can yield to efforts to help him recognize his worth irrespective of his illness. For some, but not all people, the last mentioned can come from religion.

The beginning task in the medical response to physical pain, the aspect of pain these pages will address, is to assess its cause or causes. Only with knowledge of the cause can the physician develop a preliminary plan of treatment. As part of this, he or she needs to know whether the pain is acute or chronic, localized or general, and what are its location and radiation and relation to other dysfunctions. Beyond these issues illuminating the cause of the pain, an effective treatment plan requires determining the kind and degree of pain the patient feels. Without knowledge of the cause, kind and degree of the patient's pain, the physician is left adrift in guesses as he begins and tries to monitor therapy.

Current technology and medical knowledge provides enough information in most cases for valid conclusions about cause of physical pain to be drawn.

Assessment of the kind and degree of a patient's pain poses a unique problem since pain is a personal, subjective experience.

A method had to be devised to obtain some meaningful expression from the patient about his pain—a revelation of his inner feeling—which could be quantified. Early assessment efforts began with various ways to have the patient grade his pain on a scale.

The foundation for this scaling work came in 1860 from pioneer in psychophysics, George Fechner, who postulated that sensations could have magnitude and be expressed in units [5]. The later psychophysicist, S. S. Stevens, subsequently developed and validated scaling methods for the sensory perceptions of hearing and vision [6, 7]. A scale of pain intensity, called the Dol scale, was devised in 1947 based on Fechner's and Stevens' work [8].

The Dol scale was designed with a series of pain stimuli—three seconds of thermal radiation—in ascending intensity. The subjects in the study reported each detectable increment of pain, or just noticeable difference (JND), every two of which were called a Dol. To assess pain, the subject fractionated the resulting scale of Dols—that is, he started with an arbitrary standard of eight "maximum" Dols and reported what fraction of eight any pain stimulus was to him.

Variations of this technique have been used ever since, typically with the report given in a scale of numbers from 0 to 5, or 0 or 1 to 10, or in a visual analogue scale on a strip of arbitrary length—perhaps 10 centimeters. In each current variety the respondent is asked to place a point that fits his level of pain on a scale between no pain and the worst imaginable pain.

While numerical and visual analogue scales are presumably testing the same thing, the visual scale has been found by one investigator to yield lower pain levels than the numerical [9].

Another approach to pain evaluation originated with Melzack's work in 1975 [10]. He devised a test listing many word descriptors in three categories: sensory (e.g., pricking, stabbing, tugging, wrenching); affective (e.g., dull, heavy, tiring, exhausting); and evaluative (e.g., mild, excruciating, annoying, unbearable). The patient chose words from this list that described his pain and arranged them on grids with intensity scales from 1 to 5 along the sides. He could place the test words he had selected as far up or down on the intensity scale as fit his experience. From this, Melzack took the number of words chosen and what the indicated pain intensity was on the scale of 1 to 5, and determined a pain rating index which provided quantitative information for statistical treatment.

Melzack's test was accompanied by a questionnaire which explored the locus of the pain, and how it changed with time. He felt his questionnaire was sensitive enough to detect differences of effectiveness among different methods then available to relieve pain.

Overt behaviors have also been the basis for judgments about a patient's pain, but they can provide only rough estimates for monitoring. Nurses and others observe many things about the patient as they care for him. (The best nurses are vigilant observers.) Behaviors they watch for include restlessness, muscle tenseness, pacing, guarding, holding, groaning, moaning, bracing, rubbing, and grimacing to mention a few. The drawback of this observational method of assessing pain is that the judgment of these behaviors takes an outsider's point of view rather than that of the expert—the patient [11]. That may be a mistake—and most certainly is if these judgments alone determine treatment decisions.

Indeed, agreement between observers and patients on levels of pain have not been particularly good. The significant others of cancer patients always rated patients' pain as worse than did the patient [12]. Caregivers' ratings of pain agreed well with their patients when pain was low to moderate, but poorly when pain was high [13]. Nurses judged chronic pain to be less than patients did (perhaps because they are witness to so much pain?), although their judgments of acute pain were generally close to their patients' [14].

We can conclude that others' observations have value but should not replace the patient's own view of his pain.

Many hospices now take multiple approaches to pain assessment. Patients are asked to quantify their pain on a numerical or visual analog scale; nurses identify behaviors revealing pain; in addition, patients' verbal descriptions are still taken into account, being placed into a scale of semantic ascendancy [15]. Along with these measurements, in our full pain evaluation at Hospice of Metro Denver, we are looking at the patient's coping strategies, the consequences of his pain, such as whether reactions are being reinforced or avoided, the history of his pain, the effects of his pain on the family—and other complications of it.

All of that is fed into the physician's thinking before the treatment is planned.

The evaluation of pain, once done, is not complete. It must be repeated regularly, and we open the door at every visit for the patient to let us know what and how he feels.

The protocol developed by the Colorado Cancer Pain Initiative, a state-wide cooperative task force that addressed the problem, and adopted at the Hospice of Metro Denver, has attempted to insure that our team members are aware and carry out those measures that will bring comfort to our patients. With their permission, we are reproducing the assessment part of the protocol below.

ASSESSMENT

A. BELIEVE PATIENT'S REPORT OF PAIN (emphasis is the authors'. This could not be more important!)

B. Sit, listen and reassure the patient/caregiver that in most cases pain can be controlled.

C. Take a careful pain history including duration, location and quality. Assess the effect of pain on the patient's mood and how it affects activities of daily living. Ask the patient whether pain interferes with sleeping, eating or movement.

D. Take a careful analgesic history including prior and present medications, analgesic response and side effects. Differentiate between an allergic reaction and side effects of analgesic drugs.

E. Have the patient express pain on a scale of 1 to 10, 1 being no pain and 10 being the worst pain.

F. Perform a complete physical exam.

G. Attempt to determine the cause of the pain.

H. Reevaluate pain level frequently.

I. Document level of pain and interventions on each nursing visit[1] [16].

---

[1] As published in Hospice of Metro Denver's Pain Protocol, 1995. Used by permission. Hospice of Metro Denver, 425 South Cherry Street, Denver, Colorado 80222-1234 and the Colorado Cancer Pain Initiative.

Pharmacology provides the big guns in the attack on physical pain. Non-narcotic, narcotic, and/or adjuvant analgesics may be given to the patient to obscure or block his pain. Non-narcotics include aspirin, ibuprophen, acetaminophen and similar over-the-counter preparations. Narcotics, or opioids, include morphine, the mainstay of serious pain control (which Sir William Osler, the famous physician in the early 1900s, referred to as "God's own medicine"); methadone, which equals morphine in controlling pain but has the problem of accumulating in the body; Dilaudid®, which can substitute for morphine at a considerably lower dose as it is much stronger; and heroin, a morphine derivative which cannot be used in the United States because it is illegal. Among the adjuvants are antidepressants, anticonvulsants, antihistamines, steroids, amphetamines, anti-inflammatories, etc., which address conditions related indirectly to the patients' pain—headache, muscle spasms, nausea, vomiting, bowel and bladder problems, anorexia, etc.—and may be used in conjunction with one or more analgesics [17, 18].

Certain pains do not call for opiate drugs. Headache from intracranial pressure is exacerbated by opioids; unstable fractures of long bones are better treated with surgical fixation as no dose of morphine can control this pain; some pains unrelated to the dying (i.e., toothache, joint pain, etc.) may respond well to non-narcotic or adjuvent medication.

Advances have been made in delivering narcotic analgesics to the patient with greater effectiveness. Simple, oral ingestion has been used for decades, eventually refined with timed release preparations. Transdermal patches—with and without iontophoresis (adapting the skin patch with a button that uses electrical current to push the medicine through the skin), suppositories, sublingual delivery for mucous membrane transmission, subcutaneous infusion with a twenty-four-hour pump, intramuscular injection and intravenous injection, sometimes with implantation devices for drug infusion, have followed.

Other approaches to the control of physical pain include blocking the nerve pathway so pain does not register in the brain, or in some very severe cases, surgically ablating the pain-carrying nerve entirely. Radiation is used for rapid relief of pain from bone metastases, acting through chemical mediators of pain. Nuclear radiation with radioisotope Strontium 89 provides pain relief through analgesia to these bone metastases for as long as three months after treatment, and it may also shrink the tumors.

Other less intrusive methods of reducing sensitivity to physical pain have been suggested including cutaneous modalities, positioning, and movement [19]. Stimulation of the skin, physical therapist Margo McCaffery suggests, may help in part by activating large diameter nerve fibers, thus inhibiting pain messages carried by smaller fibers, called the "gate-control" theory. The gating mechanism modulates sensory input prior to perception, with heat, cold, massage, and relaxation closing the gate, and anxiety and excitement opening the gate [20]. Stimulation of the skin may also help by increasing the body's supply of endorphins, nature's natural opiates [11].

Cold can decrease sensitivity temporarily by numbing tissue. Superficial massage, superficial heat and cold, menthol application to the skin, and the less utilized transcutaneous electrical nerve stimulation (TENS) are in the battery of offerings from physical therapy.

Yet another useful method of controlling physical pain is hypnosis, William's salvation in our story, a process to induce a state of attentive, receptive concentration with a relative suspension of peripheral awareness. As early as 1846, hypnosis was used with some success for amputations, when combined with other surgical anesthesia [21]. Since World War II hypnosis has been utilized more broadly for pain. Its effectiveness has been related to the severity of the pain, the level of hypnotizability of the patient, and his cognitive state [22]. In combination with analgesics, hypnosis can be a powerful tool for control of pain.

Compounding the patient's basic physical pain, particularly when the person is inactive, may be the common side effects of morphine use, nausea, and constipation [23]. For nausea, which is usually short-lived, there are many anti-emetics: Compazine® in oral or suppository form, Reglan®, Zofran®, and Kytril®, to name a few. At Hospice of Metro Denver, we have found a suppository containing Decadron®, Reglan®, and Benedryl® to be very effective in controlling nausea.

Narcotic-induced constipation results because the drug decreases peristalsis in the intestine, thus increasing stool transit time. At the same time, the anal sphincter becomes stronger, unable to relax in response to rectal distention. The stool, in this circumstance, becomes dry and hard, with painful impaction a possible result. The patient requires great energy to expel the waste in this state, and more pain occurs. Fifty-one of eighty dying cancer patients were found in one study to suffer constipation, twenty-five of them severe—but only about half of them received treatment [24].

Prevention of constipation is the better part of care. We use stool softeners and laxatives such as Senekot-S® and Fleets® enemas routinely when narcotics are given, and they generally are effective in keeping waste moving normally in the intestines. When impaction occurs, the only solution is the manual removal of the stool, not a pleasant experience for the patient or the nurse. (On more than one occasion the first author has been called a saint by newly referred, grateful patients when the ordeal was over! Once relieved and on a preventive regimen, these patients experienced more comfort.)

Treatment of constipation includes fiber, liquids, activity, rectal agents, and cathartics. Subcutaneous infusion of metoclopramide is done in extreme cases to increase intestinal motility [25].

Undermedication has been reported as the overwhelming problem in the care of dying patients (see p. 138). There can be no more agony than that caused by knowing relief is there but can never be yours—or your patient's—like the starving prisoner whose food is locked up, or the despairing sailor whose swamped boat cannot be seen from the steamship at its side.

Nurses from four states were asked to rate themselves on a scale of 1 to 4 (poor to excellent) on factors which, if inadequate, could be barriers to effective pain management. Their self-ratings averaged 2.6 on educational preparation, 2.3 on knowledge of legal/political issues, 3.1 on practice, 1.9 on financial issues, and 3.1 on ethical issues [26], pointing to needs in the nursing profession. They regarded undermedication, inadequate education of the prescribing physicians, and lack of a pain team service as the three most important problems facing nursing staffs.

Among the reasons why patients are often undermedicated, David Cundiff cites inadequate education of physicians and other health professionals involved in treating these patients, poor communication among patients, family, nurses and physicians, and lack of money [17].

Other reasons for undermedication are suggested: professionals may fail to recognize until late that the patient has developed tolerance for the drug and no longer gains relief from it. Physicians may fear respiratory depression will result from overmedication, so they prefer to err on the side of safety. This side effect has been found not to be likely if the drug is increased in gradual steps [27], a fact that appears not to be universally known even within the palliative- and cancer-nursing communities. Myths continue to exist about the power of morphine to lead to respiratory distress and death in morphine-tolerant patients.

Some physicians will persist in worrying about respiratory depression. According to Rousseau, they always have the option of switching the medication from morphine to an equivalent dose of another opioid such as hydromorphone or fentanyl [28].

Misconceptions about addiction held by physician, nurse, patient, or family member play a very large role in undermedication. Addiction, a compulsive abuse of drugs out of craving for no medical purpose, is often confused with physical dependence or with tolerance.

Physical dependence is an altered physiologic state in which withdrawal signs and symptoms accompany the discontinuance of the drug if dosage is not tapered off first. It poses no clinical problem if managed well.

Tolerance is the very reason respiratory depression is unlikely to occur. The patient's system builds resistance to the drug's effects with repeated exposure, so titrating dosage upward in increments according to need is not only benign but necessary.

True addiction is actually very rare in patients treated with narcotics [29].

Professionals and the public alike often do not differentiate between these legitimate and proper uses of narcotics to relieve pain and their improper use to produce a high, and are robbing the patient of comfort in order to remain pure on an irrelevant issue. We have been brainwashed with "Just Say No." The details and fine points that can modify opposition to narcotics are important to know. Some headway is being made in correcting this misconception. Goodman and Gillman, the authors of a classic textbook in pharmacology, say no patient should ever wish for death because of a physician's reluctance to use adequate amounts of effective opioids (narcotics) [30].

Patients, themselves, can impede good pain management. This is particularly true in care settings that are episodic and don't have the continuity that hospice provides, where the team gets to know the patient and his reactions and can help him understand his options.

Among these patient-generated impediments is stoicism. We have cared for the patient—and there are many—who wants to be a "good patient," who holds the pain in and refuses to complain until it becomes unbearable. This may have been an appropriate response in the medical dark ages, but today it certainly is not.

We have also seen many patients who deny pain because they don't want to learn what it signifies—for example, that it reflects progress of his cancer.

Patients sometimes fear erroneously that if their pain is controlled with morphine too early, the pain will be uncontrolled at the end.

Others may be reluctant to report pain for fear of interfering with medical treatment, or of being abandoned by their physicians; some have the misguided belief that by remaining silent, by not complaining, they will please their physicians. We know some patients whose religious beliefs do not allow them to use pain medication, or whose intellectual limitations preclude their understanding its value. Some reject it because they are afraid of side effects from the medication, or of that bug-a-boo, addiction.

There are patients who fear they will lose control under medication; even patients who refuse medication because pain convinces them, in some incomprehensible way, that they are still alive.

All of the notions described pose difficult problems for us who are trying to comfort and ease these people through their time of dying. We must watch our patients with an intuitive eye, judging what they don't say as well as what they do, what they choose not to reveal as well as what they make visible, and help them to understand and accept the comfort that can be available to them. We need to allay their fears of addiction, of loss of control, of being lesser persons. The ongoing hospice relationship, with its openness, understanding and building of trust gives us the best chance of doing these things. We can most likely provide comfort for the patient and greater ease for his loved ones.

A study of unmet analgesic needs in hospitalized cancer patients reveals something we have long felt strongly about, that increasing the patient's sense of control makes a big difference to him [31]. He can cope with pain more effectively if we provide him information about the pain and the treatment so he can understand it, if we help him set realistic goals for his remaining life, if we encourage him to express his emotions—and then accept them. We need to let him talk out his feelings and beliefs. He can then move ahead, accepting more realistically the pain he may have to suffer [32].

A helpful strategy is to have the patient set his own pain relief goal on the *no-pain* to *unbearable-pain* scale, perhaps 0 to 2 on a 0 to 10 scale, which he can tolerate, thereby setting an informed guideline for the nurse and physician as they provide pain control measures. The patient exerts control and plays an active role in his own management [33].

Leaving written instructions for care in general and the medication schedule in particular is helpful to the patient and his caregiver. With something in writing, they feel less vulnerable to uncertainty and forgetting, more competent to handle the needs. A written list, together with the reminder that their nurse is only a phone call away, can see most families through the times they are on their own.

A survey of caregivers' most often asked questions focused on why the patient suffered pain, what pain the patient would have in the future, and whether pain means death is closer. Caregivers want pain-related educational materials. They want training to be the "comfort coach" [34].

Another source of comfort to the patient and his caregiver is knowing there will be an answer to episodes of pain not controlled by regularly scheduled doses of medication. Planning ahead for this "breakthrough pain," with drugs pre-prescribed by the patient's physician and kept on hand, can avoid unnecessary trauma in the care setting.

The treatment of children in pain is a special subject, requiring special knowledge. It is a subject of importance in hospice, as the National Hospice Organization reported that 95 percent of hospices will admit children; in 1993, 2,750 children received hospice care [35].

Traditional medicine has believed in the past that infants and children do not have the neurological capacity to feel much pain, nor do they have any memory of it later, but that in any event it can't be measured accurately; that it is better to undermedicate a child because injections are hard on them or medication may cause respiratory depression or addiction; that pragmatically, pain builds character (!), and that medication might mask the symptoms. For these reasons, infants and children have very often been left to suffer pain we would never force on an adult.

These beliefs are gradually (and thankfully) being broken down. Anand and Hickey found in a landmark study that by twenty-nine weeks gestation, the fetus' neuropathways are well developed [36], and Fitzgerald and Anand dispelled the notion of inadequate memory in pointing out the ongoing psychological disturbances pain produces in children as they mature into adulthood [37].

Several studies have demonstrated that pain can be measured in children, even in infancy. Infants were noted to respond to pain with characteristic torso and limb movements, and that endorphin levels can be measured in children's spinal fluid, indicating with positive correlation their level of anxiety [38]. Infants in the zero- to three-month-old age range also reveal their pain by scrunching the face, frowning, stretching a square-mouth opening, and increasing crying with elevated pitch and more difficulty being consoled [39]. Children two to six years old exhibit hiding away, and fighting the pain [40]. Their behaviors also include crying, refusing treatment, and stalling. Their verbal descriptions vary. Children's drawings, including their choice of colors (e.g., black and deep red for pain) are projective items helpful in assessing their pain [38].

While developmental factors, previous pain experience, and parental attitudes toward the child's feelings complicate assessment, it can be done. And children do experience pain.

A consensus is growing that the ethical responsibility of clinicians working with children is to provide full treatment of pain unless 1) the pain is useful; 2) it is the best way to achieve a goal; or 3) it is necessary—that is, there are no other ways to achieve a goal, or pain is at the lowest possible level [41].

The American Academy of Pediatrics has published guidelines for pain control in children [42].

The World Health Organization published guidelines for general cancer pain management in 1986. Another publication useful to health care professionals is the Acute Pain Management Clinical Practice Guideline #1, Agency for Health Care Policy and Research, Rockville, Maryland, Publication # 92-0032, 1992 [43].

Other organizations with information about pain control include the Resource Center for State Cancer Pain Initiatives, 1300 University Avenue Room 3671, Madison, WI 53706, and the National Cancer Institute of the Federal Government. The Institute funds cancer pain education programs; they have developed a long-range plan to make educational materials available to patients and their families.

In past years, the attention of physicians was on the etiology of illness, with scant effort to understand or treat pain [44]. That is changing, thanks to pioneers in medicine and other health-related fields who have dared to look at persons rather than bodies, illness rather than disease, and pain and suffering as primary problems and not simply as symptoms of a disease process. Greater efforts have been made, and the focus has enlarged, so a major attack is being brought on pain, the greatest enemy of a good death. England and Ireland have a medical specialty now in palliative medicine—pain control [45]. The United States has its American Academy of Hospice and Palliative Care Medicine (formerly the Academy of Hospice Physicians), which includes a major focus on pain control. The University of Colorado School of Medicine began a pain control course in 1995. The University of Oregon Health Sciences Center has created a multidisciplinary comfort care team. A pain fellowship has been created by the M.D. Anderson Cancer Pain Center and The Hospice at the Texas Medical Center in Dallas, with physicians attending a six-month practice at Anderson, then six months at The Hospice. The Cleveland Clinic has announced a similar program. Evidence grows that the field of medicine and related health care disciplines are learning more, understanding more, and providing more help in the fight against pain.

There is more to do. Sachs et al., urge physicians to use the new pain control guidelines, and educate patients about palliative care. In their institutions, physicians can influence change, and teach new information and attitudes about pain control [46].

Hospice will continue to spearhead the war on pain.

REFERENCES

1. S. Stoddard, *The Hospice Movement: A Better Way of Caring for the Dying,* Stein and Day Publishing Company, Briarcliff Manor, New York, 1978.
2. J. C. Liebeskind, Pain Can Kill, *Pain, 44*:1, pp. 3-4, 1991.
3. D. B. Gordon and S. E. Ward, Correcting Misconceptions about Pain, *American Journal of Nursing, 95*:7, pp. 43-45, 1995.
4. R. E. Enck, Pain Management: An Overview, *American Journal of Hospice Care, 5*:3, pp. 17-19, 1988.
5. G. T. Fechner, *Elements of Psychophysics,* 1860, Holt, Rinehart and Winston (translation), New York, 1966.

6. S. S. Stevens and A. H. Davis, *Hearing: Its Psychology and Physiology*, John Wiley and Sons, New York, 1938.
7. S. S. Stevens, Mathematics, Measurement and Psychophysics, *Handbook of Experimental Psychology*, S. S. Stevens (ed.), John Wiley and Sons, New York, 1951.
8. C. T. Morgan and W. G. Garner, Further Measurements of the Relation of Pitch to Intensity, oral presentation to the 18th Annual Meeting of the Eastern Psychological Association. Proceedings, in *American Psychologist, 2*, p. 433, 1947.
9. J. S. Carpenter and D. Brockopp, Comparison of Patients' Ratings and Examination of Nurses' Responses to Pain Intensity Rating Scales, *Cancer Nursing, 18*:4, pp. 292-298, 1995.
10. R. Melzack, McGill Pain Questionnaire: Major Properties and Scoring Methods, *Pain, 1*:1, pp. 277-299, 1975.
11. M. McCaffrey, *Nursing Management of the Patient With Pain*, Lippincott Publishers, New York, 1979.
12. B. R. Ferrell, B. A. Ferrell, M. Rhiner, and M. M. Grant, *Report to the 1st Asian Pacific Symposium on Pain Control*, Sydney, Australia, February 1991.
13. S. A. Grossman, V. R. Sheidler, K. Swedeen, J. Mucenski, and S. Piantadosi, Correlation of Patient and Caregiver Ratings of Cancer Pain, *Journal of Pain and Symptom Management, 6*, pp. 53-57, 1991.
14. K. Teske, R. Dant, and C. S. Cleeland, Relationships between Nurses' Observations and Self-Report of Pain, *Pain, 16*, pp. 289-296, 1983.
15. T. A. Ahles, D. W. Coombs, L. Jensen, T. Stuhel, L. H. Maurer, and F. J. Keefe, Development of a Behavioral Observation Technique for the Assessment of Pain Behaviors in Cancer Patients, *Behavior Therapy, 21*:4, pp. 449-460, 1990.
16. Colorado Cancer Pain Initiative, *Pain Protocol*, Denver, Colorado, 1994.
17. D. Cundiff, *Euthanasia is Not the Answer*, Humana Press, Totowa, New Jersey, 1992.
18. R. E. Enck, Pain Management in Overview, *American Journal of Hospice Care, 5*:3, pp. 17-19, 1988.
19. M. McCaffery and M. Wolff, Pain Relief Using Cutaneous Modalities, Positioning and Movement, *The Hospice Journal, 8*:1-2, pp. 121-153, 1992.
20. S. Weinrich and M. C. Weinrich, Effect of Massage on Pain in Cancer Patients, *Applied Nursing Research, 3*:4, pp. 140-141, 1990.

21. J. Esdaille, *Hypnosis in Medicine and Surgery*, Julian Press, New York, 1957.

22. J. L. Spira and D. Spiegel, Hypnosis and Related Techniques in Pain Management, *The Hospice Journal*, 8:1-2, pp. 89-119, 1992.

23. S. C. McMillan and M. Tittle, A Descriptive Study of the Management of Pain and Pain-Related Side Effects in a Cancer Center and a Hospice, *The Hospice Journal*, 10:1, pp. 89-107, 1995.

24. J. M. Addington-Hall, L. D. MacDonald, H. R. Anderson, and P. Freeling, Dying from Cancer: The Views of the Bereaved Family and Friends about the Experiences of the Terminally Ill Patients, *Palliative Medicine, 5*, pp. 207-214, 1991.

25. R. E. Enck, Constipation: Etiology and Management, *American Journal of Hospice Care*, 5:5, pp. 17-19, 1988.

26. K. G. Wallace, B. A. Reed, C. Pasero, and G. L. Olsson, Staff Nurses's Perceptions of Barriers to Effective Pain Management, *Journal of Pain and Symptom Management, 10*:3, pp. 204-213, 1995.

27. S. Aranda and M. O'Connor, Euthanasia, Nursing and Care of the Dying, *Australian Nursing Journal, 3*:2, pp. 18-21, 1995.

28. P. Rousseau, Physician-Assisted Suicide, *Journal of the American Medical Association, 274*:4, p. 302, 1995.

29. J. Porter and H. Jick, Addiction Rare in Inpatients Treated with Narcotics, *New England Journal of Medicine, 302*:2, pp. 123-131, 1980.

30. L. S. Goodman and A. G. Gillman, *Pharmacological Basis of Therapeutics*, Pergamon Press, New York, 1990.

31. D. S. Zhukovsky, E. Gorowski, J. Hausdorff, B. Napolitano, and M. Lesser, Unmet Analgesic Needs in Cancer Patients, *Journal of Pain and Symptom Management, 10*:2, pp. 113-119, 1995.

32. J. E. Warner, Involvement of Families in Pain Control of Terminally Ill Patients, *The Hospice Journal, 8*:1-2, pp. 155-170, 1992.

33. D. B. Gordon and S. E. Ward, Correcting Misconceptions about Pain, *American Journal of Nursing, 95*:7, pp. 43-45, 1995.

34. B. Ferrell, M. Z. Cohen, M. Rhiner, and A. Rozak, Pain as a Metaphor for Illness: Cancer Care Givers Management of Pain, *Oncology Nursing Forum, 18*:8, pp. 1315-1321, 1991.

35. M. O. Amenta, Terminally Ill Children in Hospice Care, *Home Healthcare Nurse, 12*:4, pp. 66-67, 1994.

36. K. J. S. Anand and P. R. Hickey, Pain and Its Effects in the Human Neonate and Fetus, *New England Journal of Medicine, 317*:21, pp. 1321-1329, 1987.

37. M. Fitzgerald and K. J. S. Anand, Developmental Neuroanatomy and Neurophysiology of Pain, in *Pain in Infants, Children and Adolescents*, N. L. Schechter, C. B. Berde, and M. Yaster (eds.), Williams and Wilkins Publishing Company, Baltimore, pp. 11-13, 1993.
38. P. McGrath, An Assessment of Children's Pain: A Review of Behavioral, Psychological and Direct Scaling Techniques, *Pain, 31*:2, pp. 1147-1176, 1987.
39. B. J. Fuller and D. A. Conner, Effect of Pain on Infant Behaviors, *Clinical Nursing Research, 4*:3, pp. 253-273, 1995.
40. R. Woodgate and L. J. Kristjanson, Young Children's Behavioral Responses to Acute Pain, *Journal of Advanced Nursing, 22*:2, pp. 243-249, 1995.
41. G. Walco, R. C. Cassidy, and N. L. Schechter, Pain, Hurt, and Harm: Ethics of Pain Control in Infants and Children, *New England Journal of Medicine, 331*:8, pp. 541-544, 1994.
42. American Academy of Pediatrics, *Report of Subcommittee on Disease-Related Pain in Childhood Cancer*, 1990.
43. Agency for Health Care Policy and Research, *Acute Pain Management—Clinical Practice Guideline for the Management of Cancer Pain (#1)*, Pub. 92-0032, Health and Human Services Department, Rockville, Maryland, 1992.
44. R. K. Portenoy, Practical Aspects of Pain Control in the Patient with Cancer, *CA, 38*:6, pp. 327-352, 1988.
45. I. G. Finlay, J. Gilbert, and F. Randall, Response to Miller et al., *New England Journal of Medicine, 331*:24, pp. 1657-1658, 1994.
46. G. A. Sachs, J. C. Ahronheim, J. A. Rhmes, L. Volicer, and J. Lynn, Good Care of Dying Patients: The Alternative to Physician-Assisted Suicide and Euthanasia, *Journal of the American Geriatric Society, 43*:5, pp. 553-562, 1995.

CHAPTER 7

Ties That Bind

Dying is a letting go. It is a ". . . progressive series of disconnections from life which requires . . . letting go" [1, p. 26].

I have watched many patients approach their time, held their hands as they realized that their bodies were giving up—fighting it first, then giving in gradually to the fatigue of the fight. Many of them finally reach a decision that the long struggle should end and peace be allowed to come. They want to let go.

Sometimes they cannot let go until some problem is solved, some conflict resolved [2]. Their peace may wait, at least for a time.

But often they are ready. You would have to live their lives to understand how ready they can be.

What is surprising then is that sometimes death won't come. I've seen it happen over and over. A patient's body is ready; he is ready, mentally and emotionally; yet for some unknown reason he does not die. Not then.

I believe that some people are bound by ties to the people who love them—bound by their own will or that of their loved ones—in some strange way. In order to die they need some distance, some space in which to do their dying. They can't leave while people they love hover.

SANDY

"We won't play guessing games, Sandy."

The physician, looking older than his mid-forties, leaned heavily on the bed-table at the foot of his patient's hospital bed. His role of messenger carrying news of disaster had dogged him with increasing frequency these past months, and it showed. His eyes were dull with discouragement as he faced the blond, pale, slim young man before him. "The lab tests indicate your pneumonia is AIDS-related." His statement was non-negotiable, final.

Sandy stared open-mouthed at his doctor, unable to speak. He listened, but could not focus on the doctor's explanation that followed.

At twenty-three, Sandy knew despair. He had good reason. He had recognized since his childhood that he was different. Homosexual, he had struggled with himself for years. He didn't want this burden. With pain and the passage of time, he had come to accept it, a peacemaking built of compromises.

Although he had found ways to make his own adjustments, his parents couldn't understand. They would never accept him as he was. And now this, the ultimate defeat.

"It's been so hard," he had pleaded to his parents at the end of his tell-all visit in their home just three weeks earlier. "I've always felt different, like something's wrong with me. I'd watch you two, and I'd look around me, and everywhere I could see, a couple was a guy and a girl. I knew that's the way it's supposed to be. But I never felt that way. Don't you see what I'm saying? I never wanted to be a couple with a girl. When I wanted to be close, it was always with a guy."

His mother, sweet-faced and nicely coifed, wrung her hands in a gesture she made often during his visit. "God has told us that a man and a woman should cleave together." She shook her head, rejecting and at the same time trying to make sense of the news he had brought them. It fit with no part of her beliefs or experience.

Sandy watched his mother and sighed. "I know this is hard for you." Sweat ran down between his shoulder blades. "But Mom, and Dad," he turned to face his father, "I'm desperate for you to understand—at least that I haven't simply chosen to do this. It's just the way I am."

His mother looked sideways at his father, avoiding eye contact with Sandy as much as checking the reaction on her husband's face. His response would, as always, give her the direction she could not find for herself. What she saw unsettled her further.

Sandy's father, flushed during much of the discussion and flinching with each disclosure, drew his tall, spare frame back into the corner of his high-backed wing chair. His posture and expression said clearly that his son, his seed, was an aberration for whom no excuses or forgiveness were possible. Words were not needed to convey his shock and disgust.

Sandy, too, read the unmistakable message. Although his parents may have wanted to understand, they couldn't. Their religion, their pride, their fear, all stood in the way. Their responses were visceral, and the silence that covered them was transparent. The visit produced only pain for all three of them.

Defeated, Sandy left his parents with his head bowed and energy gone. He shuffled numbly to the bus stop, his worn-down running shoes catching on some of the brick pavers in the walk. He grabbed the door-rail when the bus arrived, and without looking, pulled himself heavily inside.

Two weeks later he became ill. He entered the hospital sick, worried, and depressed; the dreaded diagnosis now took him to the very bottom.

An hour after the doctor left, Joe arrived at the hospital, anxious to see his lover. He had spent the day denying his fear that Sandy might have AIDS. Too impatient to wait for an elevator up to the third floor, he took the steps two at a time. Perspiration beaded on his forehead, gleaming between a shock of black hair on top and unruly, prematurely-grey eyebrows beneath.

Joe and Sandy had met four years earlier at the library where both of them worked. Joe drove the inter-library delivery truck and Sandy was an apprentice to the librarian. A friendship developed which led eventually to their love affair.

Neither could believe they had been together for almost three years.

They were a surprising couple. Joe was as big and dark as Sandy was slight and fair. Joe was the older of the two men. At thirty, he felt responsible for Sandy. A worry line permanently creased his forehead, and it dug a deep groove as he approached Sandy's room in the hospital.

A quick stop at the nurse's station relieved Joe about Sandy's pneumonia. Only a small part of one lung was involved. Buoyed by this news Joe sprinted to Sandy's room. "Hey, fella, I've missed you long enough. Let's get out of this chamber!"

Sandy's spirits rose as he heard the warmth in Joe's familiar voice. The isolation, the dread, the despair retreated; he was human again, some spark of will fighting within him. He smiled weakly at Joe. "God, what a joy you are!"

The two touched hands silently.

"So when can you come home? What does the doctor say?"

"Maybe I shouldn't come home. It's bad news, Joe." Sandy's eyes filled with tears.

"No . . . tell me." Like a gambler who had to lose everything before he gave up his habit, Joe refused to believe his fears until he heard the proof. "Your pneumonia isn't that bad!" He raked his fingers upward through the thatch of black hair hanging over his eyes.

"It's happened . . . everything they warned us about. I've got it, Joe. I've got AIDS." Sandy started to cry.

"Hhheeeee . . ." Joe blew out a long vocal breath. The energy with which he had kept his denial intact escaped like air out of a punctured tire. The reality was both he and Sandy might be victims of this deadly disease. He reached out to Sandy. "Don't cry. I can't stand it. It'll be all right; I know it will."

Sandy clung to Joe until his control returned.

Sandy recovered from the pneumonia in a week, and Joe took him home. He was armed with AZT, an expensive AIDS drug the doctor prescribed as "the only thing we have now that's doing much good." For the next few months they pretended—and almost believed—that everything was as it had been. Sandy did the cooking, Joe the cleaning, and when both returned from the library at the end of the day, they spent a half hour race-walking in the near-by park. Their evenings were generally quiet, at home, where the two movie buffs watched videos.

Sandy went back to the clinic weekly for check-ups. He did well for a while. Then race-walking became a strain. He couldn't keep up with Joe, and he couldn't last the usual half-hour. Joe noticed, and he slowed down. He also made excuses for stopping early. Both knew what was happening, but they had the grace to play the game.

Sandy started to cough again; that was when Joe noticed his partner was thinner. "Are you eating enough?" he asked, fear driving their game out of his mind. Always short and wiry, Sandy suddenly looked smaller, his pants drooping in the seat and gathered in folds at the waist. They could have belonged to a big brother.

Sandy nodded. "My cooking's the best." He grinned. "Seriously, I do eat everything I feel like eating. Sometimes I'm just not hungry." Joe's worry line etched deeper.

Within days Sandy's cough developed once more into pneumonia, and Joe took him back to the hospital. This time they had to celebrate Christmas there. Sandy's recovery took longer, and his doctor wouldn't let him go home for the holiday, even on a day-pass. Joe set up a mini-tree on the window-sill. Sandy tried to sing "Oh Tannenbaum, oh Tannenbaum . . .", a carol from his childhood. He forgot the German words after the first line, which was good because he didn't have enough breath to sing. They laughed, then sat quietly, both men knowing nothing was funny.

The doctor finally discharged Sandy from the hospital. This time the homecoming was less jubilant, more sober. Sandy walked without help, but slowly. Race-walking was out of the question, a thing of the past. Joe carried his bag, and while Sandy took a nap, he prepared their dinner.

The weeks flowed into months. Sandy had good days and bad, hiding the bad days the best he could. He never made it back to the library. He was hospitalized again, then two months later Joe found him in the bathroom coughing hard and speaking incoherently.

"Sun shines, everyone yes, yes, son-of-a-gun . . ."

Joe froze when he opened the bathroom door. "Jeez, Sandy, what's the matter?" He reached over and touched Sandy's face. "You're hot, aren't you? Do you have a fever?"

"Fevering, fevering, fevering . . ." Sandy sing-songed, looking at Joe without appearing to recognize him.

Joe jerked forward, put an arm around Sandy's shoulders and led him out to their car, then drove as fast as the law allowed to the hospital.

"You scared the hell out of me, Sandy." Joe sat on the edge of Sandy's hospital bed two weeks later. "You didn't make much sense, the way you were talking on and on. I was sure glad to get you in here where they'd know what to do." Sandy shook his head, embarrassed. They both laughed awkwardly, then fell silent.

Sandy's doctor came into the room. He stood for several seconds at the foot of Sandy's bed, eyes averted, then cleared his throat and forced himself to look at Sandy. His first words stuck in midstream. "I'm afraid you have very little time. The signs are in your central nervous system now, and that's bad. We can continue to treat you here, or you can be at home; the outcome will be the same. You must decide what you want to do." The stillness that followed pounded in their ears.

Joe's hoarse voice broke the quiet. "How much time?"

"A month, maybe. Two months at the most." The doctor was already turning. AIDS patients were coming in more frequently, and the inevitable death tore at his heart. The Hippocratic oath had long conditioned him to seek cure, sometimes to batter his work-weary body to continue the effort for recovery; he could not deal with this pre-ordained failure.

Joe gripped the headboard of Sandy's bed. Neither man moved a muscle. Sandy finally spoke. "We'll go home, Joe. We'll be together. It'll be all right."

Joe moved Sandy back into bed at home, thunderstruck at what they faced. Dealing with Sandy's dying was hard enough; he now had to help him with bathing, dressing, and moving from place to place in the small house they shared. In addition it fell to him to cook, clean, and do the laundry, all the while working full time at the library. Much as he loved Sandy, Joe couldn't handle everything alone.

He lay awake beside Sandy that night, shifting restlessly from side to side, then finally slid out of bed. He padded directly to the kitchen where, in a drawer under the phone, he retrieved a business card given them by a woman who had visited Sandy in the hospital. Sent by his doctor, she was a hospice nurse who explained their program and offered assistance if Sandy were going to be at home.

"Janice Miller, Primary Care Nurse, Hospice of Metro Denver," he read silently when he found it. "I'll call her first thing in the morning."

Joe punched the hospice number into the phone. Perspiration popped out on his forehead as he waited. Then, finally, too full of need to make small talk, he described Sandy. Janice, on her end of the call, wasted no words either; she confirmed their address and promised to come.

She arrived late in the day, a small, mature woman laden with bags. After completing the interview and exam, she smiled at Joe. "You do have your hands full. How have you managed by yourself? It's time you called us—we can help now." She was cheerful and upbeat, and by the time she left, a bright leprechaun with her white hair and kelly green suit, they were both smiling. Her visit injected strength into both Sandy and Joe.

On that same day the mailman brought an unexpected letter to Sandy from his maternal grandmother. She lived in Florida, and he hadn't seen her since junior high school. Her handwriting brought back images of chocolate chip cookies and trips to the zoo. He had tears in his eyes when he read what she had written.

Dear Sandy,
I can't write so good, but Ted Shanks is down here on vacation and told me your sick. You had real bad luck, and I'm really sorry. I'd sure like to help you. Am not to busy to come,

would you like that? If you have another bed I can sleep on
I'll pack my bag right away. Let me know.

Love,
Grandma

P.S. I can sleep on a roll-way. I bring my own pillow.

Sandy couldn't disguise his eagerness as he phoned his
grandmother that evening to accept her offer. "I just can't
believe it, Grandma," he kept saying over and over.

Joe went to bed that night without his usual deeply etched
worry line. Professional and personal help were on the way. He
was nearly asleep when he jerked, then rose off the pillow with
a start. "Sandy . . . Sandy . . ." he prodded his partner. Sandy
roused and grunted. "No one's ever watched us, I mean, living
together. Your grandmother—what will she think?" Sandy
rubbed his eyes for a minute, then turned away, hunching the
cover up over his ears. He had no answers. The men were facing
another unknown.

Joe met Sandy's grandmother at the airport a few days later.
Short and round, she wore a simple flowered dress and smelled
vaguely of lilacs. Her movements were quick for someone in her
seventies. She looked like a grandma used to look, from her
white hair knotted on top of her head to the sensible low-heeled
black shoes on her feet.

Her eyes swept imperceptibly over Joe, coming to rest on his
face above her. "You got a heavy load, don't you?" She spoke
with consummate understanding. Joe's hand dropped from his
forehead and a smile transformed his face. He leaned forward
and hugged her. "We're so glad you're here, Grandma."

Both Janice and Grandma were answers to a prayer. Sandy's
fitness was spent. His breathing was labored. Even turning in
bed was an effort. He no longer arose, either to eat or to go down
the hall to the bathroom, and on the sixth day at home he lost
control of his bladder. This was a turning point; he became a
full-time, needy patient. It would take both women to get them
through this ordeal.

Actually there were rich moments, as Janice noted in her
now-daily visits to see Sandy. She saw little acts of courage and

thoughtfulness among the three of them as she led Joe through the bed-bath procedures and offered suggestions to Grandma for nutritious soups and drinks that Sandy could be encouraged to swallow. Joe ran out to the store for the ingredients Grandma needed; Grandma found the iron behind a chest of tools in the utility closet and did a job on Joe's clean but perpetually wrinkled shirts. Sandy didn't thrive; he was beyond ever thriving again. But he allowed. He was sweet and loving to his grandmother; he tried hard to consume the food she prepared. He fought tears or any other outward show of distress when Joe was near; he could see how pained Joe became. While it was the hardest of times, in its own strange way it was the best of times.

Some days when Janice arrived Joe hovered over her, eager to learn what he could do to help Sandy. Other times he and Grandma took the chance to tend their own personal needs, and Janice stayed with Sandy.

"Janice, do you think I'll go to hell?" Sandy's question one morning struck out of the blue.

"Someone as kind as you? No way! Why would you think that?"

"Well, you know, I'm not religious—at least not churchy." Sandy looked carefully at Janice. "And now I'm going to die and I don't know what to think." He spoke very slowly, choosing his next words. "Being gay IS different, and I know my parents hate it. They think it's a sin. It's all mixed up together, God and my parents. The more I worry about it, the less I know what to think."

Janice waited.

"Have I been bad?" he finally asked. "Am I being punished? Can't Mom and Dad love me even a little bit? It's a hell of a way to say goodbye!"

Janice sat down on the edge of the bed. Sandy lay his long, slender fingers over his eyes.

"I don't know the answers," Janice said softly. "Would you like to talk it out with someone—someone who knows about these things?"

"Maybe," Sandy said slowly.

"We have a chaplain at hospice, Sandy. Frank Gorham—he's good at this. I think you'd like him. He really cares about people, and he doesn't judge them or preach at them. He listens, and he has a lot of insight that might help. How does that sound?"

"Would he come?" Sandy's voice was shy now, and touched with eagerness.

"I'm sure he would, Sandy. I'll ask him to call you."

The plan worked. Rev. Gorham and Sandy connected. They were quickly on a first-name basis, and Sandy revealed his worries.

"Sandy," Frank began when Sandy fell silent. "I'd like to call your parents. For one thing, they may not even know you're sick. For another, they could feel as bad as you do about their break with you. Give them a chance. If they come through, you'll feel better. If they turn you down, at least you'll have done what you could to make things right between you. What d'you think?"

Sandy pursed his lips tightly, scowling. "I don't know . . . they turned me away once already."

"You're still angry, aren't you?"

"I guess," Sandy mumbled.

"Afraid, too?" Frank probed.

"I suppose."

"Are you sure you want to confront them again? It might hurt more . . ." He paused, watching Sandy struggle. "Then again," he continued, "it might clear the air." Frank pulled back and waited for Sandy to decide. It had to be his call.

"This is hell," Sandy muttered under his breath. "Damn it! I never wanted to hurt them; why couldn't they see that?"

Finally he sighed, the decision made. "Maybe I'll regret this, but yes. I want you to call them. They live in Chicago—Joe has the number. Tell them if they can come, I'd like to see them." Sweat glistened on his forehead.

Frank placed the call that evening. "I'm Frank Gorham, the chaplain at Hospice of Metro Denver," Frank said to Sandy's mother. "We need to talk. It's about Sandy."

"What about Sandy?" his mother blurted back.

"He's quite sick. It's AIDS, I'm afraid." Frank spoke as gently as he could. "He has asked me to call you."

There was silence from the other end, then Frank heard tears in her voice. "No . . . I'll get my husband."

Frank waited. He heard the couple speaking hastily in the background, then another phone click on.

"Hello, who is it?"

"Frank Gorham here. I'm the chaplain in the hospice program that's caring for Sandy. He's at home now. He's trying to sort things out in his life, and he needs to talk with you. There isn't much time."

The woman gasped at the other end of the line. Then she spoke, barely in control of her voice. "Can we go, Harry? Right away?"

Frank waited to hear Sandy's father answer. "You can," he said at last. "For the week-end."

"Will you be coming, too, sir?" Frank asked. "Sandy would like to see both of you."

"No."

"Is there anything I can say to change your mind?"

"No."

Time stopped momentarily, then Sandy's mother broke the silence. "I'll be there Friday evening."

They arranged the details, then Frank hung up. He sat for minutes with his head bowed into his hands.

Early the next morning Frank stopped by to report to Sandy. Sandy took a deep breath when Frank finished. "Thank God Mom will come. What should I do about Dad?"

"Sandy, you have to come to grips with it. You've done nothing deliberately to harm them, and you've tried your best to make it right. If your father still has a problem, you can't take it over and make it yours. Let your anger go."

Sandy's expression was sober for a minute. Then he spoke. "Yes . . . It's strange. I don't really feel angry now . . . Just so sad. . . ." A smile suddenly lit up his face. "It's good to know I'll see Mom again."

Sandy reached his hands out as he looked up at Frank. "Oh, man, thanks. You've made . . . you've made things better." His voice broke.

"She'll be here soon." Sandy's excitement and anxiety spilled out to Grandma, Joe, and Janice the next week-end. "No, Joe, I don't want you to leave. I want her to see all of me—that means you too. That's what this visit is all about—I want it based on what I really am."

"You've got guts, Sandy. Gotta hand it to you."

Grandma smiled silently and patted Sandy's feet through the mound of bed covers, then motioned to Janice to follow her. "I'm making split-pea soup for our dinner, boys," she called out as she disappeared in the direction of the kitchen.

In a vaudeville gesture, Joe cocked his head to one side, extended his open palms from his shoulders, raised his eyebrows and smiled a big smile. "Well, how about that!" Sandy laughed, and Joe tumbled onto the bed holding his stomach. They both laughed until tears came. When Joe rose he touched Sandy's face. "God, that was good."

Janice plumped up Sandy's pillow and took his hand. "You're doing very well, my friend." His thin face shone with pleasure.

"What is it, Grandma?" Janice pulled on Grandma's sleeve when she reached the kitchen.

"I can hardly stand it, I'm so excited. I have to tell someone! Ever since I got here I kept wishing Elsie would come. That's my daughter—Sandy's Ma. I kept my fingers crossed, and I said a prayer every night. Never pushed Sandy, and I never said boo to Elsie—that husband of hers would get his back up for sure if I meddled in." Grandma stopped to take a breath, her face flushed. "But here you go—she's comin'! Bless their hearts, Sandy and Elsie. I sure do hope it works okay."

"I do, too, Grandma." Janice reached her arm around her shoulders and squeezed.

Sandy and his mother greeted each other with an embrace that began hesitantly, then blossomed into a genuine, loving hug. When they separated, Sandy smiled through his tears.

Then Grandma welcomed her daughter. The welcome signaled the end of a long separation—her own, and Sandy's as well. Both women were crying when Sandy's mother spotted Joe over next to the window. She straightened up, then slowly disengaged herself from her mother and wiped her eyes. She moved mechanically in his direction, her lips parted and eyes staring. Grandma and Sandy watched, mesmerized, as she reached Joe, then stopped stock still. No one said a word.

Like two statues they stood, facing each other. Suddenly they came alive. As if controlled by a main switch, each one thrust out a hand, and simultaneously they spoke. "Hello," the stilted words came out in unison. Shock registered. Then like twin puppets, they both giggled. Nobody moved. Grandma started to laugh, and Sandy joined in. Soon, all four were laughing so hard they had to sit down. Joe and Sandy's mother sat on one side of the bed, Grandma on the other, all rocking back and forth, unable to control their laughter. As they finally gathered their composure, Sandy's mother asked, "How will I ever describe this to your father?" Sandy and Grandma started laughing all over again.

The ice was broken.

The remainder of the week-end was open and strangely filled with joy. Mother and son reminisced, and Sandy and Joe filled in the long barren gap in Elsie's memory with stories of their library work, their race-walking haunts, their favorite videos, their escapades in finding the furnishings for the house. When the time came for her to leave and goodbyes to be said, she and Sandy clung together. "My dear son," she said at the end, "thank you. I will always keep this time close to my heart." She choked up, then whispered, "I love you, you know. Forever. I will pray for you, Sandy, and for your soul." Sandy squeezed her with all the strength he could muster.

"Mother," Elsie turned to Grandma when she finally pulled away, "I can never tell you how good you are—you will surely have your reward some day in Heaven. I wish I could stay. Please do what I can't do, and I will be so grateful—I'll call you every day." They embraced, then she turned to Joe. "I don't know what to say . . . you've given my son the love he needed when we . . ."

"No, no—don't," Joe interrupted. "I don't need all that. I'm just glad you came. You made him so happy."

"Thank you, Joe." She took his hand, squeezing it between both of hers, before she let him carry her bag to the cab waiting outside.

Janice returned on Monday. "How did the visit go, Sandy?" She looked carefully at his vital signs, noting some drop in his blood pressure.

"It was wonderful. Just wonderful. I couldn't have hoped for more." Sandy looked worn out but content.

"Marvelous! I'm really pleased, Sandy. Frank will be so glad to hear this, too."

Sandy gave Janice a blow-by-blow description of the meeting between Joe and his mother the day she arrived. Janice listened, and they were both laughing as she moved about the room preparing supplies for his bath.

Ten calm days followed, with Sandy gradually growing weaker. Frank came to see him. Joe was in the room.

"Bless you, Frank," Sandy greeted him.

"I'm grateful that it worked out. You can feel your mother's love now—and God's everlasting love is all around you. Can you tell?"

Sandy nodded.

"Know that it supports you—feel it—as you take your journey to be with Him." Frank seated himself on the edge of the bed so he could face Sandy at eye level. "Would a prayer help?"

Sandy nodded quickly, without words.

Frank reached for Sandy's and Joe's hands, and they bowed their heads together to pray.

As the time drew near, Janice spoke with Joe and Grandma about the signs of approaching death. "Do you see how Sandy is sleeping more and more? You can tell his body is giving up. All of his systems are slowing down. One day he may slip into a coma, and you should be prepared. It would be a light coma at first, then deeper until he dies." Then, seeing fear on Joe's face, she continued. "I'll be here often, and you can call me at any time—for questions, or if you think he is dying. I'll come to be with you if you'd like."

"Will he know anything if he's in a coma?"

"He'll be aware of what you say and do during the light part. You'll see some response. His eyes may move under the lids; his breathing may quicken; he may move a hand or a finger. We're not sure what he's aware of when the coma deepens, but we believe the last thing to go is one's hearing. If you have something you want to say, by all means say it to him. He could very well hear you and understand, or at least know you're there."

Joe and Grandma hung onto every word Janice said. When Joe left, Grandma shook her head. "It has to be hard to be so young and so scared." Janice agreed.

Joe and Grandma began to spell each other, one or the other staying at Sandy's side at all times. He had to be diapered, then turned at intervals so his hips, heels, and elbows, already padded with sheepskin, would not develop bedsores from pressure against the mattress. Joe managed this care when Janice wasn't there.

Sandy fought harder for rapid, shallow breaths, then gradually became less responsive. It seemed he slipped into a light coma for a day, then it deepened gradually with each shift. Joe and Grandma were ready to say goodbye.

A day went by, and another and another. Five days of watching seemed forever. The bearers of the vigil ministered to Sandy, moistening his lips, turning him, talking to him.

Then, finally and suddenly, it was over. It was strange, the way it happened. Joe discovered they were running out of diapers, so at the end of his watch he went to the store. Grandma decided she would have a cup of tea during her turn. For a few minutes she was in the kitchen. In their brief absence Sandy died. He took his last breath and left. With no one there to witness or cling to him, no one to cry over him, he took his leave. In his few unattended minutes, he died. It was over at last. He was free.

NOTES:
Aids Care; Spiritual Care; Humor

Sandy and Joe's story brings three issues to the surface. One is hospice care for AIDS patients, another the role of spiritual care in the overall hospice program, and last, humor and its place in end-of-life dynamics within hospice comfort care.

AIDS Care

The specter of AIDS loomed significantly in the United States in the early 80s. Within a year or two referrals of AIDS patients to hospice began. They were met initially with some resistance from staff because so little was known about this lethal illness—even by health professionals. Fear on the part of nurses, aides, and volunteers was understandable.

Gradually, with education and encouragement, hospices were able to change these attitudes and teach the necessary skills to their workers so they could respond to the needs of this patient group [3]. At the latest census available, 1992, AIDS patients comprised 4 percent of the patients cared for by hospices in the United States [4]. The literature suggests that proportion may now be larger. Hospice of Metro Denver, for example, cares for a substantial AIDS population—sufficient to warrant the publication of a four-page newsletter devoted solely to its service to AIDS patients.

Care practices have changed along the way, reflecting this growing acceptance of AIDS patients. Where total protective clothing was de rigeur in the early care of AIDS patients, hospice nurses tend now to use only gloves and sometimes glasses, and then only when handling body fluids. (Can you imagine the isolation patients felt when their caretakers' faces were masked and all visual reactions were sterile? When no one looked kind or warm-hearted; when a smile couldn't be seen? Hospice care must have been a mixed blessing for the early AIDS patients.)

With the increase in the rate of new AIDS patients slowing remarkably in the United States (85% increase rate in the 80's vs. 5% in 1995-96), and with new combined antiviral and protease inhibitor medication efforts together with the new *viraload* labtest to determine the level of HIV in the blood, the face of AIDS may change in this country, and we hope that will happen. Control of the disease, perhaps even cure may be possible in the future. For now, however, the prognosis for AIDS remains the same for all—a death sentence. Comfort care is appropriate and necessary.

Comfort care for AIDS patients now comprises much the same process as care for any other hospice patient. AIDS patients no longer are singled out in a way that sets them apart.

While death remains the known outcome of AIDS, we make a distinct and conscious effort to shift our AIDS patient's and family's focus from laboratory results, which were paramount in importance in the early management of the illness, to symptoms. No longer do T-cell (CD4 lymphocyte) counts matter. The issues that carry weight revolve around support and comfort, the same as for any other patient [5].

Unlike our other patients, however, with some AIDS patients selective active treatment may be added to their care for reasons quite different from the others. With non-AIDS patients, active treatment may be included solely to enhance the patient's comfort. For example, radiation or hyperthermia may occasionally be given some cancer patients in hospice—not for cure but to shrink tumors causing pain. Although ordinarily considered active, in this situation for non-AIDS patients, the treatment is really palliative.

But anti-AIDS drugs are given some AIDS patients as truly active treatment—to prevent pneumocystitis carinii pneumonia (PCP) and herpes; antibiotics are given for opportunistic infections; hydration is administered for fatigue and dizziness. These decisions will depend on the patient's condition and his desire for these treatments following counseling. These active treatments given some AIDS patients in the hospice program represent a departure from the usual hospice approach.

The hospice unit in St.Paul's Hospital in Vancouver has a formal model with both active and palliative treatment [6].

AIDS is so isolating and so fraught with intense, complicating issues of self-worth and public reaction that comfort care must include large doses of understanding and acceptance—attitudes which have to be communicated by the team. Perhaps the single greatest need these patients experience is for good communication. From an openness between the hospice worker and the patient, trust is built. If ever trust is needed, this is the time.

Hospice programs have poured on in-service education for their staffs in order to break down the early fears and allow trust to grow. AIDS patients now do receive more support. Unfortunately, some fears and prejudices are overcome reluctantly, so there is room for more progress.

Even in the best of climates, hospice care of AIDS patients can be frustrating—just because of the nature of the disease. AIDS has no predictable course. Nurses have found many of the symptoms unresponsive to their usual treatments. Nausea, for example, does not reliably improve with administration of the usual anti-emetic medications. Itching does not reliably respond to the usual nursing strategies. And so it goes. Providing care to AIDS patients can be very difficult.

The intravenous-drug-user AIDS patient poses special problems. Continued drug use, increased staff stress, and difficult interactions with funeral directors are but a few of them.

Nevertheless, hospice care has become feasible and compassionate for this group [7]. With the increase in hospice service to AIDS patients, savings are reaped which are both financial and humane [8].

Professionals in hospice service have reported that their stress is greater with AIDS than with other patients. These workers have difficulty with the fact that some AIDS patients are so young, and particular problems when the patient doesn't protect others. Nurses and others cope by talking with supportive colleagues, and by practicing good infection control [9, 10].

Difficulties in serving AIDS patients can be summarized with the following observations: patients rarely have stable social and economic situations; they have far more acute physical and psychological problems than most patients; they have fractionated support systems, often with alienation from their families; they want to hang on to hope for a cure, so acceptance of palliative care is reluctant; they may be seeing several doctors unknown to each other; they may have poor or no insurance; because of fear and ignorance, hospice programs may have difficulty finding volunteers; home visits may be in dangerous neighborhoods; patients may be overwhelmed by multiple, overlapping griefs; patients may be self-medicating; and frustration is high among the hospice team because they cannot meet all of the AIDS patients' needs[1] [11].

In health care as in any arena where problem solving is important, be it business, child-rearing, inventing, the creation of art, or whatever, success achieved the hard way is often the sweetest. We have invested effort and devotion into making our care of AIDS patients worthy and responsive to their needs, despite these problems, and we can see it has flowered into something of value.

Spiritual Care

AIDS hospice chaplain, F. Driscoll, has found among his patients a deep longing for spiritual fulfillment, spiritual acceptance and belonging, spiritual meaning and purpose, and spiritual peace [12]. He agrees with Kelley and Callanan who have said that perhaps the core of hospice work (with any, not just AIDS patients—authors' comment) takes place after symptoms have been brought under reasonable control; that the important thing is helping patients integrate their lives so they can die with some acceptance and satisfaction [13].

Driscoll, and Kelley and Callanan are right. Holistic medicine says human beings have four domains: biological, psychological, sociological, and spiritual [14]. Care that leaves out any one of them is like teaching adolescents about sex without a context of love and responsibility; the results are inadequate, empty, and perhaps destructive.

The spiritual needs of our patients must be addressed. How and by whom they are addressed are open to question, perhaps because those needs differ greatly from patient to patient. The word *spiritual* itself is used very differently by theologians and philosophers.

Spiritual is a multifaceted word. It is from the Latin, meaning *breath*, and is defined by Stiles as ". . . that which gives life to physical organisms, in contrast to purely material elements" [15, p. 235].

---

[1] Drawn from M. O. Amenta and V. Shubert, Vol. 12(2), 1994, *Home Healthcare Nurse*. Used with permission of Lippincott-Raven Publishers.

Millison and Dudley offer their reading of the word as ". . . pertaining to or consisting of spirit, soul or incorporeal as distinguished from the physical being" [16, p. 65].

Oldnall has in mind the perception of meaning, purpose and fulfillment of life [14].

Harvey Pothoff, Professor of Religion at Iliff School of Theology, relates *spiritual* to one's meaning and values [17].

John Morgan, Professor of Philosophy at Kings's College and coordinator of the International Conferences on Death and Bereavement, defines *spiritual* broadly as referring to the non-material aspects of life. He includes ethics, art, music, culture, literature, and religion which transcend their material aspects, manifestating spirituality. He ties spirituality to the specialness of the human being: our search for knowledge, our attempts to feel comfortable about ourselves and our place in the world, our ability to make decisions, the sense that we are part of a larger whole [18].

"Spirituality has been described," Zerwekh observes, "as the essence of personhood, the longing for meaning in existence, experience of God, experience of ultimate values, and trust in the transcendent. Its ultimate end," she continues, "is union or connection with a reality more enduring than the individual self"[2] [1, p. 26].

Munley considers spiritual caregiving the capacity to enter into the world of others and respond with feeling—a natural event in the hospice environment [19].

One of her patients put it in concrete terms, very simply, "They (hospice workers) give spiritual support by their love and actions. A lot of times it doesn't have to be any great outspoken thing either . . . the fact that they are so giving and so caring to me is spiritual"[3] [19, p. 245].

Spirituality not only is a dimension of our humanness, but it is uniquely human. Klass regards it as an awareness of a relationship to that which is beyond our senses, a capacity not

---

[2] © 1993 *American Journal of Hospice and Palliative Care*/Prime National Publishing Co. Used with permission.

[3] Reprinted from *The Hospice Alternative* by Anne Munley, copyright © 1983 by Basic Books Inc. Used with permission of HarperCollins Publishers Inc.

shared by other species [20]. He believes the spiritual is our aid and comfort in the face of death.

You will notice none of these statements makes spirituality synonymous with religion. Morgan defines religion more narrowly as a given system of beliefs. Individuals may or may not profess a religion, he says, but all have spiritual needs and concerns [18].

Spiritual is intended by some, however, to mean religious, or at least, in the view of Klass, to understand spirituality in the context of dying, we must turn to religion, a cultural institution. It is through religion, he believes, that communities are bound together in shared symbols, ritual, myth and ethical norms which can provide the meaning dying people seek—as long as those things have not become ends in themselves [20].

In view of the many religious orientations in the United States, ranging from atheist through no religion, personal religion, personal plus institutional religion, and institutional religion [19], the service hospice provides cannot be overtly religious without offending or doing harm to some of its patients. Hospice programs (those not sponsored by any religious group, particularly) stay clear of practicing or promoting a specifically religious orientation in their care.

The National Hospice Organization endorses philosophical, moral, and religious pluralism in its programs. It must. The NHO 1979 Statement on Religious Foundations of Hospice in the United States says:

Hospice care is concerned with the dynamic process of religion, that is, with binding together, tying up and tying fast. On the intrapersonal level, hospice endeavors to support the integration of the human personality in the face of the physical deterioration in impending death. The interpersonal dimension of hospice care seeks to promote the development and continuance of significant human relationship(s) between the dying person and other human beings. And finally, in regard to the eschatological dimension of human life, hospice care affirms each person's search for ultimate meaning by respecting and responding to each individual's personal truth[4] [21].

Within that broad framework, matters of spirituality are largely left to individual hospices in the United States.

Some would argue with this position. Munley feels that by being broad enough to cover the spiritual needs of everyone, even those with no formal religious beliefs, the statement causes hospice to lack an authentic sense of the dynamics of spiritual caregiving [19]. She cites William James who said yielding to the unseen reality—which might be the structure of the universe or a personal God or any concept in between—facilitates a transition from tenseness, self-responsibility and worry to equanimity, receptivity and peace [22]. This self-surrender, James believed, empowers the religious person to experience the negative as positive—called *grace* by theologians. Resting with James, Munley appears to want more specifics than the National Hospice Organization describes [19].

Robert Miller, Medical Director of St. Anthony's Cancer Center in St. Petersburg, Florida, in his review of David Moller's book *On Death Without Dignity: The Human Impact of Technological Dying* (Baywood Publishing, 1990), refuses to split the issues of spiritualism and religion. He said we should not be content with managing pain and symptom control but rather strive to provide a death with dignity that means more than a calm, controlled acceptance of death. He said patients should be helped in a way that transforms the dying process into a final opportunity for self-enhancement, growth, and an individually inspired quest for meaning. The problem to be solved, he feels, is to remain non-denominational in hospice while finding a way to put religious and spiritual meaning into the experience of dying [23].

Whether the program is religion-sponsored or broadly oriented, few would argue with the position that the role of palliative care or hospice programs is to create an environment where the patient's spiritual orientation can flourish

---

[4] Used with permission of the National Hospice Organization, 1996.

[24]. Brescia said so poignantly, "If there is any beauty in us as humans, it is our intense ability to find meaning and wholeness in the face of adversity, and to transcend . . ." [25, p. 339].

The sense that the responsibility for providing this spiritual support belongs to the chaplain, the nurse, the social worker, the nurse's aide and the volunteer, in short, the entire hospice team, is widespread [14, 26, 27]. All may be involved, but chaplains are considered by Burns to be the primary professionals concerned with the transcendent nature of life and the integrative role that spirituality plays in care for the dying. He feels that understanding spirituality in a person's living and dying requires an understanding of religion and theology, which generally spells *chaplain*. He adds, however, that a clergyman is not limited to religious language [28].

Where Burns believes the chaplain represents a perspective based on concern for the whole person, the whole family unit, and the whole staff, and probably functions that way, Swaggard opines that the clergy often do not know how to go beyond their sectarian prisms. He suggests they should get hospice training [29].

The first author's experience with hospice confirms the importance of spiritual support which can come in many forms from all on the staff, including and particularly the chaplain when the patient wishes to see him or her.

Spiritual caregiving is a challenge to teach to the hospice team, particularly when spiritualism is separated from formal religion. The subject becomes a virtual mist of abstractions, one which is outlined or specified only with great difficulty if at all. Through interviews with hospice nurses and the families they served, Stiles identified areas of nurse behavior in which spiritual support could be found [15]. They were: the nurse's way of welcoming a stranger, ways of giving and receiving, ways of being, doing, and knowing. From the warmth and respectfulness of behaviors in these areas, which could be generalized over the entire hospice staff, came a spiritual dimension that lent personal meaning and spiritual growth to the patient and family. Stiles characterized it as *being with* rather than *doing to* the patient.

Although a spiritual commitment is not required of hospice workers, there is apparently a bonus of heightened satisfaction for those who have the capacity and succeed in providing spiritual care [16].

The refreshingly clear norms for hospice team members recommended by Munley are: "1) don't impose your personal beliefs; 2) respond to the patient out of his own background; 3) don't proselytize at the deathbed; and 4) whatever the patient asks for in spiritual support, do it yourself or get someone who can[5] [19, p. 254].

Whatever spiritual care is, Dame Cicely Saunders, the founder of modern hospice, put her stamp squarely on the basic point: Spiritual care is not an optional extra [30].

The spiritual needs and spiritual care of dying persons have been the focus of many meetings since the early 80s. For fourteen years annual Conferences on Death and Bereavement have been held at King's College, London, Ontario, the most recent titled "Exploring Death and Spirituality." The International Work Group on Death, Dying and Bereavement has been convened in major cities around the world every eighteen months over a period of twenty-two years. The 1996 meeting was held in Delphi, Greece. A consensus on the importance of spiritual care led to two Conferences on Secular and non-Secular Issues in Death and Dying at Yale University, one in 1985 and one in 1986. A Sixth World Congress on Care of the Terminally Ill was held in Montreal in 1987. The National Hospice Organization held its first Conference on Spiritual Care in Hospice in 1991. All of these meetings devoted attention to the spiritual needs and spiritual care of dying persons.

The final text on spiritual care in hospice has not been written. More meetings will be held and positions may change. The authors know that, whatever happens, hospice will continue to offer support to the patient and his family in his spiritual journey toward death.

---

[5] From *The Hospice Alternative*, Anne Munley, copyright © 1983 by Basic Books Inc. Used with permission of HarperCollins Publishers Inc.

The Role of Humor

It may seem a far leap from spiritual needs to humor, but the two have a vital link. Humor, indeed, has a bearing on all aspects of care: spiritual, biological, psychological, and social. Humor has so many wonderful things going for it. And humor has its place in hospice, in caring for the dying. The words in Proverbs 17:22 are immortal and bear repeating: "A merry heart doeth good, like medicine."

Humor is a complex phenomenon which is only partially understood. It is a spontaneous expression of one's inner spirit.

We are not talking about jokes, necessarily, or other material that might be presented in an artificial way (although efforts have been made with some good effect to structure humor into health care—see [31]). Humor doesn't need professional comedians to prompt or provide it [32]. Rather, humor is a perspective that allows a person to take himself lightly while at the same time being quite serious about his work [33]. It is a natural outgrowth of human interaction, often responding out of a keen sense of and appreciation for the incongruous, the absurd. Spontaneity and humility enrich humor, if not being essential to it. Humor may rely on expectations being upset. It is a view of life that recognizes human frailty, cosmic jokes, and the indefatigable human spirit.

There is a special value to humor in hospice care. Allen Klein observes that it helps us cope because it instantly (even if briefly) removes us from our pain. He offers an appropriate line attributed to several persons including comedian Michael Pritchard: laughter is like changing a baby's diaper. It doesn't change things permanently, but it makes everything okay for a while [34].

As Klein points out, much of the suffering we experience comes not from our difficulties, but from how we view them. Dealing with a life-threatening illness may not be so much what causes us pain as how we relate to it. While the situation in which the dying patient finds himself is often a very difficult burden, adding humor can alter his perception and lighten that burden. Think what this can do for him! What is most important to hospice workers, good humor can be learned. Fears of being inappropriate or of how it will come off with the dying can be overcome. Knowing that humor often builds a bridge and increases both listening and communication can reinforce the nurse or aide. Those benefits are a bonus, for they decrease the patient's tension.

The perspective can be contagious, and when the patient responds, he discovers that humor has given him some internal control—an incredible gift when all that surrounds him seems so out of control.

Both the hospice worker and the patient find a remarkable tool when they learn to make use of humor.

The introduction of humor in a hospice relationship is best done if rapport has already been established. Then it should be unstudied, unplanned and good-natured, recognizing the patient as a peer. It cannot be sarcastic or at someone's expense [35], and black humor, of course, is as inappropriate as liquor for a six-year-old. It is strictly forbidden [36].

Humor is one of the first signs of trust in the emerging empathy between nurse and patient, and reflects joy or comfort in the new relationship. It is—or ought to be—an integral part of the nurse's way of being and doing, of giving and receiving— an outgrowth of his or her internal energy. When humor has this natural impulse, it can yield the spiritual dimension lending personal meaning and spiritual growth to the patient that we referred to earlier [15].

Humor also becomes a kind of adjunct therapy with the potential for healing, or at least feeling better [37]. Enhanced respiratory and cardiovascular functioning result from laughter. Heart rate decreases, blood pressure drops. And who hasn't felt the deep relaxation of skeletal muscles after a good belly laugh?

Humor distracts from pain, decreases tension and has been found on laboratory studies to release endorphins, nature's pain killers, and immunoglobin A [38]. Groucho Marx is reported to have said (with more wisdom than he knew) "A clown is like aspirin—only he works twice as fast."

The clinician who responds to a dying person with humor shows the patient that he exists beyond the sick role—he is still a whole person. Such reassurance has to be soul-satisfying. The director of one hospice told the story of attending the death of a patient, trying to keep his last hours comfortable. He was sponging perspiration from his patient's face. The patient was bald; the sponging extended across the top of his head. "Be careful. . . . You'll wash my hair away," the patient said with a twinkle. The hospice relationship was clearly that of peers, and one of warmth, one which thrived on humor. Within hours the patient died, surely a "good death."

Laughing in the face of death empowers patients and their families, as well as the hospice staff, to confront a taboo subject and rob it of some of its mysterious hold over us. Robinson believes humor is so important that the human need for it is as strong as the need for love, security, or trust. He would add it to the list of basic needs [38].

Humor links people. Interpersonal relationships of considerable depth become complete when humor is possible, and when it is shared. Without it, a dimension is missing. Without it, the partners to the relationship are deprived.

Humor is, indeed, the agent for many good things during one's end-of-life scenario. It can aid the biological, psychological, social, and spiritual parts of one's life; without it, closure lacks some spice that might have made it richer.

Humor has a hallowed place in hospice care.

REFERENCES

1. J. Zerwekh, Transcending Life: The Practice Wisdom of Nursing Hospice Experts, *American Journal of Hospice and Palliative Care, 10*:5, pp. 26-31, 1993.
2. M. Callanan and P. Kelley, *Final Gifts,* Bantam Books, New York, 1992.
3. C. S. Dukes, B. A. Turpin, and J. R. Atwood, Hospice Education about People with AIDS as Terminally Ill Patients: Coping with a New Epidemic of Death, *American Journal of Hospice and Palliative Care, 12*:1, pp. 25-31, 1995.
4. National Hospice Organization, personal communication, 1995.
5. C. F. Von Gunten, J. Martinez, K. J. Neely, and J. H. von Roenn, AIDS and Palliative Medicine: Medical Treatment Issues, *Journal of Palliative Care, 11*:2, pp. 5-9, 1995.

6. D. Kuhl, Dancing across the Lines: People in Pain, *Journal of Palliative Care, 11*:1-2, pp. 26-29, 1995.
7. W. Bulkin, L. Brown, D. Fraioli, E. Giannattasio, G. McGuire, P. Tyler, and G. Friedland, Hospice Care of the Intravenous Drug User AIDS Patient in a Skilled Nurse Facility, *Journal of Acquired Immune Deficiency Syndrome, 1*:4, pp. 375-380, 1988.
8. J. J. Kelly, S. Y. Chu, and J. W. Buehler, AIDS Deaths Shift from Hospital to Home, *American Journal of Public Health, 83*:10, pp. 1433-1437, 1993.
9. H. W. Nashman and C. H. Hoare, Psychosocial Impact of AIDS on the Professional Hospice Caregiver, *International Conference on AIDS, 8*:3, p. 112, 1992.
10. M. Slone and T. Stephany, Stressors of Hospice Home Care Nurses Caring for AIDS Patients: A Pilot Study, *American Journal of Hospice and Palliative Care, 12*:1, pp. 32-36, 1995.
11. M. O. Amenta and V. Shubert, Hospice Nursing and the AIDS Epidemic, *Home Healthcare Nurse, 12*:2, pp. 54-55, 1994.
12. F. Driscoll, The New Congregation: Reflections by an AIDS Hospice Chaplain, *Journal of Palliative Care, 11*:2, pp. 61-63, 1995.
13. M. Callanan, personal communication, 1996.
14. A. S. Oldnall, On the Absence of Spirituality in Nursing Theories and Models, *Journal of Advanced Nursing, 21*:3, pp. 417-418, 1995.
15. M. K. Stiles, The Shining Stranger: Nurse-Family Spiritual Relationship, *Cancer Nursing, 13*:4, pp. 235-245, 1990.
16. M. Millison and J. R. Dudley, The Importance of Spirituality in Hospice Work: A Study of Hospice Professionals, *The Hospice Journal, 6*:3, pp. 63-77, 1990.
17. H. Potthoff, indirect personal communication, 1995.
18. J. D. Morgan, The Existential Quest for Meaning, in *Death and Spirituality,* K. J. Doka and J. D. Morgan (eds.), Baywood Publishing, Amityville, New York, pp. 3-9, 1993.
19. A. Munley, *The Hospice Alternative,* Basic Books, New York, 1983.
20. D. Klass, Spirituality, Protestantism, and Death, in *Death and Spirituality,* K. J. Doka and J. D. Morgan (eds.), Baywood Publishing, Amityville, New York, pp. 51-73, 1993.
21. National Hospice Organization, *National Hospice Statement on Religious Foundations of Hospice*, Washington, D.C.
22. W. James, *The Varieties of Religious Experience,* Collier Publishing Co., New York, 1961.
23. R. J. Miller, Book Review of D. W. Moller, On Death Without Dignity: The Human Impact of Technological Dying, *The Hospice Journal, 8*:3, p. 97, 1992.

24. P. O'Connor, Role of Spiritul Care in Hospice: Are We Meeting Patients' Needs? *American Journal of Hospice Care, 5*:4, pp. 31-37, 1988.

25. F. J. Brescia, Killing the Known Dying: Notes of a Death Watcher, *Journal of Pain and Symptom Management, 6,* pp. 337-339, 1991.

26. P. O'Connor and M. Kaplan, Role of the Interdisciplinary Team in Providing Spiritual Care, in *Quest of the Spiritual Component of Care for the Terminally Ill,* F. Wald (ed.), Yale Universiy Press, New Haven, Connecticut, 1986.

27. M. Pizzi and J. Johnson, *Productive Living Strategies for People with AIDS,* M. Pizzi and J. Johnson (eds.), Hawarth Press, Inc., New York, 1990.

28. S. Burns, The Spirituality of Dying. Pastoral Care's Holistic Approach is Crucial in Hospice, *Health Progress, 72*:7, pp. 48-52, 54, 1991.

29. V. Swaggard, On Burying Platitudes, *Hospice, 5*:1, pp. 23-24, 1994.

30. D. C. Saunders, *The Management of Terminal Malignant Disease,* Edward Arnold, Inc, London, England, 1984.

31. M. H. Ackerman, M. B. Henry, K. M. Graham, and N. Coffey, Humor Won, Humor Too: A Model to Incorporate Humor into the Healthcare Setting (Revised), *Nursing Forum, 29*:2, pp. 15-21, 1994.

32. H. A. Squier, Practice Sketch: Humor in the Doctor/Patient Relationship, *Family Systems Medicine, 13*:1, pp. 101-107, 1995.

33. M. E. Killeen, Clinical Clowning: Humor in Hospice Care, *American Journal of Hospice and Palliative Care, 8*:3, pp. 23-27, 1991.

34. A. Klein, *Healing Power of Humor,* Jeremy P. Tarcher, Inc., Los Angeles, California, 1989.

35. L. Erdman, Laughter Therapy for Patients with Cancer, *Oncology Nurses' Forum, 18*:8, pp. 1359-1363, 1991.

36. C. West, Laughable and Sociable Commentary in Medical Encounters, in *Routine Complications: Troubles with Talk Between Doctors and Patients,* C. West (ed.), Indiana University Press, Bloomington, Indiana, 1984.

37. D. F. Groves, A Merry Heart Doeth Good Like a Medicine, *Holistic Nursing Practice, 5*:4, pp. 49-56, 1991.

38. V. M. Robinson, Humor in Nursing, in *Behavioral Concepts and Nursing Intervention* (2nd Edition), C. E. Carlson and B. Blackwell (eds.), Lippincott Publishing Company, Philadelphia, Pennsylvania, 1979.

CHAPTER 8

Letters and a Diary

Sometimes caring for a family in hospice is an unmitigated joy. That may sound strange, but you have to believe me. To watch a dying person and his loved ones and see that they understand and embrace the bedrock principles of healthy living and dying, and to be part of their experience, is to know fulfillment as a hospice nurse.

Because I feel so rewarded by them, and because these kinds of people are so special, it would not be fair to exclude from this collection of stories an example of a family that truly *lived* through a death. The family members suffered their loss and experienced the pain of grief, it is true. And they went through some of the rough spots that are normal between any two or more people. But they allowed no smoke screens, no pretenses. They had the time together, and used it well. They said all the unsaid things; they shared the memories; they earned an intimacy which enriched each one.

If I were defining a healthy death by example, I would tell you about Jonathon and Rose.

JONATHON

February 19

Dear Diary,

Oh God, the worst has happened. Dr. Palmer came to the room this morning. He held our hands . . . he told us there is no hope for Jon. Six months . . . They've done all they can. I can't think . . . I can't breathe.

Don't leave me, my only love—my dearest husband. You are my breath and my strength, my song and my joy. Stay by my side . . .

February 20

What a man! Jon is helping me rather than the other way around! He said this morning, "Rose, you must accept what is happening. We'll have faith and find the strength."

I'll try. Jon says our part on this planet is temporary, to draw from and give to with all our being, and when it's time to go we should leave as much as we've taken—maybe more. He's done that—not because he is a minister, but just because he's a good human being. He's the best human being I know. He'll always be in our hearts, the girls and mine. We won't ever let him go.

How will I survive?

I must call Susan and Joan. They need to know.

February 21

Dearest Joan,

You and your sister are the fountains in my desert. Thanks for being there last night when I called. I'm glad I can turn to you—that you're both old enough to handle the news. Our old friends from the church have been wonderful, but they're not family. With you I know I'm not alone . . . we have each other.

Dad is so sweet. He doesn't complain. He's very weak, but he understands everything. I'm still in shock. It was only a bad cold and stomach ache when he went into the hospital six weeks ago. To be sent home now to die is more than I can comprehend. If Dad were old-old, like nearly ninety, I'd understand. But mid-seventies—no. It seems like only yesterday we were fishing the Blue up at Breckenridge.

We both want to be grandparents . . . Dad would have made a wonderful grandpa . . .

I'll let you know exactly what we will do.

Much love,
Mom

February 21

Dearest Susan,

How blessed it is to have daughters like the two of you! I needed you so badly last night. Your voice was just the right medicine. I hope I answered some of your questions and helped you, too.

I think we ought to start a round-robin letter. Once Dad is home, I won't have much time for writing.

I wish traveling to Denver weren't so expensive for you. Why did you have to pick a college in Chicago for your work? And Joan in San Francisco. You're both too far for my liking. Maybe you and Joan could alternate trips home, so Dad will have more visits—and at the same time the cost won't be too great for either of you. I'd like to help out with the fare, but you know about a minister's pension.

We love you, dear.
Mom

February 21

Dear, dear Mom,

The news was a shock, even though I've been halfway expecting it. Dad, bless his heart, has so many things wrong. Pancreatitis and a bad gall bladder would do in anyone, long before the blood clots that hit his lungs. He looked so bad when I was there. What's amazing is that he's still with us.

I spent the evening crying—I'm not sure how much was grief and how much relief at knowing. Please try to be strong, Mom; we are all in this together. Call me whenever you feel like it. I love you both.

Susan

February 21

Dear Dad,

I just want you to know that I know—and I love you very much. My heart is so full. I'll come to be with you and Mom at spring break.

Susan

February 22

God give me strength. I need it for the girls, for me—and most of all for Jon. This is all too fast—too harsh. My heart is breaking.

February 23

Dearest Joan and Susan,

This will be the start of my joint letters—not round robin after all. I'll take turns sending carbon copies—just so you know I'm not playing favorites. Smile. Please write as often as you can, both of you.

Your phone call, Joan, and your letter, Susan, were a great help. Dad knows you care. I'm trying to find a cheaper long distance rate—I feel like such a spendthrift when I call. What phone company do you both use?

We've started to plan because Dad will leave the hospital in a couple of days. I've called a home hospice program—do you know about that? Cousin Jennie used hospice before she died, and all of us liked their way. They'll help me care for Dad so he can be at home. I'll send you some information.

The hospice people will order a hospital bed. We'll set it up in the den. Then Dad can look out through the dining room to the garden. I'll add another bird feeder, and it won't be long before the forsythia leafs out and the crabapple blossoms. The view will be a tonic for him—for both of us.

* * * * *

So many people were in and out I didn't get this letter mailed. Now it's Wednesday.

Today the hospice nurse came. You'd like her. Janice Miller— she's small and quick-moving, and white-haired like me, but not as old. You'd never guess she was a nurse, with her emerald-green turtle-neck sweater and slacks. She wore one of those ski caps with the pointy tops, in flaming orange. She has bright, twinkly eyes, like a pixie, and her laugh ripples out a lot. It's good to hear. She's upbeat, which surprised me. Not the sad long-suffering type you might expect in this kind of work. She and Dad hit it off right away. In fact, she asked him if she should call him "Reverend Gilliam" and he said no—to call him Jon.

And I'm Rose. We'll all be first names. She'll come to the house twice a week, until we need her more. And here's good news—Medicare covers her visits!

I'm glad we'll have her. A hospice nurse knows about everything we'll need, and already I feel she'll be ours.

She'll meet us at the house when the ambulance brings Dad home tomorrow. She's going to teach me how to give him a bed bath and chart his temperature and pulse and all of that. I hope I can do everything right.

I can't wait to *do something*. Sitting by and watching all these weeks in the hospital has been awful—I've been as much use as a third leg—no good at all.

Dad doesn't complain, but he sleeps fitfully and eats next to nothing. Maybe he'll do better at home. We've talked some about the future months. We both want to use them well.

I can't wait to get him home. Be with us in spirit, okay?

Love,
Mom

February 23

My love will be home tomorrow, and we'll start down this path together. I'm on tenterhooks; my heart pounds. We've ministered to lots of people in the congregation as they approached death, and we know there's nothing to fear—dying is part of living—*but we don't know what the next six months will hold. I don't want Jon to suffer. And I can't bear to lose him.*

Please God, give me strength.

February 24

Dear girls,

Dad's home! He's happy, but exhausted. His transfer to the ambulance went okay. I rode with him. (No siren, thank you!) He looked so relieved to be home. Janice was waiting, and she helped me get him into the adjustable bed. What a great invention that is!

Janice thinks we're going to manage fine. I'm glad someone believes in me. I'll do my best, but confidence isn't my strong suit right now.

Bless Bob and Ellen next door. They came over and helped me move the wide bookcase out of the den into the back shed so I'll have more room to navigate around the bed. Little Bobby and Rachel stood outside and waved to us when the ambulance got here—they're such darling kids. It was like a party, his homecoming.

My mind won't stop racing—it goes like a car-wash rotor out of control. I'm trying to remember all the things Janice taught me today. Medicines, charts, diets . . . I wrote it all down. There's so much I didn't know. I'd never be able to do this without her.

Now I must get to bed—need to sleep while Dad does. Take good care of yourselves.

Much love,
Mom

March 1

Dearest daughters mine,

Bless you for phoning, both of you. Dad loved it . . . The comedy sketch you described, Joan, was great.

Dad's having trouble with something. I'm not sure if it's diet or medicine, but he thrashes around and twitches and can't sleep at night. Neither of us has slept much since he came home. Janice talked with me, God love her, and now she's going to have a night aide come and watch over him. Then I'll shut my door when I go to bed so I can get some rest. Janice is going to ask Dr. Palmer about changing the medication. I surely hope it works.

I brought the stereo in from the living room. Dad still loves his music (some things never change.) I think we'll wear out Four Seasons and Mozart's 41st, he wants them so often. Being home is a blessed gift.

We've started going through photo albums. We do only a few pages at a time, so we can savor the memories. Do you remember the time we drove up Hoosier Pass—you were just little tykes—and we saw that brilliant rainbow so close you both screamed—and then you wanted to get out of the car because you were sure the pot of gold was right there in front of us? Dad and I could see it all over again. Those were great days. What dear children you were!

I trust both of you are well, and that your work is going along okay. Let us know.

Must close. Dad's waking up. Love you both,   Mom

March 2

As a barber I'm a miserable failure. I sliced Jon's cheek today while I was shaving him—the crease at the corner of his mouth caught the razor, and zip I did it. With his old twinkle, he accused me of getting even for all those boring sermons. Dear Jon, he makes me laugh when I need it most.

March 8

Dearest Susan and Joan,

Bad windstorm last night. I thought the howling would never stop. This morning there were branches and leaves down everywhere. When I got up during the night to look out the windows I saw the aide fussing over Dad, who must have been as anxious as I was. (The aide is a big, solid-as-a-rock young Swedish woman, and her very presence should reassure him. It does me.)

Are you girls okay? It's not fair to give you such little attention, but for now the supply is exhausted with Dad. You would choose that, I know.

I searched for the paper on the Elizabethan period that you asked for, Susan, but I can't find it. You have several cartons of stuff in boxes here, so I can't be sure. I'll look again when I have time.

Having the night aide here is helping. I can stop my watching long enough to get some rest. The constant vigilance was hard. I felt as if some invisible genie was sucking my strength out through my eyes and ears—a little more each day. Now I'll recoup. Dad surprises me; he still isn't sleeping much, yet he functions better than he did in the hospital. He sends you his love.

You'd be proud of me. Janice is! I give Dad his bath and manage his charting, and you'd think I trained at Johns

Hopkins! Everything is going as right as we can hope for. Janice likes us, I can tell. She comes on Monday and Thursday, cheery and so welcome. The aide is here every night but Saturday.

Bobby and Rachel have been in almost every day. They bring drawings for Dad—turtles and birds and houses and stick-figure-people—and I've taped them all over the den. First I was afraid to let the children get up on the bed with Dad, but then I decided what can they harm? So now they climb right up and give him a kiss, and do you know, Dad puts an arm around each one and he loves it! He fell asleep this morning in that position, three heads propped against the pillow, and the children still chattering on. I should have taken a picture.

Only a month 'til your visit, Susan. We'll count the days. Be prepared—Dad is very thin and wan. He's not in pain, however, so we're content. Joan, maybe you can make it in May. Hope so. Must close—Bye for now.

> Much love,
> Mom

March 15

Today was a pretty good day. We went through some of the girls' school folders. Susan was so sweet and thoughtful—with her sunny, blond curls—and Joan so different—full of imagination, our black-haired livewire, no inhibitions at all. She was born for the stage. The memories are good for the soul.

I can't believe that Jon can lie there day after day. I asked him how hard it is, flat on his back, not being able to walk in the garden or work on his papers. He took my hand and told me he could live contentedly like this for a long time. He misses being active and involved, he said, but nothing hurts, and it's very special going through these old things together, remembering. He smiled through his dear blue eyes, and I couldn't help it, I started to cry. I lay down next to him, and he held me, warm and close, our tears all mixed up together.

Crying together, even when it is so sad, is like a warm cup of cocoa. It cushions the needles in my stomach. 'Specially with his arms around me, holding me close. Oh God . . .

Good night, my beau-lover.

March 25

Am I some kind of ogre? Jon is so patient, and I want to be kind and loving—but today my reserves ran out. I jabbed him, pushing the clean sheet under as far as I could before rolling him over on it—and it wasn't really an accident. How awful I am. He can't help being so slow. What's happening to me?

April 1, 4 P.M.

Rose—

I had to leave before you returned. Hope you enjoyed your respite while the volunteer was here. She and Jon were getting on fine; you should have a break more often.

The new medicine must be working. The aide reports Jon has been much calmer and sleeping longer. Let's see how you do without her one night, and then call me on my beeper, would you please?   Janice

April 1

Dear ones,

Janice brought a volunteer from hospice with her today. I hadn't been out of the house since Dad came home—neighbors have been getting the groceries for me—and I was going stir-crazy. Janice could tell. She brought this young woman to stay with Dad so I could have three hours away. I hugged Dad and Janice (she's like family now), and then I left.

I shopped for the birthdays coming up in May and June. Then I drove over to Cranmer Park, up on the hill, and just sat and looked out at those gorgeous snow-covered peaks and breathed in the almost-spring smells. We still feel winter's chill, but new life is in the air. It fills my heart—how good it will be!

Those few hours were like a month in the country.

Then when I got home, guess what! The hospice volunteer had washed the living and dining room windows. They sparkled, and now all that spring wonder can come right into our house! It is marvelous. Dad caught it, too. He had an extra gleam in his eyes when I took care of him this evening.

Susan, when you come next week, pack for both warm and cold. Dad says don't bring anything, just yourself. While we're not prepared to have you come nude, smile, Dad has his priorities straight. Our time is precious, and we should use it for the important things, not appearances.

I don't have time now for more. Oh, Susan, I found your paper. I'll save it for when you come. King Lear isn't one of my favorites, but if your students like it that's all that counts. Will you begin with that after the spring break?

It'll be great to have you here. Give us your flight schedule when you can. I'm sure Bob or Ellen will want to pick you up at the airport.

Wish you could come too, Joan. Soon, I hope. Bye now.

> Much love,
>
> Mom

April 9

Susan is home at last. I hugged her hard and could feel the strength in her slim body. How young she is—how little she knows of loss and dying. Yet somehow I know she'll be all right.

Jon had fallen asleep with the bed tilted up; he roused and his face flushed when we entered the room. Susan's voice broke, and they both started to cry. I didn't know which one to help; I just wanted to hold both of my weeping loved ones in my arms.

Susan dried Jon's tears with a tissue, then she blurted out her first words.

"You're so small."

Weird—but I guess he's all eyes and eyebrows now, and she hasn't been watching the change take place. Nobody said anything, then we all started to laugh. After that we couldn't stop talking—even after Jon fell asleep.

It should be a wonderful weekend.

April 17

Dear Mom and Dad,

Flying home, I kept thinking about you. I just had to write a quick note before I got all wrapped up in my classes.

You two and Janice are so open about your illness, Dad, and about what I still have trouble saying in words, your dying. I've never seen anyone strip away the taboos, the fears, the way you have. At first it upset me. I didn't think I could handle it—listening to you, Mom, talk about what to plant next year when you'll be alone, and Janice asking whether you, Dad, had written your request yet for no resuscitation. A part of me froze—an iceberg where my stomach should be.

But over the next few days the tightness in my chest eased, and the frog in my throat disappeared. I relaxed and enjoyed being with you . . . I could see for myself how much better it is this way.

I don't know who's responsible, but you really have achieved something remarkable. I can tell you are sharing this part of your lives and it makes your marriage richer . . . And Janice is so nurturing—the three of you made me feel warm and good. It's amazing. No secrets, no fake optimism, no working at a smoke-screen—and all your time and energy can go to the right things, to using your time.

I'm so proud of you.

Love
Susan

May 6

Janice brought a wheel chair with a water cushion today. Together we moved Jon, wrapped like a babe in swaddling, out to the back step where it was sunny. He's very thin and weak, but he looked around at the garden and beamed. Five minutes was all he could take—it was worth the effort.

May 10

Dear Joan,

Let's hope you get to see Dad in the wheel chair outside when you arrive. He can tolerate a half-hour of sitting now, and his color, his eating, and his sleeping are all better!

Bob and Ellen will pick you up at the airport on Thursday—we'll be waiting for you!

Love
Mom

May 10

I can't help it—I'm starting to hope. I know I shouldn't, but he's doing so well. His voice is stronger. Today Janice was here, and Jon teased her like he would have done a year ago—said with her handwriting, she was really a doctor, going incognito as a nurse. Tonight he asked me what was going on in the Persian Gulf. I didn't even know he knew about it! He is so much more tuned in than he was.

Bobby and Rachel saw him outside and came over to show off their cartwheels and handstands, if such they can be called. "We do cobatics," Rachel shouted as they approached. In her three-year-old mind, I'm sure she considers herself and her brother skilled acrobats. Jon applauded when the show was over.

Those two children adore Jon . . . he laughs at their antics, and it warms my heart.

May 13

Joan arrived today. She scares me sometimes; she is so poised and worldly. Nothing rattles her. She launched right in after the hellos with her replay of a day at the TV station, and she had us in stitches. She dresses like a career woman in magazine pictures, and I marvel that we could have produced such a child.

May 20

Joan carries on as if nothing is happening here. I don't understand—she has to be frightened. She tells her stories and jokes and she's always washing her hair and fussing over her make-up. You'd never know she's going to lose her father pretty soon. I want to scream at her, don't you see he's dying? Can't you make him feel special?

I guess it wouldn't do any good. Joan is Joan. She has to find her own way to deal with this. I just hope she can cut through the cover before it's too late.

May 21

Susy—

Will leave Denver tomorrow. Pop's pretty cool—likes to sit outside in the sun. Mom and I took him out in the wheelchair for a little while each day. He watches the iris grow and dreams about his corn and tomatoes, I guess. Doesn't say much, so I put on a show about my job. You know, "let me entertain you." (Sing it, Susy.)

Hey—send me a video of your King Lear.

Cheers . . . J

June 18

Susan's here, thoughtful as ever. She plans to stay the whole week, and Jon and I are up for a good, relaxing time together. He remains interested in everything, and while he has no endurance, he loves having Susan around.

I baked four pies today. They smell so good out in the back shed. "Jondear," I called from the kitchen, "you'll never guess what I've made." He rang his little bell, and when I got in to the den he was smiling like a contented cat. "Cherry pie," he gloated. The aroma had filled the whole house. I couldn't surprise him.

Tomorrow we'll have a party.

June 19

I brought the first Peace roses of the season in from the garden today. Their blush of color—their perfection—catches my breath. Jon took one look at them and started to cry.

He's doing that a lot lately—crying. He gets over it quickly, but it upsets me.

Susan is with him for long periods. She reads to him, or they talk, and sometimes they just sit, holding hands. She is a gift. . . .

June 24

Dear Joan,

Susan will be leaving tomorrow, and Dad's spirits have thrived with her visit. Now we're eager to see you. Three weeks roll by very quickly, so it won't be long.

Dad hasn't changed much since you were here. His face is still thin; his eyebrows don't seem as bushy. More single grey hairs spike way out over his eyes like wire. And they're not as blue as they used to be—his eyes. They've faded, more like a reflection of what once was. He has lost a little more weight, I guess—his appetite is fair—and he still wants to know what's going on in the world. I think you'll have a good visit.

Be sure to bring the press clippings from your last show. We'll both love to see them.

Much love,
Mom

June 26

Joannie,

When you get home, would you see whether you could take Mom out to lunch or something? . . . She needs a treat. Ask Janice to get a volunteer in to stay with Dad. I'd be grateful if you would.

We had a good visit. Dad looks forward to seeing you. You bring some sparkle into his life that only you can make.

School's back in full swing . . . My classes aren't too full this term. English majors must do a lot of traveling in the summer—or working, one.

Have a good trip. Let me know how it goes.

S.

June 26

Jon told me we should get a financial advisor for me. We were trying to decide whether to put the bonds in the girls' names now. I just don't know what to think; I know so little about money mattters.

Why must you die, dear heart? Can't you see I need you?

July 7

I wonder if I'm making life more difficult for Jon. I do all the things Janice tells me to do, but is it right? Maybe I'm just dragging his life out—keeping him forever in limbo. He cries, he lies there by the hour, he can't do the things that used to mean so much to him. It breaks my heart.

Am I being selfish? Am I hanging on, at his expense? Should I let him give up, and give up myself? This has been going on so long, I don't know what's right any more.

July 9

Today Jon tried to reach for the photo album before I could get there. It fell and dumped pictures all over the floor. He started to cry, and I tried to cover it all over the best I could. He fell asleep with tears on his cheeks.

I can't stand this. What can I do to make him feel better?

July 10–3:30 P.M.

Oh dear God. I did it.

I just had to talk with Janice. When Jon took his afternoon nap, I sneaked out the back door and drove over to her home. I let it all out—I told her about his crying so much, and maybe I'm taking such good care of him that he'll drag on and on, and what should I do?

She heard me out. Then she suggested I ask Jon what he wants. She reminded me he has no tubes, no artificial feeding, no adrenalin shots—just a blanket of love and reasonable comfort—and death will come when nature takes its course. She thinks I'm doing just right. His crying is common, and I shouldn't be distressed, she said. Just accept it and go on. She was so reassuring. This funk I've been in, suddenly it evaporated.

But when I got home, Jon was awake. He was angry because I hadn't answered his little bell or left him a note (where was my mind!) and he worried the worst things—an awful accident—on the basement steps, in the bathtub, maybe in the car. He was frantic.

In his terror, he spilled the urinal into the bed. Everything was soaked when I got there. He saw me and fell apart. He swore, he cried—it was awful.

I lied·to him—God help me. I said we were out of his laxative so I had to run to the store. The excuse didn't help. I tried to apologize. He accused me of not caring . . .

NOT CARING? That's all I needed to hear after all I've done for the past five months. I slammed my purse down and walked out of the den.

I know I did wrong, but I'm angry—I'm hurt—I've never been so miserable.

* * * *

How could we get into such a mess? I just want to hide, I am so ashamed.

* * * *

10 P.M.

I can't go to sleep without adding this note. The tempest blew itself out, thank the good Lord. After I calmed down and could think straight, I returned to Jon with a pot of tea, to make amends. And Jon reached out for me, holding my hands when I sat down on the edge of the bed. He apologized and kissed me, and we both tasted tears. I told him about my talk with Janice. What a relief to let him in—to share it all. As it turns out, he wants to live out each day left to him—just what we're doing.

I will NEVER hide my concerns or try to make decisions without him again. Everything must be out front where we can think it through together.

July 11

Hey, Joan,

Last night Mom called me in tears. I don't know what's going on, but I thought you should know before you get there. I hope you can give her a boost.

Have a good visit.

Love
Susy

July 11

Rose—

As sick as Jon is, he still thinks about others. When I walked in today he asked about my daughter—the one who fell last month up at Bergen Park. I told him she's doing better, and he said to take one of his Peace roses to her. He has to be 90 percent saint!

Sorry I missed you . . . The aide said you'll be back soon. I'll stop in tomorrow.

Janice

July 12

Janice,

I can only say, thank goodness for the other 10 percent! Smile . . .

R

July 14

Rose—

Joan is struggling. I saw her leaking tears right through her shell after you left the house today . . . She protested when I approached, but I put my arms around her anyway. . . . That's all it took—she broke down completely. I urged her to cry, to let it out. My, what a deluge. It would have done your heart good.

When she quieted, I led her to the back deck where we could sit and talk. "I've tried so hard to make him happy," she told me. "I never let him talk about being sick. I just make it fun . . . but I . . . I . . . I can't anymore. I can see . . . I know he's going to die." And she burst into tears.

I let her go on until she got it out . . . Then I said I thought it would be good to tell her dad how she felt—how hard she found it to deal with his illness. I said they might feel closer, and relieved to have it out in the open. She looked alarmed, then thoughtful.

I felt you ought to know . . . .

Call me if I can do anything. J

July 14

Joan showed a crack today, finally, and Janice, bless her heart, was there to help her. All it took, I guess, was to show Joan it was all right to let the feelings out.

I had a good talk with her later. She is scared, and she's finally admitting it. I held her and confessed I'm afraid, too. That seemed to help. I urged her to try to talk to Jon; to just let out what she feels.

She said, "I can't. I guess I want to, but I look at him and my throat closes up. All that comes out is silly stuff. I can't say what I feel."

I told her he would be honored by her opening up, and they both would feel closer—and better. She should remember how it was when she learned to dive, I said—take a deep breath and jump right in—fast—before her fear could stop her. I also warned her as gently as I could that later she might regret not taking the chance she has now.

It's up to her. I hope she can get through her barriers—my dear, talented, tied-in-knots daughter.

July 18

Joan left today. I shall miss her. And I'll worry about her. I don't know what she managed with Jon. I couldn't tell a difference.

July 18

Susy—

Just got in from the airport. I did get Mom out for a lunch spree—(Cliff Young's; she protested the elegance but loved it), and then we spent an hour at the Tattered Cover browsing the gardening books—her choice, as you might guess. When we got home Dad was asleep and the volunteer was cleaning up the kitchen, so it all turned out well. 'Twas a good idea, my fair maid.

Now—I'm having a problem. Help me, Suz. Janice and Mom are at me to talk with Dad—straight talk—admit he's dying—let out the gorilla in the pit of my stomach that won't let me be honest with him. Mom knows how I feel. She says just jump in. But I couldn't do it—not this trip. I tried, I really did. What am I going to do? You've always been so good at this, while I always seem to be on stage. Why can't I be like you?

J.

July 19

Dear Mom and Dad,

Home safe. Thanks for everything. Please tell Janice she is a jewel. Next time we'll really do it up right, Mom—lunch at the Brown Palace. Big hugs for both of you.

Love,
Joan

August 1

Dear girls,

Dr. Palmer gave Dad six months, and they're almost over . . . I can't believe it. The days flow into weeks, and the weeks become months . . . I am lulled into the feeling that we'll just keep talking and looking at pictures and listening to music and having you visit, endlessly. In my head I know that's crazy . . . but if I don't think about it, that's the way it feels.

Janice has added a quickie Saturday visit to her Monday/Thursday schedule here. I phone her any other time we have questions. Life goes on.

There is no news. My letters are dull, I'm sure. Bobby and Rachel keep us entertained—although they haven't been here for a few days. Colds, I guess. Take good care . . .

We love you,
Mom and Dad

August 2

Jon seems very quiet today. Says he feels okay, just tired. Hope all is well.

August 3

Damn! Damn! Even that isn't strong enough! Jon is sick. Why did I let the children in last week? I should have known they could get sick—all kids catch bugs. Ellen says they have flu. Why did I let them get up on the bed, so close to Jon, and kissing him, of all things?

Janice called Dr. Palmer, and he just said aspirin and lots to drink. She's coming out in the morning, unless his temp gets up to 100—then I'm to call her right away.

August 4

We'll take it day by day, Janice says. In Jon's condition, flu is a blow we don't need. He looks awfully sick—deep, dark hollows around his eyes, which he barely opens—scarcely any voice— unable to lift his head . . . Last night was tough—he slept only for snippets. And when I got him ready for sleep tonight, he started to cough. Temp is up, and he complains his ears hurt and he aches all over. I wish I could make it go away . . . I am so tired. . . .

August 4

Dear girls,

I don't want to alarm you, but Dad has the flu. He needs your prayers more than ever. He's not in much shape to fight it by himself. Janice is coming every day, so we're doing everything we can. There is no miracle antibiotic for flu, but we're pouring on the TLC.

I'll let you know if I think you should come home.

Meanwhile, I'm hanging on to the plan for a birthday party for him on the 24th, so keep your reservations. It will mean so much for you both to be here. Think positively—Dad is holding fast so far. I'll stay in touch . . . Much love,

Mom

August 8

Dear girls,

We're heartened—Dad's still pretty sick, but Janice says the first few days were the test. She thinks he may pull through this.

Your calls were a great help to me. Your support means more than I can say . . .

Much love,
Mom

August 12

I don't know whether to be happy or not. Jon's fever has left him, but so has his interest in the world. He's kind of blahh. . . . He survived the flu, but Janice says it would take a healthy person a long time to recover—and he doesn't have that much time.

He told me today he is ready to die whenever his body decides to give up. I can still feel the lump that knotted up in my throat. It hurts to breathe. And I thought I was prepared. . . .

August 18

My dear girls,

Ken Graham, Marge Kaplan, and Sylvia Rhode have all visited Dad this week (Sylvia is as absent-minded as ever). He enjoys seeing old friends, although he fell asleep each time after only a few minutes. He pays attention only briefly, then drifts off. The flu took a lot out of him, I'm afraid.

Everything is still go for his birthday. It will be quiet, but good. Bob and Ellen will meet your planes.

Much love,
Mom

August 24

What a strange birthday! After we sang and blew out the candles, Jon asked Janice to sit with all of us, and tell us exactly what lay ahead. In her own loving way, she put it all out on the table. I sat on the edge of the bed, Susan and Janice were on chairs facing the bed, and Joan stood vigil at its foot. None of us moved a muscle as she spoke—her voice strangely calming the turmoil inside me.

She said Jon's body had gradually slowed down, and the flu had stripped him of what reserves he had left, so his death could come soon. He nodded his head, and I reached to hold his hand. She said he would sleep more and more, then probably slip into a coma. At first he would look unconscious, but still have moments of hearing and knowing, and we should feel free to talk to him and touch him. He asked if he would feel pain or discomfort, and she said no. We should keep his lips and mouth moist with some special sponges she has, and turn him frequently, and he will be fine. His relief showed, and by now my tears were partly gratitude.

As the end approaches, she said the color would leave his face and skin, and his breathing would become shallow and irregular, and as he reaches total release, all tension would disappear from his muscles and we would likely see a beautiful expression of peace on his face. She has seen it many times. I'm glad she said that; it comforted me some.

We were all quiet for moments, then Susan broke the silence.

She asked how long the coma would last. Janice couldn't predict, but she said maybe a few minutes and maybe a day—she didn't think much longer.

Then Susan asked if she and Joan should extend their stay. Janice couldn't advise them but said it could be two weeks or more before Jon died.

I glanced at Joan. She stood riveted to the footboard, her lips parted, staring at Janice. I rose and moved to her side and put my arm around her shoulders. She trembled slightly, but continued to stare. I couldn't get her to shake loose.

Then Jon rallied; he raised his hands and reached for Janice. When she approached him, he drew her face near and kissed her on the cheek. "Bless you," he said, and sank back on the pillow. In moments he was asleep.

Janice hugged each of us, reassured us we could call her, and left.

I give thanks that there was time for a birthday, and that the girls could be here. And I'm glad we could have this

extraordinary help from Janice. Jon is content, I am more ready,
and Susan told me she feels calm—that she will cope. Joan
remains the question. I'll try to help her.

Happy birthday, my dearest one-and-only beau-lover.

Sept 1

Dear girls,

It is good you chose not to stay on after Dad's birthday.
Things haven't changed much. Dad is about the same—asleep a
great deal of the day, able to focus on things for only brief
periods, and generally weak but content. We can still share
some lovely moments—like a glorious sunset last night. Dad
called it a preview, and smiled.

I have thought so much about you both. You were able to say
goodbye while Dad was still responsive. He knows you love him,
and you know how much he loves you. That is a richness many
people don't have, and you can always cherish it.

Janice comes every day. She asked about you. I've thanked
her for all of us.

I will let you know of any change. You can decide when you
want to return.

We love you,
Mom and Dad

September 14

I haven't had a minute . . . Even now, the girls will arrive any
moment and I may not be able to write much . . .

Jon died last night. He had been in a deepening coma for over
a week. I stayed at his side most of the time, spelled by Janice
and for brief periods, by a volunteer who promised to call me if
there were any change.

I talked to him sometimes, sometimes I just sat and held
his hand. Several times I think he heard me—a flicker of his
eyelid, a change in breathing . . . I bathed him, I shaved him
each day, I moistened his lips and mouth and I turned him every
couple of hours. I did all the things I felt like doing, and it was
good. I have loved him for all these years, and this was no
different . . .

I thank God for his love—that I could be his mate, early on and all the way through, to the time I laid his hands across his chest and said goodbye. I thank God I had the strength to stay by his side, giving him my love until the end.

I thank God, too, for Janice who took me when I was frightened and unknowing and showed me I could do it . . . who believed in me, who came when I called, who offered the resources that made our final odyssey possible, who helped guide Susan and Joan through their struggle with losing their father. They can look back now, and feel tender and warm.

Jon did not want to leave me . . . I know, because it took him so long to die. I know because he hung on and hung on, until finally I told him it was all right. I spoke into his ear and told him to go with love because we had completed our work, and I would be okay. Only then, when I kissed him, did I feel him let go. God bless his dear, sweet soul . . .

Joan asked to do a eulogy at the funeral. It may be just the right thing . . . her chance to get it out . . . .

September 16

You all have known my father, but not quite like I knew him. I studied him, unconsciously, all my life. That is my job as an actress, but it has always been my nature to find out about a person's character, under the skin. And what a wonderful character my father was!

You saw him as a preacher and a scholar, an intellectual who each and every week could construct a sermon worthy of publication. He was a scholar, but he was also a man who could laugh—and cry. I've seen his tears—with a beautiful sunset or painting, with a symphony or choir, with a finely tuned phrase, with a moving interaction between people. He was a man with a capacity to feel, and to feel deeply.

You saw him as a community activist. Did you know he was shy, pushing himself to do what he knew to be right, sometimes with acute discomfort at being in the limelight? He would often rather have been fly-fishing—he loved it with a passion.

Speaking of fly-fishing, did you know he sometimes picked up homeless men down at the viaduct to share some of his fishing trips? He looked at them as people, not statistics, and in exploring, he learned two or three of them used to fish as boys. He fed them and took them up into the mountains with him. For him, it was not a big deal.

He tried to teach me to fish, but I was never very good at it. That probably disappointed him.

He loved ideas, he loved music, he loved nature, he loved to laugh, and perhaps most of all, he loved people—and he always expected you to share his feelings. He couldn't understand your shock, for example, when he advised you from the pulpit to miss church if necessary to get up in the hills to glory in the wonder of the aspen when it turned to gold. The willow, too. Remarkably, like a child, he assumed everyone would feel the same thing.

I will miss my father very much, but I will always carry with me the essence of his spirit. It will be renewed every time I step onto a set or a stage, every time I try something new, every time I am challenged. He gave it freely, many times in my life, and he would give it to you.

You will understand when I tell you this. From the very first time I played a role in a play, when the kids in the neighborhood put on Little Red Riding Hood and I was Little Red, until the last show I did on TV, Dad always wished me the actor's best wish—"Break a leg, Joan." Each time it warmed my heart, and I do believe I went on with an extra flourish because of it. When I said goodbye to my father three weeks ago, we looked each other in the eye and neither of could say what was in our hearts. Finally, from both of us at the same time, it came. And we both understood. He would say it to you, every time you need it.

"Break a leg."

NOTES:
A Good Death

> Do not go gentle into that good night,
> Old age should burn and rave at close of day;
> Rage, rage against the dying of the light.
> Dylan Thomas[1] [1, p. 128]

---

[1] Poems of Dylan Thomas, Copyright © 1952 by Dylan Thomas. Reprinted by permission of New Directions Publishing Company.

Death is un-American.

Arnold Toynbee [2, p. 131]

Dylan Thomas was a poet. Toynbee was not. No matter. They have said the same thing—that death is to be denied, hidden, ignored, rejected. Each has expressed in his own way this message that has pervaded attitudes in Western civilization since the beginning of the twentieth century. We all know intellectually that life cannot go on indefinitely. Death is out there, back behind the bushes, coming one day to all of us, yet we live—or try to live—with the illusion that the reality of death will not have to be faced. Until it is here we should not think about it, plan for it (hard-numbered estate planning and pre-paid funerals being the exceptions), waste energy worrying about it. We should protect children from exposure to it. We certainly should avoid speaking about it, and if we read related materials we ought to do it in private and hide the books under a best-seller so our friends won't think we are morbid. As Lewis Thomas said in his classic, *The Lives of a Cell: Notes of a Biology Watcher*[2] "We continue to share with our remotest ancestors the most tangled and evasive attitudes about death. . . . We have as much distaste for talking about personal death as for thinking about it. It is an indelicacy, like talking in mixed company about venereal disease or abortion in the old days" [3, p. 55].

It was not always so. There was a very long time, prior to the twentieth century, when death was considered part of life. Disease and accidents were expected along the way, and if the available care produced no cure, the natural outcome was death. The response was not one of panicky avoidance; rather, saddened families, friends, and the community at large accepted the reality and provided what comfort there could be until the death occurred. Birth and death were the most natural events on the landscape of living. Both were simply parts of life.

A fifteenth-century religious treatise, "Ars Moriendi," demonstrates this accepting attitude. It put into writing what is

[2] The Long Habit., copyright © 1972 by the Massachusetts Medical Society, from *The Lives of a Cell* by Lewis Thomas. Used by permission of Viking Penguin, Penguin Books USA Inc.

needed for a beautiful death. The dying person is told that when death is upon him he must come to it without resistance or anger or defiance. Those attending the dying person are told not to give priority to medical over spiritual aid.

It is difficult for us in today's Western civilization to understand such a belief and tradition. It is foreign to us. We call the doctor with every hurt and fever. We rely on medical wonders to bring us back to health from the most extreme illness or injury. We do not countenance death as an outcome.

The same blessings that allow us to have this attitude bring us our biggest problem at life's end. We cannot accept death when it comes. While we rightly embrace life and want to live it to its fullest, we in Western civilization have lost the will to adapt when death approaches. Avoiding and denying it until its breath is upon us does not protect us from the pain of loss when it occurs. Rather, denial robs us of the wealth dying could bring in closeness, spiritual and emotional growth, and understanding of the mystery of life.

What accounts for this remarkable shift in perspective in just the last fifty to one hundred years—such a short stretch in the long run of humanity? How did we get from there to here?

The answer has to lie in the technological revolution of the twentieth century, perhaps with seeds from the industrial revolution a century earlier. Its remarkable achievements have changed our lives—our expectations and values—our view of the world. That revolution has led us to believe that there are no limits to what is possible—that we human beings can do anything. That good revolution has also led us to deny death.

Technology has drastically altered our lives and perspective. In transportation, for example, design and engineering of our cars, trains, and airplanes permit us ever more speed, comfort, and safety. In our homes, every year we have new miracles in security, entertainment, cleaning, and cooking. This metamorphosis has taken place in every aspect of our lives. Is it any wonder that we think all things are possible, that we can do anything—that we should always have convenience and efficiency, and never have to wait or get our hands dirty?

The technological revolution has been particularly startling in the field of medicine. Organisms causing illness have been identified; their vulnerabilities are known. Medications have been found or designed which effectively kill most of these organisms so health can be restored. Organs that no longer work can be replaced. Unwanted genetic traits can be avoided or altered so as to produce healthier and better-functioning infants. Burned and mutilated bodies can be restored to adequacy and in some cases to virtual normalcy. Abnormal appearance, that is, literally, appearance that doesn't conform to the norm, can be transformed into what is contemporaneously considered beautiful. The miracles even extend to machines which can breathe and circulate blood for near-moribund patients. We can almost say that no longer does one have to die until the decision is made to let life end.

Medical scientists have succeeded in producing a mind-boggling array of technological improvements. These discoveries and inventions continue to come, often improving our lives, always strengthening the notion that man can control his destiny.

In many respects the advances in technology are positive. No one would choose to go back to ancient and medieval times when health care was unknowing and primitive at best, when there was so little chance of recovery even from the most common illnesses. Now is a great time to be alive. So many opportunities exist to do wondrous and exciting things. We are the beneficiaries of improved tools for living, of electronic advances, of scientific knowledge that make our lives longer, easier, safer, and more productive. We would not give that up.

But inevitably, along with the extended life-span, convenience and life-at-ease to which twentieth-century Western civilization has become accustomed came a distaste for the ugly, the imperfect, the painful. This distaste caused us to give up some qualities and ways that were of great importance to people. The slower pace, quieter dialogue, traditional mores and customs and social togetherness of those earlier less sophisticated times had value that we have lost.

For persons living before the twentieth century, the acceptance of death as part of life probably heightened and fine-tuned their sense of the present [4]. It kept the door open to communication. It made the days more precious, being always aware that they were limited. Persons today who have experienced life-threatening illness or accident, who have had to face and accept the possibility of death, frequently report this insight.

That earlier prevailing attitude of accepting death built into the community common rituals and behaviors that supported its members during times of illness and stress. Being with the dying, taking care of them, seeing to their needs and bringing them comfort had earlier been something everyone knew how to do. It was expected, something children witnessed around them and understood as they grew up. These ways and the opportunities they offered have been vanishing like dry ice during the past century.

No longer do families want to deal with dying. They don't want its disruption in their bedrooms, their living rooms, particularly as the end nears. Dying at home, almost always the practice before this century, has virtually disappeared. Today 80 percent of the deaths in the United States take place in hospitals, away from the dying person's familiar surroundings and sources of support. Fifty years ago that rate was 50 percent; one hundred years ago it was 0 percent [5, 6]. The trend has been a natural—perhaps inevitable—result of our twentieth-century change in attitude.

To the extent traditional hospitalization of the dying has grown, death has become a sterile isolating event. Removed from the community instead of occupying the position of honor in his home, the dying person is placed at the lowest priority in an institution dedicated to curing people. Health-care professionals hurry past him to serve others who can respond. The isolation is devastating to his morale and self-esteem, for it removes him from society, no longer valued, finished.

How much better to have one's final months, days and hours enveloped in the comfort of nurturing surroundings, at home or in a dedicated hospice facilty, supported and honored by family and friends who can share the rituals of farewell in a natural way! Only recently are we seeing the introduction of hospice rooms in hospitals, providing a promise of this better kind of death to persons who cannot be at home.

Isolation is not the only problem to be solved. Others that arise to challenge us are related, complex, and circular. Denial of death together with our belief in the power of medical technology and our growing intolerance of the imperfect has resulted in demand for more technology, overtreatment, and overtesting [7], at the very high price of personal suffering, frustration, more denial of death, and rising costs of health care.

We consumers of health-care services cause this excess because we demand it, relying on the expectation that another test, another treatment will solve the problem. We cause it, but we are not alone in creating the excess. What demand does not come from patients and their families often comes from physicians, for many of them are disinclined to give up treating patients in what surgeon and medical professor Sherwin Nuland calls "their fascination with biotechnology" [5]. They are even carrying out life-prolonging treatment when their patients wish to avoid it, according to an unprecedented $28 million, eight-year study reported at the close of 1995 [8]. Despite structured efforts in five teaching hospitals in the United States to avoid relentless heroic measures when they were not wanted by the patient, medicine obeyed its culture's tradition of regarding death as defeat, of continuing its patching, fixing, going from crisis to crisis in the ongoing conspiracy of silence about death. This effort to deny death, particularly strong in tertiary care hospitals [9], permeates our society.

With physicians' interests naturally focusing on practical, technical, medical treatment matters, their interaction with dying patients rarely includes discussion about dying. Their training and work orientation lead them to their medical priorities. With this focus, it is too easy for them to provide care without facing and responding to the emotional and interpersonal turmoil that are part of the human experience of dying. Psychosocial care is not found often enough in medicine; it's an unexpected gift when you get it [10]. The last hospitalization often ends up a frantic effort to perform drastic life-saving measures, however difficult or painful, rather than a time to rally the resources of support for a caring last goodbye. Again, this depressing picture may brighten with the recent introduction of medical school courses in death, dying and palliative care (see Appendix A). A recent report of care of patients over eighty-five years of age does show progress. In this study, few CPRs were given, and the care was comfort oriented [11].

We would like to believe that the values we need to preserve can co-exist with the benefits of technology. Perhaps even with the medical advances we can stop the sanitizing, the dehumanizing of death which has occurred with our generation's sophistication. We would like to see, in contrast to the common medical model described above, the chance for more people to experience a "good death," a peaceful death, a process that can move past the shock and denial to acknowledgment, then to acceptance, resolution of matters that were incomplete, emotional and spiritual growth, and finally to closure in a supportive environment. A "good death" may seem an oxymoron. As seen in the lives of many of our patients, including Jonathon and Rose in "Letters and a Diary," it is anything but.

Consider this recent description of a good death: ". . . dying in comfort, supported by and connected to important persons in one's life, resolving interpersonal and spiritual conflicts, gaining an understanding of the meaning and purpose of life, and accepting death"[3] [12, p. 1250]. Or this: ". . . a death that someone might choose for himself, had he a choice . . ."—one beginning when the patient realizes nothing more can or should be done, then proceeding at its own pace and including care, control over decision-making, composure, communication, continuity of as many normal functions as possible, and closure [13, p. 41]. Or this: ". . . compassionate care and relief from pain, . . . and time to experience our dying" [4, p. 320]. In all descriptions, a good or peaceful death is in striking contrast to a bad one, with the unresolved conflicts, incomplete farewells, and unfulfilled search a bad death implies.

The diagnosis of a life-threatening illness is a terrible blow to the patient and his loved ones. Both will suffer loss—one of his own life and dreams, the other of the patient's presence and companionship, and any dreams they had of a future with him. No one asks for a blow like this, yet it takes place in the lives of

[3] Drawn from *The Archives of Internal Medicine*, Vol. 155(12), pp. 1250-1254. Copyright 1995, American Medical Association.

thousands of people every day. When it happens, the dying person and his family must choose how they will cope, how they will adapt. Their choice may be healthy or it may be unhealthy. They may either accept or deny, they may make themselves ready or remain unprepared, they may be peaceful or resistant [14].

A healthy death requires first that the dying person and his family adjust their goals and perspective about the future. Instead of plans for travel or building, the patient must think ahead of wrapping up, of leaving a legacy. Perhaps that legacy is love and memories; perhaps it is also something material—financial resources, creative works, a project to complete before leaving. Whatever it will be, the goal and view of the future must change in order to do this planning. The dying patient must choose to make this adjustment.

Such a choice is a healthy one. It is cognizant of reality. It is constructive. It will lead to further healthy adaptation to the impending death, and to an easier bereavement for the family. It is in stark contrast to the all-too-common preference for hiding the facts, for pursuing futile treatment beyond all reason, for pretending until it is over and all chance for communion is lost.

In addition, a good death, like the quality of life one would prefer, must be personally defined [15]. The patient himself should be given the opportunity to talk about his intent, his view of the dying he would choose [16].

This talking, communicating, is essential to a peaceful death, but the opportunity is often not afforded the dying patient. The pervasive denial, the pretense imposed by the physician's silence and caregivers' reluctance to talk out anxieties and plans, leads to inhibition of the patient's expression. Too often the people around him believe speaking openly would rob him of hope, not realizing his hope can and must lie in something other than an expectation of cure. His hope lies rather in not suffering, in not being abandoned, in living so a good legacy is left, in faith, in reaching a milestone, in having control. These are the hopes they should keep alive [5], and to do so requires open acknowledgment of the dying.

Instead the patient is given to believe that he must not open the topic. Doing so is silently forbidden. The avenue of openness and release of questions, concerns, and feelings is effectively closed, and a healthy adjustment becomes less accessible— maybe even placed behind a solid wall.

Then again, the failure may originate not with the physician or caregiver, but with the patient, himself. He may be unwilling to put words to his gut-level feelings, perhaps out of fear of dying, perhaps out of hoping silence will make the dying disappear or at least keep it at bay, perhaps out of some desire to protect others from the knowledge they surely have. The family members, then, feel pressure to remain silent, their distress locked inside.

Either way, this destructive avoidance of communication can generate a complete circle of silence. Dying in this kind of climate, if not changed before it is too late, is a tragic way to end a life.

Some small improvement in this situation has been recorded in recent years. In the mid-seventies, 78 percent of caregivers of late-stage cancer patients were found not to have discussed with them the possibility of dying [17], whereas in a study a decade later that figure dropped to 60 percent [18]. There is evidence in the recent formation of the American Academy of Hospice and Palliative Care Medicine and new medical journals addressing death, dying, and palliative care that more doctors also are now discussing death with their patients. We know some of them, and can see the heart-warming results of their work.

One of the beauties of hospice care is that team members can change and are changing this failure of communication. They can teach caregivers how to introduce the subject and how to respond, through both coaching and example. In our care of Henrietta (Chapter 5: What's Best for Me), the team was left to talk with her alone, as her husband refused to acknowledge her dying, but in many families hospice has been able to help ease these discussions between the patient and his loved ones so a peaceful death like Jonathon's can occur. More than any other feature of hospice care of patients, families point in their acknowledgment letters to the change team members wrought in their desire and ability to talk openly. This change helped them cope with the dying, even helped them find enrichment and acceptance in the patient's final weeks. In their letters and conversations they often reveal the tension they had felt, with death's presence filling every waking moment, the fear forcing normal thought processes out of their heads. They recall their reluctance to give voice to their fears, describing at the same time the inner urge to lay open the subject of dying. They express their gratitude for being given permission, for being shown the way.

Hospice team members and physicians can see the signs of decline in their patients which call urgently for dialogue, if that has not previously begun. Those signs include weight loss and lowered bodily function and often include a disinclination to eat and drink [6]. Sleep time may increase [19, 20]. At the very latest, by the time these signs are observed some communication about the impending death should commence. Most often, deep within them, the patient and the family want this release and linkage.

In an attempt to bring more knowledge to this deeply emotional process, human adaptation to dying has been studied. Marjorie Dobratz developed a "Life Closure Scale" [21] with which to identify and measure factors that help human beings adapt to death. She found that patients' cognitive efforts to search for meaning and to maintain hope were useful. The dying who directed positive attitudes toward their illness and found meaning which allowed them to transcend their limited images of themselves were better able to cope [22]. Coping required changing oneself, one's viewpoint and plans, in order to fit the circumstances of dying better, and those patients who succeeded in reorienting themselves diminished their fear of dying. Dobratz concluded that factors of older age and good social support are often present in patients who adapt well to their dying; when pain is present adaptation is often poor.

Another evaluation tool was devised to examine a patient's adaptation to dying. The McCanse Readiness for Death Instrument looks at the ways patients react physiologically, psychologically, sociologically, and spiritually to their impending deaths. Indicators of adaptive responses, drawn from earlier research reports and validated by experienced hospice nurses from different locations, were grouped into test questions relating to four concepts: 1) withdrawal from the environment, comprising attention to food, pain, temperature, noise and light; 2) decreased social interaction, including desire for companionship, verbal interaction, responsibility toward others, and need for approval; 3) increased death acceptance behavior, covering sleep time, time perception, reminiscence, talking about death and deceased loved ones and the value of personal possessions, and visualizing one's future after death; and 4) increased admission of readiness to die, addressing the patient's fear of death and his feelings of peacefulness and willingness to let go of life [23].

The patient's answers to these questions may provide a basis for hospice workers to judge what steps will be helpful to his adjusting as he moves toward the end of life. While the twenty-eight-item questionnaire may be too formidable to administer in its entirety, the hospice worker can judge the patient's likely responses to many of the items informally by his behavior and conversation. The resulting assessment may suggest what can be done to help him—what will make it easier for him to die peacefully. Direct questions, to the extent the formal assessment can be comfortably administered, may spark some discussion that would not otherwise take place, thus bringing a positive value to the patient.

The concept of a good death, one that is peaceful because it has included warmth, closeness, comfort, and closure, lies at the core of hospice philosophy. Jonathon's and Rose's experience in "Letters and a Diary" comprised all the elements hospice knows will result in such a peaceful death: absence of or minimal pain, acknowledgment and acceptance of the dying, reoriented thinking and planning, resolution of old issues, communication, and closure. They rarely occur in the same constellation, but the hospice team can guide and teach in that direction, offering more people the comfort and growth a peaceful death can provide.

REFERENCES

1. D. Thomas, *Collected Poems*, New Directions, New York, 1953.
2. A. Toynbee, *Man's Concern With Death*, McGraw-Hill Publishing Company, New York, 1968.

3. L. Thomas, *The Lives of a Cell: Notes of a Biology Watcher*, Bantam Books, New York, 1974.
4. J. Viorst, *Necessary Losses*, Ballantine Books, New York, 1986.
5. S. Nuland, *How We Die*, Alfred A. Knopf, New York, 1994.
6. J. D. McCue, The Naturalness of Dying, *Journal of the American Medical Association, 273*:13, pp. 1039-1043, 1995.
7. E. Friedman, A Sense of Loss, *Healthcare Forum Journal, 38*:2, pp. 9-12, 1995.
8. A. F. Connors, for the SUPPORT Principal Investigators, A Controlled Trial to Improve Care for Seriously Ill Hospitalized Patients, *JAMA, 274*:20, pp. 1591-1598, 1995.
9. G. A. Annas, Sex, Money and Bioethics: Watching ER and Chicago Hope, *Hastings Center Report, 25*:5, pp. 40-43, 1995.
10. D. W. Moller, *On Death Without Dignity: The Human Impact of Technological Dying*, Baywood Publishing, Amityville, New York, 1990.
11. K. A. Hesse, Terminal Care of the Very Old, *Archives of Internal Medicine, 155*:14, pp. 1513-1518, 1995.
12. T. E. Quill and R. V. Brody, You Promised Me I Wouldn't Die Like This, *Archives of Internal Medicine, 155*:12, pp. 1250-1254, 1995.
13. A. Weisman, *On Death and Dying*, Behavioral Publications, New York, 1972.
14. M. E. Rogers, *Introduction to the Theoretical Basis of Nursing*, Davis Publishers, Philadelphia, Pennsylvania, 1970.
15. P. Ebersole, Quality of Life: What is It? *Geriatric Nursing, 16*:2, pp. 49-50, 1995.
16. D. Tomezak and L. Quig, Needed: A Conceptual Model for a Comfortable Death, *Caring, 13*:5, pp. 8-9, 78-79, 1994.
17. M. J. Krant and L. Johnston, Family Members' Perceptions of Communications in Late Stage Cancer, *International Journal of Psychiatry in Medicine, 8,* pp. 203-216, 1977-78.
18. W. R. Moore, Perceptions of Terminal Illness by Family Physicians and Relatives, *Omega: Journal of Death and Dying, 14,* pp. 369-376, 1983-84.
19. E. Kübler-Ross, *On Death and Dying*, Macmillan, New York, 1969.
20. M. E. Rogers, *Oral presentation at Texas Women's University*, Dallas, May 1985.
21. M. C. Dobratz, The Life Closure Scale: A Measure of Psychological Adaptation to Death and Dying, *The Hospice Journal, 6*:3, pp. 1-15, 1990.

22. M. C. Dobratz, Causal Influences of Psychological Adaptation in Death and Dying, *Western Journal of Nursing Research, 15*:5, pp. 708-729, 1993.
23. R. P. McCanse, The McCanse Readiness for Death Instrument (MRDI): A Reliable and Valid Measure for Hospice Care, *The Hospice Journal, 10*:1, pp. 15-26, 1995.

CHAPTER 9

Beginnings and Reflections: One Nurse's Personal Story

When people reach my age, they seek answers to the big questions about life. At seventy-two years of age, after fifty-one years of nursing, I want to know what my life and career were all about. What value have they had? I've worked so hard, so long. Why has hospice become such a driving force in my life? Why can't I let it go?

I am aware that my questions and my answers have particular relevance to me, and some might say only to me, but I believe they can have broader meaning, too. They may shed some light on the *why* of the stories. They can illuminate the dynamics and motivations of one specific hospice nurse. They can help some readers understand—the ones who ask, "How can anyone do hospice nursing?"

I must go back to my early years to start my search for answers. The important people and experiences in my childhood likely set the course I have followed; at least it is a place to begin.

I grew up the youngest of five children in the only Jewish family in a poor Catholic neighborhood. The Depression was a disaster for us. No one I knew had extra shoes in the closet. Meat appeared on the table maybe once every week or two, if we were lucky—and we ate a lot of potatoes. I never knew, and certainly never expected anything more than the simple lives we led.

Three sisters, Lett, Helen, and Kate, lived near us. Helen and Kate were nurses—plain, good people, the kind often described as "salt of the earth." Helen delivered me when I was born. They were saints, these women, giving food and other help to our neighbors and their patients even though their own lives were barren of any extras. It was true generosity, coming from their own scant stores. I loved them unreservedly.

We naturally didn't celebrate Christmas in our family, but I used to go to their home each year to help trim their tree. Afterward I went along to midnight mass. I begged to hang a stocking in my own home on Christmas Eve, just like they did. I wanted to do everything just like they did. I visited the women frequently, staying for supper whenever my mother would give permission. My parents made major concessions to their Jewishness in allowing me this friendship.

When Kate died, I remember going to the viewing at the funeral home. I was about ten years old, and I had never seen a dead person before. I can still feel the sudden dryness in my throat as I walked to the casket, the cold sweat on my palms. There she lay, my "second mother," waxy and still, like the gardenias fastened to her dress. Their heavy fragrance lingered; to this day I choke up when I smell gardenias.

Some years later, Helen had a stroke. I visited her in the hospital. She was in a coma and I could see nasty bedsores on her heels and elbows from lying for hours in the same position. The sight of those raw ulcers made me sick to my stomach. Then I got angry. Why didn't they turn her? How could anyone in a hospital care so poorly for my dear Helen?

I knew then that I would become a nurse. I don't believe I made a deliberate decision—I just knew. I would become a super-nurse, worthy of these three sisters . . .

Kate and Lett and Helen affected my life critically, but they weren't the only ones. My mother did, too—deeply, and in a very different way. She suffered because my father couldn't seem to earn a living, and my aunt provided for us—with visible resentment. Both of them humiliated Mother, and watching her, I wanted to cry. I ached for Mother. I wanted to banish the problems—make her rich and happy. But when I grew older and my nurses' training concluded—when I could have helped—I made no offer. I had fallen in love, and chose instead to marry. Mother lived two more unhappy years, then died of a coronary. I had failed her, and my grief weighed heavy with guilt.

I needed to say "I'm sorry."

Since Mother died I have been doing for others, in as close and personal a way as I could find. Intensive care and hospice nursing are close and personal, and in them—particularly hospice—I have found my way.

I suppose, then, by inspiration and guilt, Helen, Kate, Lette and my mother led me to nursing and ultimately to hospice.

Beyond that, some of my nursing colleagues have helped to shape my career. I remember a head nurse in the Intensive Care Unit (ICU) to which I was attached when I was quite young. She was a kind, overworked ex-nun who set no limits to her caring for patients. She found time to listen when they needed to talk. She closed her eyes to visiting hours; she allowed children to slip in for quick visits. There were few rules she wouldn't break if she thought it important to the patient or his family.

I'll never forget the time she stood up to a surgeon who seemed to enjoy humiliating the people working around him. Each of us had been the butt of his nasty demeaning remarks at one time or another. One day he berated a co-worker of mine loudly in the hall. The poor young nurse tried to protest her innocence, then ran away in tears. Our head nurse walked over, planted herself in front of him and announced in a clear, firm voice, "Sir, we will lose all our nurses if you continue to treat them this way. Then you'll have no one to care for your patients, and I'll be forced to inform the administrator that you have caused the problem." The surgeon looked stunned, then backed away. He never behaved badly to us again.

A burning pride rose in my throat as I watched her take a righteous stand for us. She became part of my psyche, this fine nurse who modeled the role I would attempt to fill throughout my career. Her values, her principles, became mine.

Another person remains engraved in my memory. He was a physician in the Intensive Care Unit. You must keep in mind that the ICU was a battlefield for lives. We took care of people who were critically ill, some too sick to pull through in spite of everything we did. We committed ourselves to saving everyone in the ICU, so when anyone died, by definition we had failed. I took every death as a personal failure.

I was thunderstruck one day when I first heard this man say about his suffering, dying patient, "We're not helping. . . . Let's see if the family will allow us to turn off the ventilator and just find a way to keep him comfortable." Here was a new view of the universe: an approach to medical care and dying that was humane, one that had been unthinkable in my mind until that moment. In that instant a whole world opened up. I suddenly saw that death could be a friend, and even a right.

That doctor changed my life. He could not transform the system—because he stood alone. But he planted a seed in me. I began to look at intensive care differently.

I started to question and sometimes to doubt the wisdom of what I saw in the ICU. I saw patients who had suffered such terrible damage that saving their lives was the final blow. Sometimes I would spend entire shifts managing the artificial feeding and toileting of patients who would never speak or understand or walk or do anything meaningfully again. I had been trained to keep them alive at any cost, using all human and technical resources at our command, but I watched their families go through agony over their endless trauma and pain. And I wondered which was better, this frantic demand that a patient continue to live, no matter what, or an acceptance that his life was coming to an end. Maybe death wasn't always so bad.

The problem was that our system offered little help when it was clear the patient would die. In fact, his impending death was a signal to turn our attention to others, to leave him alone. Sometimes we moved him to the most distant room. Conveniently, then, we didn't have to be reminded over and over of our failure.

As for the patients' families, we found less and less to say to them. I can see their eyes still, the pain and sorrow leaping out as they sought help from us. We could not utter the simple words of support they needed to hear: "It must be very hard to stand by as your husband—or wife—or child—or friend—dies." To do so would have been an admission of failure.

I was ready to listen when news of the first modern hospice program filtered out of England in the late sixties. Like my physician-friend in the ICU, people there accepted death when it was inevitable. That made sense to me. I wanted to be able to comfort a patient and his family when they had had enough, or when attempts to cure had been exhausted. Just help them. Understand them and be kind to them. Show them the closeness dying can bring, so they can carry away warmth instead of horror.

Gradually I reached the conclusion that I couldn't continue my work in the ICU. It was too narrow-minded. In 1975, I asked the hospital to reassign me to its special cancer unit.

During that next year, Dr. Sylvia Lack came to Denver to present a three-day seminar about hospice. She was genuinely an authority, for she had worked with the pioneer of the modern hospice movement, Dame Cicely Saunders, who began the first program at St. Christopher's Hospital in London back in 1967. Dr. Lack had established the first hospice in the United States in 1975 in New Haven, Connecticut, and was proselytizing the hospice message around the country. I attended the seminar, and by the time it concluded I knew that hospice was where I belonged.

I was surprised to learn that the concept of hospice was anything but new. Hospice had its roots in ancient and medieval Europe when medicine was very primitive. Sick or injured people in those times were expected to die. Instead of pursuing a cure for very long, people just turned to each other for help to get through the remaining days.

Beginning almost two thousand years ago, Dr. Lack explained, groups sprang up to offer care to sick and dying strangers who had no one else to attend them. Some of these groups were religious, others secular.

One of them in the 1200s, the White Cross Knights, put the group's ideas into writing. Distilled to the essence, they were *acceptance, assistance, caring,* and *respect.* Those principles still hold, Dr. Lack said. They moved me.

I listened spellbound as Dr. Lack described her first group in New Haven. Later I learned that a second program had begun in Marin County, California. By 1977, nearly thirty hospice programs were operating in the United States. That was sufficient evidence for me; with the help of two cancer patients and another nurse, I decided to try to start something in Denver.

I quit my job at the hospital and wrote to the existing programs. Some of them wrote back, answering my questions. The San Diego Hospice was most helpful, generously providing information their staff had gathered in their short experience.

Three colleagues and I drafted a proposal to create "Hospice of Metro Denver." Dr. George Curfman, a local oncologist, presented it on February 28, 1978, to the Denver chapter of the Cancer Society. The Cancer Society agreed to pay $37,000 for one year of trial operation, provided we report our activities to them every three months. We were only too happy to promise; we would have given them anything they asked. Amazingly, we were in business.

When we began we had one patient. By the end of the week we had five. In some ways we were poorly prepared. Our first director had never witnessed a death. I was the only staff nurse, paid a pittance and not reimbursed for my travel from patient to patient. I was also asked to handle public relations: I, who could not speak to a group larger than two without hyperventilating!

Despite these formidable conditions, we grew. We were hellbent to make it work. We learned by doing, and we had the help of some marvelous people. The Boulder, Colorado Hospice had opened eighteen months earlier; they referred our first patient and allowed me to attend their team meetings. Dr. Evelyn Paley, a psychologist-friend, taught me how to control my speaking anxieties. We approached problems with a practical, if not an expert view. Armed with a vision of what was needed and little more, we proceeded with our program.

It was slow at first, but over the years we have become a large broad-spectrum hospice. We have always had a home-care structure. We provide home nursing and social-work service, and since 1994 also have had our own free-standing live-in hospice facility. We offer personal help and chaplains and specialty therapists when needed. We train volunteers to assist with personal and household duties that otherwise would not be done, and to add continuity to the hospice presence in the home. We provide support groups for parents, spouses, children, and friends. All of this is for the patient and his family while he lives, and for the family during their bereavement later.

For the dying persons who need it, we provide special care and pain medication. Beyond that, and sometimes far more important, we listen to them, giving all of them and their families understanding and help with their attitudes and feelings, and with their expectations. We show them by our own behavior how to accept the inevitable. Our example eases their adjustments. Indeed, our families have often found some rewards, some beauty, some fundamental truths about life in this final human act of dying.

For nineteen years since we started, I have tried to make that happen. I am proud of what we have done.

I've made mistakes, but looking back, I can see how much I have learned. I am a different nurse now. I am a changed person.

After caring for and about so many people, I have grown in my own understanding of myself. I have become aware of a universal self-knowledge from all my patients and families, a kind of transcendent view of life, which has enriched my life.

I view dying differently. I began my hospice work accepting death as part of life, but over the years it has become more. I have developed a respect for death. When my patient dies, I feel I am in the presence of something larger than anyone or anything. I have learned neither to trivialize it, nor to be overwhelmed by it. I have learned to regard death as the profoundly significant event it is in the lives of the patient and his circle of family and friends. I have watched its effects on countless people, and their experiences fill me with awe.

I have learned that I don't need to blow up when things go wrong. I've been blessed with many teachers. Minnie's daughter, Jane, in Chapter 2, for example, dealt with all of the problems of impending death in her household with an even temper, giving Minnie acceptance and love and allowing Amy to work through her difficult reactions to her sick grandmother. Other families, too, have shown me what love and stability really mean. My handling of difficult people and situations, in hospice and in my personal life, has become more reasonable as I see how noble the human spirit can be.

I've also learned I can't make assumptions about people—either about what they mean, or about what they understand. I discovered that Aggie's and Ray's uncommunicative gruffness (Chapter 1) didn't mean they didn't care about each other. I was shocked to learn that both Joseph (Chapter 4) and Sandy (Chapter 6) thought their dying might be punishment for wrongdoing in their earlier lives. I never should have assumed they understood their illnesses rationally. Even among my colleagues I have learned not to assume anything. They may not understand what I understand. That was certainly true in the staff meeting after Henrietta's death (Chapter 5), when I reported my plan to strip the dressings off of her chest if her husband called Emergency. One physician charged that was immoral—which hurt keenly until I realized he couldn't understand. He was not part of the commitment to Henrietta. I should not have assumed he would see it in the same light.

I've learned to be careful of what I say. My quick tongue has gotten me into trouble more than once. Very early in my work, I described a patient's problems to his friend—violating a confidence. I knew better. In that moment I destroyed a trusting relationship. I'll regret my mistake forever, and I've never, ever repeated it.

People always ask me how long it will be until someone dies. I don't know, I can't know with any precision, but I've sometimes answered as though my experience made me an authority. Then my predictions created expectations that turned out to be incorrect. What a mistake! A deathwatch that extends beyond its predicted bounds can be a terrible thing. The family wears out, even getting angry with their dying member when he doesn't die, when their emotional energy can't last beyond the expected time. It's as if each one's reservoir of patience and will is programmed, emptying its contents within a planned period. Never again will I put an hour or a day on the line! I've learned people do better without a measure in place.

Another lesson I've learned over time is to apologize. I have made mistakes, and will undoubtedly find new ones to make. I can say "I'm sorry" now—something I found difficult during the first few years. An apology can clear the air and let us get a fresh start.

I discovered that dying persons need reassurance that they are still important and worthy. They often withdraw, unwilling or afraid to burden others with their illness. One way we can reassure them is simply to touch them. Touching is direct; it includes. I learned to touch a lot, holding hands, stroking cheeks, embracing shoulders. Giving a bath is a full cornucopia of wonders—touch and closeness, scent, relief to aching muscles and the delight of feeling clean. I've learned to tell how much touching is good, and where to draw the line; how to be close in a way that is accepted. I've learned that the secret of a good hospice nurse is to be a friend who is at the same time close and objective.

Religion is another area in which I've grown. Some hospice programs are sponsored by a religious group; ours is not. It is true we have clergy who will aid our families if that help is requested, but our clergy function without denominational limits. I join the families when they ask me, sometimes holding hands while hearing the prayers they offer and sharing the spiritual moments of their grief and joy, whatever their religion. When I am with a family I respect their wishes about religion, and do not impose anything from my own Jewish beliefs.

I've fallen into some strange and sometimes funny situations over the years. Our very first patient, in 1978, was a born-again Christian, and his ultimate expression of gratitude to me while I was caring for him was, "You are wonderful—you are such a good Christian!" I know he meant it as a compliment. I wonder what he would have thought had he known I was Jewish.

In my ignorance of other religions' practices, I once unknowingly insulted a Buddhist patient, walking into his house wearing shoes which should have been removed at the door. Then his family tried to tell me in Korean words I couldn't understand that I should disconnect his intravenous tube before he died. Their religion demanded it. What a scramble went on around me before I finally understood and complied!

I have had trouble sometimes with religion, but I have tried in these circumstances not to let my feelings interfere. One attitude that gives me particular problems is that an illness or death is "God's will." Especially when the patient is young, or the illness harsh and painful, I cannot accept this belief. I try to be nonjudgmental when this is the family position, remaining quiet during their religious practice.

I have had difficulty with my own religion on occasion. I recall a dear old man with a beard and blue eyes who looked like he'd stepped out of a rabbinical portrait. I felt very close to him, even confiding to him one day that he was the father I wished I had had. The rabbi of his synagogue learned that my patient had a colostomy, and promptly refused to let him touch the Torah. This uncompromising blow to my devout friend who had always participated in the service seemed to me cruel and unnecessary. Again, I held my tongue and left the religious issues to the family and their clergyman.

While I have learned to avoid discussion of religion, I still react privately against some things that are said and done in its name. Having said that, I must add that these years in hospice have strengthened my own personal belief in God.

One more lesson I have learned over the years is that there are limits to what I can give, even when I want to give more. I realize that when the load gets too heavy, I must reduce it. I have known what it is to be bone-weary and emotionally wrung out. When I reach this point I cannot sleep. I think about the families and cannot seem to let go. One's wellspring should never get that empty. I cut back now, caring for five or six families instead of eight, until I feel my body and spirit have recovered.

Looking back, there are things I would do differently if I could do it all over again. But I have given it my best.

People often ask me how I could stand it all these years, taking on one patient after another knowing they all would die; saying goodbye over and over and over—as one life after another ended.

Every hospice nurse faces this; it is not unique to me. We grow close to the patients and their families during the time we have with them. The relationship is special and intimate. Rarely are people as open, as unguarded and honest, as when death is near. With most of our families we build a bond; rarely does this fail to happen.

I feel close enough that, if my patient's condition is critical, I hate to turn him over to the on-call nurse on my days off. After weeks or months of helping the patient and his family prepare, I want to be part of the dying, if that is to happen. I try to attend the funerals, and I always attend the memorial celebrations our hospice holds twice a year for the patients who have died. Their families come, and we want to see each other again.

It is true—I lose a friend when my patient dies, sometimes a dear friend. I hurt when I say goodbye. Often I cry. But then I turn around and take on another family, another patient.

I do so because I feel sure and strong about what I do; it's so right. I feel rich. I've been rewarded. When I head out to see a new patient, even after all these years, my heart still beats faster. My senses heighten, wondering what he or she and the family will be like, what our relationship will be, and what opportunity I will have to aid them. It is something like a first date . . . only different. The patient may welcome me, or he may start out angry at me and the world for his fate. He may reject me entirely, accepting only that I will aid his spouse. Most often, along the way, these negatives turn positive with some twist of interaction, some event or humor that transforms his attitude to acceptance. When some of these special, one-of-a-kind things happen in the patient's home, my being swells with the privilege I've had at being there—at being part of them—at making a difference for them. When my patient dies, I feel the fullness of life—its deepest, most intense meanings. No flatness, no emptiness in this career I have chosen. My life is often hard, but it is rich and rewarding. I earn this life by doing what I do, by being a hospice nurse.

If I've done my job well, I feel the warmth and the closeness . . . I share the laughter and love . . . I know I've made the time better. I've changed the dying from something that's feared, that's the enemy, to a natural part of life—maybe even a friend. The families tell me this, and I know it even without their saying a word. This is powerful; it is beautiful. . . .

After considering all of this, I may never know the entire answer to the questions about my life's value, and the role hospice has played in my life. But a fire still burns in me after all these years, and I would pass it on to any who can hear the message behind the words of the theologian, Howard Thurman:

> I share with you the agony of your grief. The anguish of your heart finds an echo in my own. I know I cannot enter all you feel, or bear with you the burden of your pain. I can but offer what my love does give: the strength of caring, the warmth of one who seeks to understand the silent storm-swept barrenness of so great a loss.
>
> This I do in quiet ways that, on your lonely path, you may not walk alone . . . [1].

REFERENCE

1. H. Thurman, indirect personal communication, n.d.

APPENDIX A

One Nurse's Perspective: Hospice Strengths and Weaknesses; Recommendations for Hospice

In my nineteen year tenure with hospice, I have seen the movement and individual hospice programs go through important growing pains. My vantage point as a long-term nurse has given me a historical view and some awareness of our future needs.

Since the beginning of our program I have seen many changes. Some, such as in pain control, are technical. For example, we started out giving liquid morphine by mouth, but because it was bitter, we put it into an alcohol solution. Patients who weren't eating couldn't tolerate this, so we found a solution—we injected the morphine. But morphine didn't work at all for some people because of allergic reactions; a substitute, methadone, was used. That, too, had its problems. Methadone isn't excreted fully and can build up in the blood, causing liver damage. It must be monitored carefully, and sometimes had to be discontinued.

Around 1989 we started using Roxonal® and MS-Contin®, morphine-based medications, which are administered in either immediate- or time-release capsules. Then a new Duragesic® patch became available which seeps medication continuously through the skin. For urgent relief of pain we now place two or three drops of concentrated morphine under the tongue which absorb immediately into the mucous membrane, or alternatively, we can hook up a constant drip into the tissue under the skin of the belly. A more drastic method had been a drip through the sub-clavian vein, but that's a serious step since it requires the insertion of a catheter, a minor surgical procedure done by a physician. To avoid the risks of the sub-clavian drip, a PICC line is now inserted into a vein in the elbow and threaded into the vena cava of the heart through which to drip the medication after placement is confirmed by X-ray. If all else fails, we add the hypnosis and imaging that William used so successfully. We rarely if ever give morphine injections, an all-at-one-time method, anymore.

Pain control has grown a brand new face in these nineteen years.

Generally our pain control methods have become more effective. But I remember one thirty-five-year-old woman with ovarian cancer who, in spite of all we did, continued to suffer pain. We built her up to massive doses of morphine, trying drops under the tongue, then a pump into the sub-clavian vein, and finally a catheter directly into her spine, but we still couldn't control her pain. When she died on the Fourth of July, I held her mother's hand and said, "She finally gained her independence!" Her mother nodded yes through her tears.

It is wrenching, but some few persons may have intractable pain despite our best efforts. We have not yet solved all pain problems.

While some physicians are becoming quite sophisticated in their management of pain, our nurses have often provided guidance to others who are not familiar with pain control for dying persons. Some are still surprised to learn that patients can handle as much medication as they need. The twin specters of addiction and respiratory depression often deter physicians from prescribing adequate pain medication; they do not always distinguish between physical dependence, psychological dependence or addiction, and tolerance, and they do not always recognize that careful increases of dosage for patients who have developed tolerance will not depress respiration.

We nurses applaud the physicians who have made the effort to update their knowledge of pain control and have come to understand these principles. But we continue to strain with some physicians to get adequate medication for our patients, and sometimes it is a losing battle.

In general, nurses have gradually shown more initiative and become more assertive over the years. This reflects a broad maturation in the nursing profession as well as our unique need and capacity to fill in where the patients' physicians cannot or do not choose to become much involved.

Our nursing staff has benefitted in recent years by the addition of support for us as we carry on our daily efforts with our families. Our stresses and hurts and our own fatigue have caused some of us to burn out, and we cried for help. A social worker and our chaplain now attend our team meetings, and they are available to us when we need them.

With the referrals of AIDS patients, we have evolved new strategies of care unique to them. At the beginning, total protective gear was required for all nurses and nurses' aides, but now we wear only glasses and gloves when in physical contact. Newly hired personnel must agree to serve AIDS patients, whose needs we have grown to meet. The AIDS program at Hospice of Metro Denver is now very active.

The funding of hospice has also changed. In the beginning we relied heavily on grant money and donations, supplemented by small payments from patients who could afford them. In 1985, Medicare finally realized that costs of care for terminally ill patients could be reduced by providing a final six-month hospice benefit, and with that, private insurance companies, too, began to offer hospice riders on their policies. At that time Medicare covered 210 days of nursing visits per year for a patient, but since 1990 nursing visits have been unlimited. The length of stay under hospice care has also been made more flexible by a rule change allowing coverage for up to six months of hospice care *if the disease follows its normal course*. Unusual events can lengthen or shorten the approved-for-funding care. During the period covered, Medicare pays the hospice program a flat per diem rate for all services.

In the present climate of budget-cutting, the per diem rates negotiated by Medicare are generally low, and hospice programs are faced with challenging decisions about how to deal with resulting shortfalls. The temptation is clearly present to limit services, perhaps more than can be tolerated; some hospices may be doing that. Other options are to find ways to provide all needed service more efficiently, and to seek grants or contributions or have money-raising projects like thrift shops to supplement the funding base. When making these decisions, boards and administrators respond out of their understanding or lack of understanding of the hospice mission. Some judicious combination of the options must, and we believe can, keep the program viable while maintaining fidelity to the mission. (After all, if the heart of hospice were lost, there would be no point to the entire venture.)

The Medicare payment does not cover our cost of serving seniors at the Hospice of Metro Denver, so in addition to implementing some new efficiencies, we seek charitable gifts to supplement the payment. We have several dedicated program funds to which our friends may contribute.

Younger, non-Medicare patients may have private insurance coverage; they pay the part of the bill that is not reimbursed by their insurance. If payment cannot be made, our hospice calls on contributions to make up the shortfall. One thing hasn't changed: we never turn patients away because of lack of money.

An unfortunate but realistic sequel to the budget pressures has slipped in that I regret to see. That is the inevitable heightening of our focus on business, dollars, and numbers. Sometimes this priority seems so strong that I worry whether we can keep the quality and training up to the standard we have always held. Stress has always existed between health professionals and administration over fiscally-based issues in health care settings; that is a chronic fact of life. Health-care people have a vision of how to promote health and serve patients; administrators have a vision of how to keep the operation going. Despite the need for accomplishing both goals, those visions can frequently be in conflict, or seem to be. With the money-crunch of the past decade, the stress over differences between the priorities of the two groups has been exacerbated. Unusual skills are needed to bring the two viewpoints into agreement.

I wish for several changes in the current hospice picture nationally. I would like the hospice of the future to be active in every community, providing home-care and in-patient service so that all persons needing help from hospice can get it. There remain many unserved persons where hospices exist; there are many communities and rural areas with no hospice program at all.

For hospice to become available to the population that should have its service, we need several things. One is a larger pool of potential hospice nurses. Another is a change in the philosophy of medicine regarding the care of persons at the end of life (along with a change in the medical education that underlies that philosophy).

To increase the pool of hospice nurses, schools of nursing must offer their students more exposure to hospice concepts and practices. The University of Miami provides a clinical experience for their Master of Science in Nursing students in which they spend one day a week for sixteen weeks with a local hospice program, attending team conferences, participating in assessment and intake and accompanying team members on home visits. This kind of curriculum should be emulated elsewhere if we are to become available across the country [1]. The University of Colorado Nursing School is now offering a course in hospice care, and there may be others by the time this book is published.

The more basic change required is in philosophy. We know that persons suffer, not bodies, but medicine has for so long regarded patients as bodies with disease which must be diagnosed and cured that the practitioner cannot truly view much less understand the person's experience of illness and dying. The patient's perception of pain and suffering and his complex psycho-social response to his illness and dying, which the physician must appreciate in order to respond effectively, remains largely unknown and out of his mental framework. As long as this is true, patient care will be technical and incomplete and referral for hospice care will be impeded. Until medical education teaches young doctors to listen to and actually enter the world of their patients, making their experience the primary focus of care and to respond to the entirety of their suffering—not just their symptoms—hospice service will be hobbled. We look with hope to emerging discourse on this issue, for the old narrow philosophy may indeed be changing.

I'd like all medical students to receive special training in care of the dying, including some time with us, so they can understand the values and mechanisms of hospice. If they work with our symptom control approaches, for example, and understand the importance of early referrals to hospice so families have time to learn to trust us, and grasp the real nature of the end stages of life, they will be better physicians when they practice medicine. (Studies of health-care delivery to hospice home-care patients show that more timely referrals help to optimize the use of hospice from both patient and societal perspectives—[2]).

The historic reluctance of medical schools to bring their students into competence in the care of the dying reflects their priorities for diagnosis and treatment of disease, but may also have originated in part in the turf battles that took place in the '70s and '80s between physicians and hospices [3]. Undoubtedly viewed as "losing a patient," referring patients to a hospice program back in those years was not a decision of choice made by many physicians. Medicine, long in charge of all matters of health care, may have been offended by the nursing model of hospice begun by Dame Cicely Saunders, although she was a physician, herself. Organized medicine fought Medicare coverage of hospice, using the financial argument that it would not save the government money. They lost their fight in 1985 when hospice coverage was begun. (When the caregivers are family members, and volunteers handle many other needs, as is true with hospice, and when the traditional response of medicine to a crisis is no longer used, end-of-life care has to be less costly than traditional medicine) [4].

The experience of Kaiser Permanente (see page 61) has found substantial savings on a per-patient basis [5]. Emanuel and Emanuel reported an estimated $29.7 billion in overall combined savings in 1992 from hospice and the use of advance directives, savings they regarded as insignificant [6]. Ezekial Emanuel has reported again, this time in 1996, summarizing previous studies on hospice care and advance directives, finding no more than $10 billion savings to Medicare, and most of that occurring during the last month of life[1] [7]. Hardly insignificant, the 1992 savings could have funded all uninsured Amercans' health insurance that year [8], and if the 1996 report is valid, even $10 billion is an amount worth saving. As Senator Everett Dirksen is reported to have said, "A billion here, a billion there, and pretty soon you're talking about real money."

Christakis and Escarce studied the survival of Medicare patients after enrollment in hospice programs, and they conclude that cost savings from hospice care would be even greater if referrals were made earlier. They found that most patients enter hospice late in the course of their illness, many having just had expensive acute in-hospital care which could have been supplanted with hospice care [9].

But money is not the only concern—or even the primary one. Essentially, medical education must change, and must move beyond its plodding pace. In 1970, fewer than 10 percent of United States medical schools offered death education at all. As long ago as 1972, concerns were voiced about medical students' scanty exposure to dying. Schoenberg and Carr expressed the belief that inadequate education in care of the terminally ill ". . . probably represents one of the greatest failures in professonal education" [10, p. 9]. By 1975, 80 percent of the schools included occasional lectures in their curricula. In 1987, 96 percent of 102 medical schools who responded to a survey reported they offered some kind of classroom instruction, most commonly an elective; in a few schools, a week of a required course focused on death and dying [11]. These were meaningful, if small, steps in the right direction.

Another survey of medical schools in 1989 revealed similar results, with eighteen out of the 111 responding schools then offering an elective lecture course [12]. A report that year identified four deficiencies in physicians' practice of medicine that were amenable to education: failure to treat patients as people, inadequate communication, failure to recognize the family role,

---

[1] It should be noted that Emanuel supports hospice as the appropriate answer to end-of-life care for quality of life reasons despite his conclusions about financial issues.

and a shallow understanding of death and dying [13]. Consciousness of this issue was rising.

In 1990, Rhymes deplored the lack of training most physicians and nurses had in caring for the terminally ill. He found many of these professionals were not comfortable in that role [14]. Even with the progress noted above, an American Medical Association survey reported in 1995 that only 8 percent of medical schools in the United States have a required course in death and dying, and only 8 percent of family medicine residency programs required exposure to terminal care in hospices [15]. How can we expect a fuller and more effective response from physicians to the needs of their dying patients if their education does not prepare them any better than that?

The University of Pennsylvania Medical School pioneered something helpful—an elective hospice preceptorship for first- and second-year students in which students were assigned to a patient's home for one term. Students attended weekly preceptorship meetings, and also attended the volunteer training provided by hospice [13]. Yale University initiated a somewhat different elective seminar in which students were paired with patients for interviews. The goals of the seminar were: 1) learn to talk with and listen to sick persons; 2) establish a professional relationship without the intrusion of friendship; 3) discover compassion without sentimentality, and the need for humility; and 4) learn of human frailty, finality of death and the common need for companionship when nearing death. The stated goals recognized implicitly the weaknesses of the usual finished product of medical education [12]. These two courses were more reality-based than the earlier lectures.

The problem with any elective course in this subject is obvious: those who elect it are probably already sensitive to the needs of the dying. The instructor is doing what the old saw refers to as preaching to the choir. Those who do not elect the course are probably the very ones who need it. Nevertheless, I view the emergence of these courses in medical education as positive.

An example of what I believe is far better, and should be emulated broadly, is St. Anthony's Hospice and Life Enrichment Program in Amarillo, Texas, which has initiated a clinical rotation within its program for third-year medical students. The rotation is part of a medical student family-practice clerkship, and every student takes it. Twenty-four hours of total time are split in several ways: The medical director lectures, then leads rounds of hospice patients, demonstrating appropriate communication, body language, and touch. The bereavement coordinator lectures on grieving, then each student visits a patient and his family. The chaplain lectures, then the student makes a home visit with a nurse. Finally, students participate in a discussion, sharing their experiences with the medical director [16].

The teaching goals for St. Anthony's program are: 1) learn and be able to describe hospice concepts; 2) describe effective pain management techniques; 3) describe effective management of common problems; 4) recognize and know how to deal with symptoms of grief; 5) recognize common psychosocial problems of patients and families; 6) recognize common psychological and spiritual issues of patients and families; and 7) evidence greater comfort and less anxiety around the terminal patient[2] [16].

These goals reflect substantial and practical realities in the care of dying patients, and it is not surprising that the administrators found significant growth in the students' acceptance of palliative care and positive attitudes about hospice care after the rotation [16].

One of the unfortunate deficiencies in medical education and in the practice of medicine, I believe, is that doctors do not attend the deaths of their patients. They read the charts and they hear the truncated reports from nurses, but rarely do they learn from their own experience what a profound event it is when their patients' lives wind down. *Solving the riddle* of diagnosis and treatment, the engine pushing medical technology to which surgeon and medical professor Sherwin Nuland refers in *How We Die*, consumes many of today's physicians who then have little time or energy for patients' circumstances and needs when the cure has failed and life departs [17]. Their long-standing role-definition prescribes ceaseless, sometimes heroic

---

[2] © 1992 *American Journal of Hospice and Palliative Care*/Prime National Publishing Corp. Used with permission.

effort with active treatment when it can help, but little or no time devoted to supportive care when treatment is futile and life is ending. That is wrong, and certainly not what Hippocrates had in mind. I'd have more of them attend a death from time to time. They should know and appreciate the events and feelings of the lives they care for—all the way to the end. That experience, repeated periodically, would give them an anchor point, a deeper sense of what their careers are all about. It would help them put into perspective the decisions and actions they take for their patients on a daily basis.

Besides nursing and medical education, I'd pour energy and funds into other kinds of education—elementary, middle and high schools, college programs, adult education, legislators, and the public—so society's view of dying can change; death can come out of hiding. With new attitudes which embrace the principles of hospice, more people can achieve the fullness of their entire life experience.

With the changes I envision, I would hope that full funding for hospice programs would come. The bottom line would still be important, but frantic fear of deficits would not rule the programs' priorities. Quality of care could keep its proper place.

Within hospice we could make improvements. We could do more than we do to instill confidence in the family members who are caring for their sons, daughters, spouses, or parents at home. It is a frightening challenge they face, and we are not sufficiently skilled in the psychology of the support and encouragement they need.

We would also be more effective if our understanding of religious, ethnic, and cultural differences in the families we serve were better. The beliefs and customs of our patients and their families play an essential role in their adjustments to illness and dying, and we in the hospice relationship need to understand and appreciate them. Misunderstandings and impediments to trust could be avoided if we did. Unfortunately, there is much we do not know.

Generalizations cannot be considered the rule, but, for example, Reformed Jews believe that the present life is all we know, while Orthodox Jews believe in recompense, immortality, and resurrection. Conservative Judaism views only figuratively the liturgy regarding immortality and resurrection [18]. Where the patient stands in these beliefs will obviously color his coping with terminal illness, and we on the hospice team should reinforce his coping; we certainly should not contradict it.

Christians believe in one way or another that life is a prelude to a better (after)life. It is helpful for the hospice worker to know that Roman Catholics base this on God's (Jesus') death and resurrection which they believe is a promise for their own passage, guided by certain rituals and upon receipt of certain sacraments, directly into Heaven—not, as was thought in the medieval Catholic church, first through purgatory. Certain anxieties seen in Catholic patients may best be handled by their own clergymen who can ease them in a way consistent with their beliefs [19].

Protestants also accept Jesus' death and resurrection as God's promise that, if they as individuals have faith, by authority of the scriptures and not the Pope, they will be taken into heaven upon their death. The Protestant role is either to endure without complaint (as in the patience of Job) or even to choose suffering to remove sin and evil (as in Jesus) in order to be fit to go to Heaven [20]. The Protestant's faith and his bonds to his church (congregation) support him as he faces death. We in hospice will do well to recognize this patient's needs and responses.

While Muslims believe in predestination, they also expect that leading good lives will admit them to heaven. Islam regards the soul as immortal. One is rewarded or punished upon death for the kind of person he or she has been in life. The reward is to spend eternity in Heaven; the punishment for the wicked is eternal damnation in Hell—a place of fiery torture. This final judgment is much like the Judeo-Christian, except for an additional concept that at the end of time and the end of the world, there will be a resurrection of bodies and a universal judgment [21].

Too few of us in American hospice programs know much about Eastern religions, whose adherents tend to believe that death is a transition point or event leading to rebirth. Hindus look on one's acts through life (his *karma*) as the determinant for what the next life will be—good acts leading to an improved life after death, bad acts to a poorer life. Buddhists add the concept of *nirvana*, a changed state of consciousness in which pain stops when the person gives up his desire to resist death [22].

Confucian thinking holds ritual as essential to enhance and maintain relationships, especially in the family and with ancestors. The dead are kept alive in memory by followers of Confucius [22].

Taoists accept the never-ending change they see in life; they take life (including death) as it comes [22].

Asians generally value social ritual and public formalities. They bear their troubles in silence to maintain their dignity, which sets a good example for others and contributes to their good reputation after death [22].

How much better it would be if these and other differences in religious belief and custom were understood by hospice staff-members! Helpful to any health worker, such understanding is particularly valuable in the hospice setting where relationships have continuity and contribute critically to the patient and family's adjustments.

Persons without conventional religious beliefs deserve special mention. They, too, need and follow some pattern of interpretation of what is happening in order to find meaning in death, theology professor Paul Irion has reminded us [23]. These secularists must find a pattern that fits with current knowledge and a scientific world view, such as immortality that is biological (genetic) or social (being remembered, or leaving some works or deed behind.) Because they have no institutional or metaphysical support, they have no rituals—but they seek, nevertheless, some way to transcend their own mortality. One way Irion suggests is that they regard life as a part of nature, making them subject to death (as all living things die). In this way, their lives are episodes in the extended process of nature, and therefore are meaningful.

The caregiver or hospice worker who holds beliefs different from his secularist patient, Irion says, must lay aside the assumption that the only real comfort is through a religious belief system. His suggestion to the caregiver is to offer his own religious beliefs only on request, and then in terms of what was found helpful to him, not in terms of an eternal truth [23].

A knowledge of religions may not be within the conventional definition of health-care skills, but hospice deals with people, not disease, with dying, not cure. Religion may play a very large role in the behavior and attitudes of dying persons and their loved ones, and it behooves the hospice team—all of its members—to know and understand the basic belief structure leading to their responses.

Differences other than religious exist among our patients, and we should be familiar with them too. The following are just a few.

According to some, pain may be dramatized in the Italian culture; American Protestants are often more self-contained, not asking for help. Not uncommon among Blacks, Greeks, and Chinese is a family and cultural pride that can lead to rejecting outside help. Puerto Ricans welcome comfort to a patient's spirit as it begins the journey to its afterlife [24]. We all recognize, of course, that these are generalizations which do not always hold true.

Among the Muslims, washing and burial customarily follow very promptly after death—usually by the next day [25]. If at all possible, the funeral of a Jew is held the next day (unless the next day happens to fall on the Sabbath).

Many Americans observe a short grieving period—perhaps three days—while the Jewish *Shiva* is one week in length for everyone, with thirty days of ritual mourning for the immediate family of the deceased during which entertainment is forbidden, and a full year of mourning if the deceased is a parent [18]. Chinese survivors observe a forty-nine-day grieving period [24].

Knowing these kinds of things could help us respond appropriately and helpfully instead of blundering into awkward communication-destroying gaffes.

Then there is the matter of program direction in hospice. Our program has demonstrated that when on-line hospice workers say what they think about policies and practices, problems can be resolved and creative improvements can follow. As in most endeavors, experience in the field is a critical adjunct to the wisdom of managers and directors who are at least once removed from the playing field. My vision for the future includes a corporate approach for hospice programs which bases all important decisions upon such combined input.

I would like to see the volunteer trustees or directors of hospice programs receive special training so that boards can function armed with specific knowledge about both hospice and trusteeship that is equal to their good intentions.

New ideas will arise. Some may be mine. But the publishing of this book cannot wait until the last bell has rung. There is a need now for a broader understanding and use of hospice, the achievement of which has been the purpose of this book.

C. J.

REFERENCES

1. E. A. Sorrentino, Hospice Care: A Unique Clinical Experience for MSN Students, *American Journal of Hospice and Palliative Care,* 9:1, pp. 29-33, 1992.
2. N. A. Christakis, Timing of Referral of Terminally Ill Patients to an Oupatient Hospice, *Journal of General Internal Medicine,* 9:6, pp. 314-320, 1994.
3. R. E. Enck, Physicians, Palliative Care and Health Care Reform, *Caring, 13*:9, p. 12, 1994.
4. A. Mitchel and G. E. Stroud, Cost Savings at the End of Life, *New England Journal of Medicine, 331*:7, p. 478, 1994.
5. T. Ryndes, New Beginnings in Hospice, *Healthcare Forum Journal, 38*:2, pp. 27-29, 1995.
6. E. J. Emanuel and L. L. Emanuel, Economics of Dying, *New England Journal of Medicine, 330*:8, pp. 540-544, 1994.
7. E. J. Emanuel, Hospice Cost Savings, *Journal of the American Medical Association, 275*:24, p. 1907, 1996.
8. J. J. Mahoney, Cost Savings at the End of Life (corres.), *New England Journal of Medicine, 331*:7, p. 477, 1994.
9. N. A. Christakis and J. J. Escarce, Survival of Medicare Patients after Enrollment in Hospice Programs, *New England Journal of Medicine, 335*:3, pp. 172-178, 1996.
10. B. Schoenberg and A. C. Carr, Educating the Health Professional in the Psychosocial Care of the Terminally Ill, in *Psychosocial Aspects of Terminal Care,* A. C. Carr, B. Schoenberg, and A. Kutscher (eds.), Columbia University Press, New York, 1972.
11. H. Edelman, Mortal Lessons, *Hospice, 4*:2, pp. 20-23, 1993.

12. A. C. Mermann, D. B. Gunn, and G. E. Dickinson, Learning to Care for the Dying: A Survey of Medical Schools and a Model Course, *Academic Medicine, 66*:1, pp. 35-38, 1991.
13. B. R. Cassileth, C. Brown, C. Liberatore, J. Lovejoy, S. A. Parry, C. Streets, K. Watkins, and D. Berlyne, Medical Students' Reactions to a Hospice Preceptorship, *Journal of Cancer Education, 4*:4, pp. 261-263, 1989.
14. J. Rhymes, Hospice Care in America, *JAMA, 264*:3, pp. 369-372, 1990.
15. R. MacDonald, Dying Patients Deserve a True Continuum of Care, *Geriatrics, 50*:9, p. 12, 1995.
16. C. F. Knight, P. F. Knight, M. H. Gellula, and G. H. Holman, Training our Future Physicians: A Hospice Rotation for Medical Students, *American Journal of Hospice and Palliative Care, 9*:1, pp. 23-28, 1992.
17. S. Nuland, *How We Die*, Alfred A. Knopf, New York, 1994.
18. E. A. Grollman, Death in Jewish Thought, in *Death and Spirituality*, K. J. Doka and J. D. Morgan (eds.), Baywood Publishing, Amityville, New York, pp. 21-32, 1993.
19. E. G. Miller, A Roman Catholic View of Death, *Death and Spirituality*, K. J. Doka and J. D. Morgan (eds.), Baywood Publishing, Amityville, New York, pp. 33-49, 1993.
20. D. Klass, Spirituality, Protestantism, and Death, in *Death and Spirituality*, K. J. Doka and J. D. Morgan (eds.), Baywood Publishing, Amityville, New York, pp. 51-73, 1993.
21. B. Lewis, *Islam and the Arab World*, B. Lewis (ed.), Alfred A. Knopf, New York, 1976.
22. D. Ryan, Death: Eastern Perspectives, in *Death and Spirituality*, K. J. Doka and J. D. Morgan (eds.), Baywood Publishing, Amityville, New York, pp. 75-92, 1993.
23. P. E. Irion, Spiritual Issues in Death and Dying for Those Who Do Not Have Conventional Religious Belief, in *Death and Spirituality*, K. J. Doka and J. D. Morgan (eds.), Baywood Publishing, Amityville, New York, pp. 93-112, 1993.
24. E. J. Rosen, Ethnic and Cultural Dimensions of Work with Hospice Families, *The American Journal of Hospice Care, 5*:4, pp. 16-21, 1988.
25. J. A. Williams, *Islam*, J. A. Williams (ed.), George Braziller Publications, New York, 1962.

APPENDIX B

Care Giver and Nursing Gems:[1]
A Collection of Practicalia

Caring for a patient with a life threatening illness includes meeting his needs of the moment. These needs may seem small—a matter of more comfort—or they may be crucial to preventing a problem of great significance. If some needs are tended to promptly, big concerns may be avoided. Sometimes the problems are so ordinary as to be ignored, yet the solution may make the difference between a good day and a nightmare. We have assembled a list of practical tips, ideas which may see the patient through an otherwise more difficult time. Perhaps one day these suggestions can help you.

CONSTIPATION
(The All-Too-Common Evil Companion of Morphine)

1. Recipe for "Black Magic": ½ pound raisins, ½ pound pitted prunes. Cook fruit, soak overnight. Mix in blender, adding 4 oz. senna powder, cinnamon, and nutmeg cloves. Chill or freeze. Give 1 tablespoon at bedtime. If diarrhea results, stop the Black Magic for 1 day, then resume with a smaller, 2-teaspoon dose. Caution: Use no other laxative simultaneously.
2. Use Senekot® or cascara to loosen stool in the colon and small bowel; Colace® for the colon.

---

[1] These helpful ideas were gathered from nurses, nurse's aides, volunteers, and a physical therapist at Hospice of Metro Denver. We are grateful for their contribution.

3. When using suppositories, wet with water, not K-Y Jelly®.
4. Give enema of 1 part hydrogen peroxide to 10 parts water. OR prepare a coffee enema (1 pot of strong coffee to a quart of water) and give to prevent impaction. Pray that it works.
5. If rectal disimpaction is necessary, use vegetable shortening, vaseline, or Chapstick® for lubrication.
6. For bloating and gas, use Mylicon 80®.

NAUSEA

1. Have patient sip mint tea or peppermint tea made with 1 or 2 drops of oil of peppermint (from the pharmacy) in 1 cup of water.
2. Use wash basin for vomiting episodes instead of the small, kidney-shaped emesis basin. Fewer mishaps!

URINARY PROBLEMS

1. Drinking a small glass of cranberry juice may help to keep kidneys flushed.
2. If patient has difficulty voiding, put 2 or 3 drops of oil of peppermint into the toilet or bedside commode.
3. For yeast infection, douche with plain yogurt.

ORAL PROBLEMS

1. Remove secretions from the back of the patient's throat with a turkey baster or a Foley catheter with a 3 cc syringe attached.
2. Nausea-accompanying thick secretions caused by radiation can be loosened by squirting a solution of 2 tablespoons of salt, 2 tablespoons of baking soda and 1 teaspoon of pediatric Benedryl Elixer® into the back of the patient's throat with a squirt bottle. The patient can be encouraged to gargle, cough and spit the material out.
3. Dry mouth can be helped by sucking ice chips, popsicles (fruity ones are best,) hard lemon or lime candies, or by chewing sugarless gum.

4. A refreshing rinse can be made of ¼ teaspoon of salt, ½ teaspoon of baking soda and 16 ounces of warm water. This swish-and-spit solution can leave a pleasant after-taste.
5. For the mouth-breathing patient with dried secretions coating his tongue, try Coca-Cola® on a toothette.

INSOMNIA AND RESTLESSNESS

1. Have the patient drink camomille tea.
2. Elevate the leg rest part of a recliner with a 2 × 4 or other base under the legs in order to provide the most supportive position for rest. The patient may find it easier to sleep for some periods in the recliner with legs elevated.
3. To help the caregiver, equip the patient's room with a baby monitor so worry-free vigilance from another part of the house can be maintained. Caregivers have needs too.

BREATHING DIFFICULTY

1. For a patient with asthma or sinus problems, have him or her drink regular hot tea or coffee, not decaffeinated.
2. For a patient with chronic obstructive pulmonary disease, direct a fan fully toward his face. When the patient uses a walker, clamp a battery operated fan onto the walker. In the absence of powered fans, put visitors to work using hand-held Japanese type fans. Besides helping the patient, the visitors can feel they have done something useful.
3. For the patient who is short of breath, encourage exhaling through pursed lips when walking, blowing the breath out like athletes do when training.

SKIN PROBLEMS

1. Use Vitamin E lotion for dry skin.
2. For patient incontinent of stool, use gobs of lotion in place of soap to clean the area.
3. For itching, boil oatmeal in a large amount of water. Cool oatmeal and strain so that the "juice" remains. Bathe area

with the juice. OR use Questran® 3 times a day and at bedtime.

4. For the "liver itch" that accompanies liver disease, Tagemet®, Vistaril®, and Questran® are all helpful.
5. For chapped lips, use Neosporin® ointment, K-Y Jelly®, Vaseline®, or Bacitracin® ointment.
6. For herpes, try Zovirax® cream (except inside the mouth!)
7. For decubitus (bed sores) slice papayas thin (like potato chips) and lay on the raw area while patient lies in the sun. Or sponge aloe plant juice directly onto the open area.
8. Use thin Duoderm® bandages rather than tape on irradiated skin. Duoderm® is easier on the skin and can be removed more easily than tape.
9. For radiation burn, prepare a solution of 1 cup vinegar, 1 cup alcohol, 4 aspirin dissolved, and 1 tablespoon of salt. Soak toweling in solution and place on burn. A substitute solution can be made with Domeboro® (a commercial preparation of aluminum sulfate and calcium acetate.)
10. For shingles, make a tea of ½ cup chickweed powder to 2 quarts of water. Soak cloth and place over skin.

ODORS

1. Add small amount of cinnamon and allspice to some water and place on stove over low heat. OR buy ozium product in a pet store (you'll know it by its black and white bottle with a signature skunk on the label). Put 1 or 2 drops in water in a small container in the patient's room.
2. For odors emanating from open wounds, cover area with plain yogurt, or try washing area with solution of ½ teaspoon vinegar in 1 pint of water.

MISCELLANEOUS

1. Put a drop of food coloring into patient's clear liquid medication to make its measurement easier.
2. When a cat cannot resist playing with the oxygen tubing of the patient with whom it shares a home, place a length

of old, split tubing around the tube to prevent claw-holes. Threading the tubing through the cardboard rollers on which wrapping paper and paper towels come will also protect the tubing.

3. For hiccoughs, find the bony notches under eyebrows with fingers and press, thus blocking a branch of the Vagus nerve.

4. To prevent slipping and falling, spray Puff-a-Lump® (available in craft shops) on socks.

5. When no clamp is available for tubing or Foley® catheter, fold tube back onto itself, and keep in place with tape or a rubber band.

6. If possible, patient should walk daily, sustaining a comfortable pace with good arm swing to relax muscles around the spine.

7. Patient should stretch gently and slowly at the start of each day and repeat several times later in the day to enhance circulation and mobility.

8. Patient should not clasp arms around the caregiver's neck to be lifted from seat. Rather the patient should scoot to the front of his seat and push off and up with his hands, with caregiver's support at one arm. Elevating furniture will help the patient to get to his feet. Bed and chair legs can often fit well atop the center hole of a standard 3-hole brick, which offers more stability than wood blocks. Styrofoam toilet seat boosters can be purchased in medical supply stores.

9. Wheelchair ramps should be limited to 1 foot rise per 12 feet of length. Anything steeper is unsafe.

10. Do not store the wheelchair in the trunk of the car, as lifting it in and out can injure the caregiver. Rather store in the space behind the driver's seat, first detaching the foot rests and rubber-banding the handgrips together behind the wheelchair seat. The job then is one of tilting and rolling rather than lifting. Best idea of all, when this will suffice: use the wheelchair to get the patient to the car, then leave the wheelchair at home, arranging to borrow another at the destination. All hospitals and many doctors' offices can oblige. Call first!

11. Walkers with front wheels are often easier for a patient to manage than those without, particularly if the patient can stand up tall and close to the walker.
12. To reduce narcotic intake, decrease each dose 25 percent during the first twenty-four-hour period, another 25 percent the next twenty-four-hour period if desired, and so forth until goal is reached.
13. Do a prothrombin blood test 6 hours after giving heparin in order to complete the blood report.

RECORDKEEPING

1. Place a spiral notebook near the patient for all who intervene in any way to log in their activity and comments about the patient. This will keep a record of what actually happened and when—sometimes a crucial help.

NUTRITION–
BOOSTERS AND OTHER IDEAS

1. Prepare a shake with a large scoop of vanilla ice cream, ¾ cup of flavored Ensure® (a nutritional supplement) and a couple of ice cubes. Instant breakfast or milk enriched with ¼ cup of instant, dry milk can substitute for Ensure®. Use as afternoon snack.
2. Another high nutrition shake: ½ cup cottage cheese, 1 tablespoon vegetable oil, 1½ tablespoons honey, and ½ orange, banana or other fruit. Yum! (Non-caloric Polycose® can substitute for the honey).
3. Serve small amounts of food on small plates.
4. Serve liquids in small glasses.
5. To clean a feeding tube, irrigate with cranberry juice instead of water.
6. Canada Dry Water® with lime will substitute for Alka Seltzer®.

APPENDIX C

Compassion Groups and Other Support

Current lists of bereavement groups can be obtained from:

Bereavement Magazine
8133 Telegraph Drive
Colorado Springs, CO 80920
719-282-1948

National Self-Help Clearinghouse
Graduate School and University Center
55 West 42nd Street
New York, NY 10036
212-840-1259

AIDS Action Council
2033 M Street N.W., Ste 802
Washington, D.C. 20036
202-293-2886
    Provides education and leadership for efforts to fight HIV and AIDS.

American Association of Suicidology
2459 South Ash Steet
Denver, CO 80222
303-692-0985
    Provides information about Colorado resources for survivors of suicide.

American Psychological Association
1200 17th Street N.W.
Washington, D.C. 20036
202-336-5500
   The professional association for psychologists, providing education, research and leadership.

Association for Death Education and Counseling
638 Prospect Avenue
Hartford, CT 06105-4298
203-586-7503
   Promotes death education and counseling through conferences, networking and resource referral.

Canadian Foundation for the Study of Infant Death
586 Eglinton Avenue East, Ste 308
Toronto, Ontario M4P 1P2, Canada
   Provides education and support for families who have lost infants.

Canadian Mental Health Association
880 Ouellette Ave, Ste 901
Windsor, Ontario N9A 127, Canada
   Among other supports, bereavement specialists provide counseling.

Candlelighters Childhood Cancer Foundation
1901 Pennsylvania Avenue N.W., Ste 1001
Washington, D.C. 20006
202-659-5136
   In local groups, provides support to parents, publications and community outreach programs.

Center for Attitudinal Healing
19 Main Street
Tiburon, CA 94920
415-435-5022
   Provides support and educational service based on the philosophy of power of love and positive thinking.

Center for Death Education and Research
University of Minnesota
1167 Social Science Building
Minneapolis, MN 55455
Provides a broad program of service as well as informational materials to both professionals and the public.

Center for Living and Dying
554 Mansion Park Drive
Santa Clara, CA 95054
Provides educational programs for students and parents, offering service to schools in order to meet the needs of grieving students.

Center for Loss and Life Transition
3735 Broken Bow Road
Fort Collins, CO 80526
970-226-6050
Provides professional services for the bereaved.

Compassionate Friends
P.O. Box 3696
Oak Brook, IL 60522-3696
708-990-0010
International group with local chapters providing support to parents whose children have died. They offer publications about parental and sibling bereavement.

Compassionate Friends of Canada
Les Amis Compatissants du Canada
685 William Avenue
Winnipeg, Manitoba R3E 0Z2, Canada
Provides support for bereaved parents, as above. This organization has programs in Australia, Israel, the Netherlands, South Africa, and Switzerland as well as in the United States and Canada.

Concern for Dying
250 West 57th Street
New York, NY 10107
212-246-6962
   Provides information on dying-related issues, and free copies
of living will and durable power of attorney forms.

Continental Association of Funeral and Memorial Societies
20001 S Street, N.W., Ste 630
Washington, D.C. 20009
202-462-8888
   Provides information about simple, inexpensive funerals.

Counseling and Research Center for Sudden Infant Death
1700 West Wisconsin Avenue
P.O. Box 1997
Milwaukee, WI 53201

The Dougy Center
P.O.Box 66461
Portland, OR 97286
   Offers support service and a directory of support group and
services for bereaved children.

Elisabeth Kübler-Ross Center
South Route 616
Head Waters, VA 24442
703-396-3441
   Provides advocacy, clinical and educational services as well
as written and audio-visual materials.

Exceptional Cancer Patients
1302 Chapel Street
New Haven, CT 06511
203-865-8392
   Bernie Siegel, M.D., organized this clinical service with an
emphasis on healing powers within the individual.

Families and Friends of Missing Persons and
Violent Crime Victims
P.O. Box 27529
Seattle, WA 98125
Provides support for persons who have suffered the loss of a loved one through crime or unexplained absence.

Families and Friends of Murder Victims
P.O. Box 80181
Chattanooga, TN 80181
Provides support for families and friends of murder victims.

Fernside, A Center for Grieving Children
P.O. Box 8944
Cincinnati, OH 45208
Provides peer-group support to bereaved children and their families.

Foundation for Thanatology
630 West 168th Street
New York, NY 10032
Provides workshops and seminars as well as educational materials for professionals working with the dying and bereaved.

Friends for Survival, Inc.
5701 Lerner Way
Sacremento, CA 95823
Provides support to persons who lost loved ones to suicide.

Good Grief Program
Judge Baker Guidance Center
295 Longwood Avenue
Boston, MA 02115
Provides crisis intervention to schools and community groups, supports and trains staff members to assist their own group members and offers educational materials and directories for use by these groups.

Heartbeat
2015 Devon Street
Colorado Springs, CO
719-596-2575
A self-help group with local chapters, Heartbeat offers monthly meetings for family and friends of suicide victims.

Make Today Count
P.O. Box 222
Osage Beach, MI 65065
314-346-6644
A national support group for persons with life-threatening illness and their families.

Mothers Against Drunk Driving (MADD)
511 E. John Carpenter Freeway, Ste 700
Irving, TX 75062
214-744-6233
1-800-438-MADD
Provides support to victims, families and friends as well as public education and political support for change in drunk driving policies. Local groups, many publications.

National Association of Social Workers
750 1st Street N.E., Ste 7
Washington, D.C. 20002
A professional association providing education, leadership and support to social workers.

National Center for Death Education Library
Mount Ida College
777 Dedham Street
Newton Center, MA 02159
617-928-4649
An educational center offering materials and directories.

National Committee on Youth Suicide Prevention
230 Park Avenue, Ste 835
New York, NY 10169
Provides research, education and leadership in suicide prevention among teen-agers.

National Hospice Organization
1901 North Moore Street, Ste 901
Arlington, VA 22209
703-243-5900
The organization to which most hospice programs belong. It offers leadership, research, support and referrals.

National Organization for Victim Assistance
717 D Street, N.W.
Washington, D.C. 20004
202-232-8560
24 hr hot line: 202-393-6682
Provides advocacy for victims, help for crime victims, service to local programs and 24-hour telephone crisis counseling.

National Victim Center
307 West 7th Street, Ste 1001
Fort Worth, TX 76102
817-877-3355
Provides services and information to victims of violent crime. It maintains a national data bank about victims' rights and criminal justice issues.

National Funeral Directors Association
11121 West Oklahoma Avenue
Milwaukee, WI 53227
414-541-2500.
Provides information about funerals and body disposition.

National AIDS Hotline
American Social Health Association
P.O. Box 13827
Research Triangle Park, NC 27709
1-800-342-AIDS
   Provides recorded information 24 hours a day, literature and referrals to medical and test centers.

National Association for People with AIDS
2025 I Street, N.W., Ste 1101
Washington, D.C. 20006
202-429-2856
   Provides information and technical assistance to local AIDS groups.

National Association for Widowed People
P.O.Box 3564
Springfield, IL 62708
   Provides support programs for widowed persons.

National Gay and Lesbian Crisis Line
800-221-7044
   Provides crisis counseling for AIDS patients.

National Hemophilia Foundation
Soho Building
110 Green Street, Room 206
New York, NY 10012
   Provides support and educational resources for families of hemophilia victims.

National Sudden Infant Death Syndrome Alliance
1314 Bedford Avenue Ste 210
Baltimore, MD 21208
1-800-221-SIDS
   Promotes research, provides services and education to families who have lost a child to SIDS.

National SIDS Clearinghouse
8201 Greensboro Drive Ste 600
McLean, VA 22102
703-821-8955
Provides information and referrals to national and local support groups.

Omega
2711 Washington Street
Somerville, MA 02143
Provides support for families of loved ones lost to suicide.

Parents of Murdered Children
100 East Eighth Street Room B41
Cincinnati, OH 45202
1-800-327-2499, X 4288
513-721-5683
A national group with local chapters, POMC provides support and resources to families whose children have been murdered.

Parents Without Partners
8807 Colesville Road
Silver Spring, MD 20910
301-588-9354
Provides services to single parents and their children: crisis intervention, education, and social programs.

Pregnancy and Infant Loss Center
1415 East Wayzata Boulevard, Ste 22
Wayzata, MN 55381
Provides services and education to families who lose infants, either during the pregnancy or after birth.

Afterwards: A Letter For and About Suicide Survivors
c/o Adina Wrobleski, Editor
5124 Grove Street
Minneapolis, MN 55436
Quarterly newsletter.

Resolve Through Sharing
Lutheran Hospital-LaCrosse
1910 South Avenue
LaCrosse, WI 54601
608-791-4747
Offers educational programs, certification courses for counselors, and support for bereaved families.

Rothman-Cole Center for Sibling Loss
1456 West Montrose Avenue
Chicago, IL 60613
Provides support and facilitates growth of brothers and
sisters of dying children.

SIDS Network Newsletter
873 Crowells Street
Oshawa, Ontario L1X 1X8, Canada
Provides information to persons concerned with Sudden
Infant Death Syndrome.

Source of Help in Airing and Resolving Experiences (SHARE)
St. Elizabeth's Hospital
211 South Third Street
Belleville IL 62222
618-234-2415
Provides educational materials to bereaved parents and
health-care providers about miscarriage, still-birth, ectopic
pregnancy, and early infant death.

Sudden Infant Death Syndrome Institute
6065 Rosewell Road, Ste 876
Atlanta, GA 30328
404-843-1030
1-800-232-7437
Provides research, clinical service, education, and support to
families who have lost infants to SIDS.

Suicide Research Unit
National Institute of Mental Health
5600 Fishers Lane, Room 10C26
Rockville, MD 20857
Conducts research and disseminates information about suicide.

Survivors of Suicide
Suicide Prevention Center, Inc.
184 Salem Avenue
Dayton, OH 45406
A national group offering service to suicidal persons and to their loved ones.

They Help Each Other Spiritually (THEOS)
1301 Clark Building
717 Liberty Avenue, Ste 1301
Pittsburgh, PA 15222
412-471-7779
Provides support and education to the widowed and their families.

Teens in Grief: Educate, Rebuild, Support (TIGER)
521 Garden Court
Quincy, IL 62301
Provides support to teen-agers who have suffered loss.

Victims of Violence
P.O. Box 393
Boulton, Ontario L7E 1A0, Canada
Provides support to the families and friends of victims of violence.

Widowed Persons Service
American Association of Retired Persons
601 E Street N.W.
Washington, D.C. 20049
202-434-2260
Provides programs to the newly widowed along with information and audiovisual resources.

GRIEFNET
Internet access address:

Cendra Lynn at
\grief@Rivendell.org\

Provides resource listings, bibliographies, and electronic mailing lists where subscribers may discuss grief-related topics.

DEATHNET
800-331-3055
HTTP://www.islandnet.com/deathnet

Right to die information about end of life issues available on the internet.

Bibliography of Additional Readings

Adams, J. P., M. J. Hershater, and D. A. Moritz, Accumulated Loss Phenomenon among Hospice Caregivers, *American Journal of Hospice and Palliative Care, 8*:3, pp. 29-37, 1991.

Ahles, T. A. and J. B. Martin, Cancer Pain: A Multidimensional Perspective, *The Hospice Journal, 8*:1-2, pp. 25-48, 1992.

Alligood, M. R., Empathy: The Importance of Recognizing Two Types, *Journal of Psychosocial Nursing, 30*:3, pp. 14-17, 1992.

Amadeo, D. M., Hospice Nurses and Approaching Death, *American Journal of Hospice and Palliative Care, 10*:5, pp. 10-12, 1993.

Baker, M., Cost-Effective Management of the Hospital-Based Hospice Program, *Journal of Nursing Administration, 22*:1, pp. 40-45, 1992.

Beach, D. L., Caregiver Discourse: Perceptions of Illness-Related Dialogue, *The Hospice Journal, 10*:3, pp. 13-25, 1995.

Beresford, L., *The Hospice Handbook*, Little, Brown and Co., Boston, Massachusetts, 1993.

Billings, J. A., Medical Education for Hospice Care: A Selected Bibliography with Brief Annotations, *The Hospice Journal, 9*:1, pp. 69-83, 1993.

Bonica, J. J., Cancer Pain, in *The Management of Pain*, J. J. Bonica (ed.), Lea and Febiger, Philadelphia, Pennsylvania, pp. 400-460, 1990.

Butler, R. N., For Dying Patients, There is Much You Can Do, *Geriatrics, 50*:2, p. 9, 1995.

Buxman, K., Making Room for Laughter, *American Journal of Nursing, 91,* pp. 46-51, 1991.

Byock, I. R., Patient Refusal of Nutrition and Hydration: Walking the Ever-Finer Line, *American Journal of Hospice and Palliative Care, 12*:2, pp. 8, 9-13, 1995.

Byock, I. R., Cancer Chemotherapy and the Boundaries of the Hospice Model, *American Journal of Hospice and Palliative Care, 9*:2, pp. 4-5, 1992.

Callahan, D., Response to Miller et al., *New England Journal of Medicine, 331*:24, p. 1656, 1994.

Chambers, C. V., J. J. Diamond, R. L. Perkel, and L. A. Lasch, Relationship of Advance Directives to Hospital Charges in a Medicare Population, *Archives of Internal Medicine, 154*:5, pp. 541-547, 1994.

Charlton, R., The Philosophy of Palliative Medicine: A Challenge for Medical Education, *Medical Education, 26*:6, pp. 473-477, 1992.

Cherny, N. I. and R. K. Portnoy, Management of Cancer: Practical Issues in the Management of Cancer Pain, in *Textbook of Pain,* P. D. Wall and R. Melzack (eds.), Churchill Livingstone, Edinburgh and New York, 1994.

Clark, M., *Health in the Mexican-American Culture,* University of California Press, Los Angeles, California, 1970.

Colburn, K. and D. Hively, Hospice Phenomenon, *Caring, 12*:11, pp. 4-12, 1993.

Cooke, M. A., The Challenge of Hospice Nursing in the 90's, *American Journal of Hospice and Palliative Care, 9*:1, pp. 34-37, 1992.

Coolican, M. B., J. Stark, K. J. Doka, and C. A. Corr, Education about Death, Dying and Bereavement in Nursing Programs, *Nurse Educator, 19*:6, pp. 35-40, 1994.

Council on Ethical and Judicial Affairs, American Medical Association Guidelines for the Appropriate Use of Do-Not-Resuscitate Orders, *Journal of the American Medical Association, 265*:14, pp. 1868-1871, 1991.

Counts, D. R. and D. A. Counts, *Coping With the Final Tragedy: Cultural Variation in Dying and Grieving,* Baywood Publishing, Amityville, New York, 1991.

Covinsky, K., L. Goldman, E. F. Cook, R. Oye, N. Desbiens, D. Reding et al. for SUPPORT Investigators, Impact of Serious Illness on Patients' Families, *Journal of the American Medical Association, 272*:23, pp. 1839-1844, 1994.

Davis, T., A. W. Miser, C. L. Loprinzi, J. S. Kaur, N. L. Burnham, A. M. Dose, and M. M. Ames, Comparative Morphine Pharmacokinetics following Sublingual, Intramuscular, and Oral Administration in Patients with Cancer, *The Hospice Journal, 9*:1, pp. 85-90, 1993.

Dobratz, M. C., Analysis of Variables that Impact Psychological Adapation in Home Hospice Patients, *The Hospice Journal, 10*:1, pp. 75-88, 1995.

Doyle, D., Have We Looked Beyond the Physical and Psychosocial? *Journal of Pain and Symptom Management, 7,* pp. 302-311, 1992.

Dufault, M. A., C. Bielecki, E. Collins, and C. Willey, Changing Nurses's Pain Assessment Practice: A Collaborative Research Utilization Approach, *Journal of Advanced Nursing, 21*:4, pp. 634-645, 1995.

Emanuel, L. L., M. J. Barry, E. J. Emanuel, and J. D. Stoeckle, Advance Directives: Can Patients' Stated Treatment Choices be Used to Infer Unstated Choices? *Medical Care, 32*:2, pp. 95-105, 1994.

Emanuel, L. L., Reexamining Death, *Hastings Center Report, 25*:4, pp. 27-35, 1995.

Emanuel, E. J. and L. l. Emanuel, Response to Cost Savings at the End of Life, *New England Journal of Medicine, 331*:7, pp. 478-479, 1994.

Eng, M. A., The Hospice Interdisciplinary Team: A Synergistic Approach to the Care of Dying Patients and Their Families, *Holistic Nursing Practice, 7*:4, pp. 49-56, 1993.

Ewer, M. S., Decision Making in Critical Illness: Who Knows Best? *MD Anderson Oncology, 36*:1, pp. 1-5, 1991.

Fainsinger, R. L., Dehydration and Palliative Care, *Palliative Care Letter, 7*:1, 1995.

Feinstein, D. and P. E. Mayo, *Rituals for Living and Dying: How We Can Turn Loss and Fear of Death Into an Affirmation of Life,* Harper Press, New York, 1990.

Ferrell, B. R., C. Wisdom, M. Rhiner, and J. Alletto, Pain Management as a Quality Care Outcome, *Journal of Nursing Quality Assurance*, 5:2, pp. 50-58, 1991.

Ferrell, B. R. and M. Rhiner, High Tech Comfort: Ethical Issues in Cancer Pain Management for the '90's, *Journal of Clinical Ethics*, 2, pp. 108-115, 1991.

Foley, F. J., J. Flannery, D. Graydon, G. Flintoft, and D. Cook, AIDS Palliative Care—Challenging the Palliative Paradigm, *Journal of Palliative Care*, 11:2, pp. 19-22, 1995.

Foley, K. M., J. J. Bonica, and V. Ventafridda, Proceedings of the 2nd International Congress on Cancer Pain, *Advances in Pain Research and Therapy*, K. M. Foley, J. J. Bonica, and V. Ventafridda (eds.), Volume 16, Raven Press, New York, 1990.

Foley, K. M., in *Current and Emerging Issues in Cancer Pain: Research and Practice*, Raven Press, New York, 1993.

Fox, S. S., *Good Grief: Helping Groups of Children When a Friend Dies*, New England Association for the Education of Young Children, Boston, Massachusetts, 1988.

George, L. and L. Bearson, *Quality of Life in Older Persons: Meaning and Measurement*, Human Sciences Press, New York, 1980.

Gibson, B., Volunteers, Doctors Take Palliative Care into the Community, *Canadian Medical Association Journal*, 153:3, p. 332, 1995.

Gonda, T. A. and J. E. Ruark, *Dying Dignified: The Health Professional's Guide to Care*, Addison-Wesley Publishing Co., Menlo Park, California, 1984.

Gould, D., Empathy: A Review of the Literature with Suggestions for an Alternative Research Strategy, *Journal of Advanced Nursing*, 15:10, pp. 1167-1174, 1990.

Greene, P. E., The Pivotal Role of the Nurse in Hospice Care, *CA Cancer Journal Clinic*, 34:4, pp. 204-205, 1984.

Greenlaw, J., Let's Get Rational about Suicide, *Internist*, 33:3, pp. 8-9, 1992.

Greer, D. S. and V. Mor, An Overview of National Hospice Study Findings, *Journal of Chronic Diseases*, 39:1, pp. 5-7, 1986.

Grey, A., The Spiritual Component of Palliative Care, *Palliative Medicine*, 8:3, pp. 215-221, 1994.

Grollman, E. A., *What Helped Me When My Loved One Died*, Beacon Press, Boston, Massachusetts, 1980.

Grollman, E. A., *When Your Loved One is Dying*, Beacon Press, Boston, Massachusetts, 1980.

Grollman, E. A., *In Sickness and In Health: How to Cope When Your Loved One is Ill*, Beacon Press, Boston, Massachusetts, 1980.

Grollman, E. A., *Living When a Loved One Has Died*, Beacon Press, Boston, Massachusetts, 1987.

Grollman, E. A., *Talking About Death: A Dialogue Between Parent and Child*, Beacon Press, Boston, Massachusetts, 1990.

Grollman, E. A., *Explaining Death to Children*, Beacon Press, Boston, Massachusetts, 1967.

Grothe, T. M. and R. V. Brody, Palliative Care for HIV Disease, *Journal of Palliative Care*, 11:2, pp. 48-49, 1995.

Hackler, J. C. and F. C. Hiller, Family Consent Orders Not to Resuscitate, *Journal of the American Medical Association*, 264:10, pp. 1281-1283, 1990.

Hanrahan, P. and D. J. Luchins, Access to Hospice Programs in End-Stage Dementia: A National Survey of Hospice Programs, *Journal of the American Geriatric Society*, 43:1, pp. 56-59, 1995.

Hardy, J. D., H. G. Wolf, and H. Goodell, Studies on Pain: An Investigation of Some Quantitative Aspects of the Dol Scale of Pain Intensity, *Journal of Clinical Investigation*, 27, pp. 380-386, 1948.

Hare, J., C. Pratt, and C. Nelson, Agreement between Patients and Their Self-Selected Surrogates on Difficult Medical Decisions, *Archives of Internal Medicine*, 152, pp. 1049-1054, 1992.

Hilberman, M., Cost Savings at the End of Life, *New England Journal of Medicine*, 331:7, pp. 477-478, 1994.

Hinton, J., Which Patients with Terminal Cancer are Admitted from Home Care? *Palliative Medicine*, 8:3, pp. 197-210, 1994.

Hinton, J., Can Home Care Maintain an Acceptable Quality of Life for Patients with Terminal Cancer and Their Relatives? *Palliative Medicine, 8*:3, pp. 183-196, 1994.

Hinton, J., *Dying,* Penguin Press, New York, 1972.

Honeybun, J., M. Johnston, and A. Tookman, The Impact of Death on Fellow Hospice Patients, *British Journal of Medical Psychology, 65*:Pt 1, pp. 67-72, 1992.

Howarth, G. and K. B. Willison, Preventing Crises in Palliative Care in the Home. Role of Family Physicians and Nurses, *Canadian Family Physician, 41,* pp. 439-445, 1995.

Hull, M. H., Hospice Nursing: Caring Support for Caregiving Families, *Cancer Nursing, 14*:2, pp. 63-70, 1991.

Irion, P. E., *Hospice and Ministry,* Abingdon Press, Nashville, Tennessee, 1988.

Jacox, A., D. B. Carr, and R. Payne, New Clinical Practice Guidelines for Management of Pain in Patients with Cancer, *New England Journal of Medicine 330*:9, pp. 651-655, 1994.

Kamisar, Y., Are Laws against Assisted Suicide Unconstitutional? *The Hastings Center Report, 23*:3, pp. 32-41, 1993.

Kapp, D. S., R. S. Cox, T. A. Barnet, and R. Ben-Yosef, Thermoradiotherapy for Residual Microscopic Cancer: Elective or Post-Excisional Hyperthermia and Radiation Therapy in the Management of Local-Regional Recurrent Breast Cancer, *International Journal of Radiation Oncology and Biological Physiology, 24*:2, pp. 261-277, 1992.

Kapp, D. S. and J. L. Meyer, Breast Cancer: Chest Wall Hyperthermia-Electron Beam Therapy, *Frontiers of Radiation Therapy Oncology, 25,* pp. 151-168, 1991.

Karlin, N. J. and P. D. Retzlaff, Psychopathology in Caregivers of the Chronically Ill: Personality and Clinical Syndromes, *The Hospice Journal, 10*:3, pp. 55-61, 1995.

Kass, L. R., Suicide Made Easy, *Commentary, 92*:6, pp. 19-24, 1991.

Kass, L. R., *Toward a More Natural Science: Biology and Human Affairs,* Free Press, New York, 1985.

Kelley, P. and M. Callanan, in F. Driscoll, The New Congregation, *Journal of Palliative Care, 11*:2, pp. 61-63, 1995.

Kelly, M. R., A Modern Argument Against Legalizing Active Euthanasia, *Internist, 33*:3, pp. 11-12, 1992.

Kirschling, J. M., B. J. Stewart, and P. G. Archbold, Family Caregivers of Post-Hospitalized Older Persons and Persons Receiving Hospice: Similarities and Differences, *Home Health Care Service Quarterly, 14*:4, pp. 117-140, 1994.

Knight, J., The Need to Laugh, *Nursing, 20*:8, p. 20, 1990.

Koop, C., Decisions at the End of Life, *Issues in Law and Medicine, 5*:2, pp. 225-233, 1989.

Kramer, A. M., Health Care for Elderly Persons—Myths and Realities, *New England Journal of Medicine, 332*:15, pp. 1027-1029, 1995.

Kuhse, H. and P. Singer, Euthanasia: A Survey of Nurses' Attitudes and Practices, *Australian Nurses' Journal, 21*:8, pp. 21-22, 1992.

Lakshmipathi, C., A. Grenvik, and M. Silverman, Intensive Care for the Critically Ill Elderly: Mortality, Costs and Quality of life, *Archives of Internal Medicine, 155*:10, pp. 1013-1022, 1995.

Lawlor, E. F., Medicare's Adoption of Hospice, *Public Policy and Aging Report, 3*:1, pp. 1-3, 1989.

Lee, D. S., M. L. McPherson, and I. H. Zuckerman, Quality Assurance: Documentation of Pain Assessment in Hospice Patients, *American Journal of Hospice and Palliative Care, 9*:1, pp. 38-43, 1993.

Leete, E. B., Becoming a Hospice Volunteer, *American Journal of Hospice and Palliative Care, 11*:2, pp. 27-32, 1994.

Loxterkamp, D., A Good Death is Hard to Find: Preliminary Reports of a Hospice Doctor, *Journal of the American Board of Family Practice, 6*:4, pp. 415-417, 1993.

MacDonald, D., The Hospice World View: Healing Versus Recovery, *American Journal of Hospice and Palliative Care, 7*:5, pp. 40-45, 1990.

MacLeod, R. D. and A. Nash, Teaching Palliative Care in General Practice: A Survey of Educational Needs and Preferences, *Journal of Palliative Care, 7*:4, pp. 9-12, 1991.

MacLeod, R. D., Teaching Hospice Medicine to Medical Students, House Staff and Other Caregivers in the United Kingdom, *The Hospice Journal, 9*:1, pp. 55-67, 1993.

Magno, J. B., The Hospice Concept of Care: Facing the 1990's, *Death Studies, 14*:2, pp. 109-119, 1990.

Martin, E. W., In-Patient Hospice Care, *Rhode Island Medicine*, *78*:4, pp. 118-119, 1995.

Martin, J. P., Making Terminal Care Decisions, *Caring*, *10*:7, pp. 42-45, 1991.

Marwick, C., Should Physicians Prescribe Prayer for Health? Spiritual Aspects of Well-Being Considered, *Journal of the American Medical Association*, *273*:20, pp. 1561-1562, 1995.

May, C., To Call It Work Somehow Demeans It, *Journal of Advanced Nursing*, *22*:3, pp. 556-561, 1995.

McCaffery, M. and A. Beebe, *Pain: Clinical Manual for Nursing Practice*, C. V. Mosby, St. Louis, Missouri, 1989.

McClung, J. and R. S. Kramer, Legislating Ethics: Implications of New York's Do-Not-Resuscitate Law, *New England Journal of Medicine*, *323*:4, pp. 270-273, 1990.

McGlashan, T. H., F. J. Evans, and M. T. Orne, The Nature of Hypnotic Analgesia and the Placebo Response to Experimental Pain, *Psychosomatic Medicine*, *31*, pp. 227-246, 1969.

McGuire, D. B., Comprehensive and Multidimensional Assessment and Measurement of Pain, *Journal of Pain and Symptom Management*, *7*, pp. 312-319, 1992.

McMillan, S. C. and M. Mahon, A Study of Quality of Life of Hospice Patients on Admission and at Week 3, *Cancer Nursing*, *17*:1, pp. 52-60, 1994.

Melvin, T. A., I. N. Ozbek, and D. E. Eberle, Recognition of Depression, *The Hospice Journal*, *10*:3, pp. 39-46, 1995.

Millison, M. and J. R. Dudley, Providing Spiritual Support: A Job for All Hospice Professionals, *The Hospice Journal*, *8*:4, pp. 49-66, 1992.

Moinpour, C. M., L. Polissar, and D. A. Conrad, Factors Associated with Length of Stay in Hospice, *Medical Care*, *28*:4, pp. 363-368, 1990.

Morgan, E., *Dealing Creatively with Death*, Celo Press, Burnsville, North Carolina, 1988.

Morgan, J. D., Death and Bereavement, *Death Studies*, *12*:2, pp. 85-89, 1988.

Moroney, E. C., What is Death with Dignity? *CHAC Review*, *19*:1, pp. 10-13, 1991.

Morrison, C., Delivery Systems for the Care of Persons with HIV Infection and AIDS, *Nursing Clinics of North America, 28*:2, pp. 317-333, 1993.

Newton, R. A., Contemporary Views on Pain and the Role Played by Thermal Agents in Managing Pain Symptoms, in *Thermal Agents in Rehabilitation*, S. L. Michlovitz (ed.), F. A. Davis Company, Philadelphia, Pennsylvania, 1990.

Ogden, J., Palliative Care: Voluntary Benefits, *Nursing Times, 90*:25, pp. 64-66, 1994.

Oleson, J. R., Adjuvant Hyperthermia for Recurrent Breast Cancer, *International Journal of Radiation Oncology and Biological Physiology, 24*:2, pp. 381-382, 1992.

Olsen, D. P., Empathy as an Ethical and Philosophical Basis for Nursing, *Advances in Nursing Science, 14*:1, pp. 62-75, 1991.

O'Neill, M. T., Caring at the End of Life, *Journal of Health Care Chaplain, 4*:1-2, pp. 103-109, 1992.

Padilla, G. V., B. Ferrell, M. M. Grant, and M. Rhiner, Defining the Content Domain of Quality of Life for Cancer Patients with Pain, *Cancer Nursing, 13*:2, pp. 108-115, 1990.

Paice, J. A., S. M. Mahon, and M. Faut-Callahan, Factors Associated with Adequate Pain Control in Hospitalized Post-Surgical Patients Diagnosed with Cancer, *Cancer Nursing, 14*, pp. 298-305, 1991.

Peterson, L. W. and M. J. Nitsch, A Therapeutic Program for Bereaved Children, *Archives of Family Medicine, 3*:1, pp. 76-83, 1994.

Podrid, P. J., Resuscitation in the Elderly: A Blessing or a Curse? *Annals of Internal Medicine, 111*:3, pp. 193-195, 1989.

Polin, H. B., In Support of Initiative 119, *Internist, 33*:3, pp. 13-15, 1992.

Portenoy, R. K., Pharmacologic Approaches to the Management of Cancer Pain, *Journal of Psychosocial Oncology, 8*:2-3, pp. 75-107, 1990.

Pugsley, R. and J. Pardoe, Too Tired to Think: The Physical Energy Requirements of Emotional Work, *American Journal of Hospice and Palliative Care, 7*:5, pp. 36-39, 1990.

Quig, L., Positive Aspects of Hospice Social Work, *Caring, 12*:11, pp. 59-61, 1993.

Quill, T. E., Doctor, I Want to Die: Will You Help Me? *Journal of the American Medical Association, 270*:7, pp. 870-873, 1993.

Quill, T. E., Oregon Death with Dignity Act, *New England Journal of Medicine, 332*:17, pp. 1174-1175, 1995.

Quill, T. E. and C. K. Cassel, Nonabandonment: A Central Obligation for Physicians, *Annals of Internal Medicine, 122*:5, pp. 368-374, 1995.

Rando, T. A., *Grief, Dying and Death*, Research Press, Champaign, Illinois, 1984.

Rando, T. A., *Treatment of Complicated Mourning*, Research Press, Champaign, Illinois, 1993.

Rapoport, N., *A Woman's Book of Grieving*, William Morrow and Company, New York, 1994.

Raudonis, B. M., The Meaning and Impact of Empathic Relationships in Hospice Nursing, *Cancer Nursing, 16*:4, pp. 304-309, 1993.

Reed, P. G., Toward a Nursing Theory of Self-Transcendence: Deductive Reformulation Using Developmental Theories, *Advances in Nursing Science, 13*:4, pp. 64-77, 1991.

Reese, R. and C. Reese, Guidelines for Developing a New Standard in Hospice Care, *Caring, 13*:9, pp. 8-9, 69-72, 1994.

Robb, V., Working on the Edge: Palliative Care for Substance Users with AIDS, *Journal of Palliative Care, 11*:2, pp. 50-53, 1995.

Sandelowski, M., Telling Stories: Narrative Approaches in Qualitative Research, *Image: Journal of Nursing Scholarships, 23*, pp. 161-166, 1991.

Sankar, A., *Dying At Home: A Family Guide for Caregiving*. Johns Hopkins University Press, Baltimore, Maryland, 1991.

Schneiderman, L. J., R. Kronick, R. M. Kaplan, J. P. Anderson, and R. D. Langer, Effects of Offering Advance Directives on Medical Treatment and Costs, *Annals of Internal Medicine, 117*:7, pp. 599-606, 1992.

Schonwetter, R. S., T. A. Teasdale, P. Storey, and R. J. Luchi, Estimation of Survival Time in Terminal Cancer Patients: An Impedance to Hospice Admissions? *The Hospice Journal, 6*:4, pp. 65-79, 1990.

Seckler, A. B., D. E. Meier, M. Mulvihill, and B. S. Cammer-Paris, Substituted Judgment: How Accurate are Proxy Predictions? *Annals of Internal Medicine, 115,* pp. 92-98, 1991.

Seegenschmiedt, H. M., U. L. Karlsson, R. Sauer, L. W. Brady, Jr., M. Herbst, B. E. Amendola, A. M. Markoe, S. A. Fisher, and B. Micaily, Superficial Chest Wall Recurrences of Breast Cancer: Prognostic Treatment Factors for Combined Radiation Therapy and Hyperthermia, *Radiology, 173*:2, pp. 551-558, 1989.

Sheehan, C. and A. Thomas, Volunteer Hospice, *Caring, 12*:11, pp. 20-23, 1993.

Silbert, D., Assessing Volunter Satisfaction in Hospice Work: Protection of an Investment, *American Journal of Hospice Care, 2*:2, pp. 36-40, 1985.

Simon, H. B., Hyperthermia, *New England Journal of Medicine, 329*:7, pp. 483-487, 1993.

Singer, P. A. and M. Siegler, Advancing the Cause of Advance Directives, *Archives of Internal Medicine, 152*:1, pp. 22-24, 1992.

Singer, P. A. and F. H. Lowy, Cost Savings at the End of Life, *New England Journal of Medicine, 331*:7, p. 477, 1994.

Smith, M. A., Primary Caregiver Options in Hospice Care, *American Journal of Hospice and Palliative Care, 11*:3, pp. 15-17, 1994.

Smith, G., Recognizing Personhood and the Right to Die with Dignity, *Journal of Palliative Care, 6*:2, pp. 24-32, 1990.

Smith, D. C. and M. F. Maher, Achieving a Health Death: The Dying Person's Attitudinal Contributions, *The Hospice Journal, 9*:1, pp. 21-32, 1993.

Soutter, J., S. Bond, and A. Craft, A Children's Hospice: Philosophy and Facility, *Nursing Standard, 9*:11, pp. 22-23, 1994.

Spencer, J., Caring for the Terminally Ill Person with Pain, at Home, *Cancer Nursing, 14*:1, pp. 55-58, 1991.

Spiritual Care Work Group of the International Work Group on Death, Dying and Bereavement, *Death Studies, 14*:1, pp. 75-81, 1990.

Spross, J. A., D. B. McGuire, and R. M. Schmitt, Oncology Nursing Society Position Paper on Cancer Pain, *Oncology Nursing Forum, 17*:4, pp. 595-614, 1990.

Sprung, C. L., Changing Attitudes and Practices in Forgoing Life-Sustaining Treatments, *Journal of the American Medical Association, 263*:16, pp. 2211-2215, 1990.

Steel, R. K., M. Musliner, and P. A. Boling, Medical Schools and Home Care, *New England Journal of Medicine, 331*:16, pp. 1098-1099, 1994.

Stephany, T. M., Assisted Suicide: How Hospice Fails, *American Journal of Hospice and Palliative Care, 11*:4, 1994.

Stephany, T. M., Aids and the Hospice Nurse, *Home Healthcare Nurse, 8*:2, pp. 11-14, 1990.

Stephens, M. A. P., J. M. Kinney, and P. K. Ogrocki, Stressors and Well-Being among Caregivers to Older Adults with Dementia: The In-Home Versus Nursing Home Experience, *The Gerontologist, 31*:2, pp. 217-223, 1991.

Stetz, K. M. and W. K. Hanson, Alterations in Perceptions of Caregiving Demands in Advanced Cancer During and After the Experience, *The Hospice Journal, 8*:3, pp. 21-34, 1992.

Taylor E. J. and M. Amenta, Midwifery to the Soul While the Body Dies: Spiritual Care among Hospice Nurses, *American Journal of Hospice and Palliative Care, 11*:6, pp. 28-35, 1994.

Tearnan, B. H. and C. H. Ward, Assessment of the Terminally Ill Patient with Pain: Example of Cancer, *The Hospice Journal, 8*:1/2, pp. 49-71, 1992.

Teno, J., J. Lynn, R. Phillips et al., Do Advance Directives Save Resources? *Clinical Research, 41*:2, p. 551A, 1993.

Thomas, L., *Fragile Species,* Scribners, New York, 1992.

Thorpe, G. J., Teaching Palliative Care to U.K. Medical Students, *Palliative Medicine 5,* pp. 6-11, 1991.

Tsevat, J., E. F. Cook, M. L. Green, D. B. Matchar, N. V. Dawson, S. K. Broste et al., Health Values of the Seriously Ill, *Annals of Internal Medicine, 122*:7, pp. 514-520, 1994.

Tsevat, J., L. Goldman, G. A. Lamas, M. A. Pfeffer, C. C. Chapin, K. F. Connors et al., Functional Status Versus Utilities in Survivors of Myocardial Infarction, *Medical Care, 29*:11, pp. 1153-1159, 1991.

Turk, D. C. and C. S. Feldman, Noninvasive Approaches to Pain Control in Terminal Illness: The Contribution of Psychological Variables, *The Hospice Journal,* 8:1-2, pp. 1-23, 1992.

Uhlmann, R. and R. Pearlman, Perceived Quality of Life and Preferences for Life-Sustaining Treatment in Older Adults, *Archives of Internal Medicine, 151,* pp. 495-497, 1991.

Vachon, M. L. S., L. Kristjanson, and I. Higginson, Psychosocial Issues in Palliative Care: The Patient, the Family and the Process and Outcome of Care, *Journal of Pain and Symptom Management, 10:2,* pp. 142-150, 1995.

Van Allen, E. J., *You Decide: Using Living Wills and Other Advance Directives to Guide Your Treatment Choices,* Irwin Professional Publishing Company, New York, and American Hospital Publishing, Chicago, Illinois, 1994.

Von Roenn, J. H., C. S. Cleeland, R. Gonin, and K. J. Pandya, Results of a Physician's Attitude toward Cancer Pain Management Survey by ECOG, *Proceedings of the American Society of Clinical Oncology, 10,* 1991.

Waller, A., M. Hershkowitz, and A. Adunsky, The Effect of Intravenous Fluid Infusion on Blood and Urine Parameters of Hydration and on State of Consciousness in Terminal Cancer Patients, *The American Journal of Hospice and Palliative Care, 11,* pp. 22-27, 1994.

Walsh, T., Oral Morphine in Chronic Cancer Pain, *Pain, 18,* pp. 1-11, 1984.

Watson, M., S. Greer, J. Pruyn, and B. van den Borne, Locus of Control and Adjustment to Cancer, *Psychological Reports, 66:1,* pp. 39-48, 1990.

Wilkie, D. J., N. Lovejoy, M. Dodd, and M. D. Tesler, Concurrent Validity of Three Tools: Finger Dynamometer, Pain Intensity Number Scale, Visual Analogue Scale, *The Hospice Journal, 6:1,* pp. 1-13, 1990.

World Health Organization, *Guidelines for Cancer Pain Management,* 1986.

Yalom, I. D., *Existential Psychotherapy,* Basic Books, Inc., New York, 1931.

Zenz, M., T. Zenz, M. Tryba, and M. Strumpf, Severe Under-treatment of Cancer Pain: A Three Year Survey of the German Situation, *Journal of Pain and Symptom Management,* *10*:3, pp. 187-191, 1995.

Zerwekh, J., Laying the Groundwork for Family Self-Help, *Public Health Nursing,* *9*:1, pp. 15-21, 1992.

Index